TURNING
THE
HIRAM KEY

MAKING DARKNESS VISIBLE

Also by Robert Lomas

Turning the Solomon Key
Turning the Templar Key
The Invisible College
Freemasonry and the Birth of Modern Science
The Man who Invented the Twentieth Century

with Christopher Knight
The Book of Hiram
Uriel's Machine
The Second Messiah
The Hiram Key

with Geoffrey Lancaster
Forecasting for Sales and Material Management

TURNING
THE
HIRAM KEY
MAKING DARKNESS VISIBLE

ROBERT LOMAS

www.robertlomas.com
www.bradford.ac.uk/webofhiram/
www.knight–lomas.com

Lewis Masonic

Dedicated to

The late Worshipful Brother Irene Peters

of Lodge Anwyl, No 256, Mold,

and

Lodge of the East Gate, No 160, Chester,

who introduced me to Freemasonry and

to her daughter, my wife

First published in hardback 2005
This paperback edition 2007

ISBN (10) 0 85318 279 5
ISBN (13) 978 0 85318 279 5

Cover design by Martin & Trevor Jackson of www.tracingboards.com

Published by Lewis Masonic

an imprint of Ian Allan Publishing Ltd, Hersham, Surrey KT12 4RG.
Printed and bound in Great Britain by Mackays of Chatham, Chatham, Kent

Visit the lewismasonic website at www.lewismasonic.com

Comments about *Turning the Hiram Key*

"These mystics haven't really given up sex, it's just a different form of orgasm. This analysis [by Lomas] forms the basis of the fifth book in the Hiram Key series, which has produced controversial theories on the mindset of man from pre-history to the present day. *Turning the Hiram Key* looks like keeping to that tradition, with detailed discussion on how masonic ritual contains the elements needed for inducing mental ecstasy." - *The Scotsman*

"Lomas... has no qualms about mixing and matching hardcore science and mathematics with ancient belief systems, a dash of folklore, and a bucketful of astronomy. And he doesn't mind asking himself, and the rest of us, some rather pertinent questions about the result." - *The Daily Mail*

"One of the practical aims of Freemasonry is to teach people how to be in control of their own lives. *Turning the Hiram Key* makes an admirable starting point for this process... Lomas gives the impression of enormous energy and intellectual vitality - a man who is in control of his own life, and has the gift of being able to teach others to follow his example." - *Colin Wilson, author of The Outsider, Atlantis to the Sphinx, and Dreaming to Some Purpose.*

"Not since W. L. Wilmshurst's books and lodge papers of the 1920s and 30s has there been such a positive and serious study of Freemasonry as a system of spiritual philosophy." - *W. Bro. Douglas Inglesent. P.P.J.G.W. Custodian of the Wilmshurst Collection*

Acknowlededgments

This book would never have been written had Lewis Masonic not recruited an eager young Mason to take over its line of traditional Masonic books. Martin Faulks, who was attracted into Freemasonry after reading *The Hiram Key*, thought that the Craft needed a serious book about its spiritual aspects. Without standing on ceremony, he emailed me and started a correspondence in the course of which he teased out of me my views on the spiritual side of Freemasonry. Before I knew it, I'd agreed to put together a synopsis for a book exploring the deep feelings that Freemasonry evokes in me. Soon after that, Martin arranged for me to meet David Allan, Managing Director of Lewis Masonic, and I found myself agreeing to write this book.

For me, this is a totally new genre. Masonic history I know, but this is a venture into an area which stirs deep emotions in me, and I wasn't at all sure anybody else would be interested in how I felt about Freemasonry. David and Martin both assured me the book was a good idea, so I went away and wrote a full outline. At this point my American editor, Paula Munier of Fair Winds Press, rang me up and asked me what I was working on. I told her about this project, and she asked to see the outline. After she'd read it she got back to me saying she thought it was a great idea, and could I do a simultaneous launch in the United States and Canada, as well as the UK? I am grateful to all three of them for their encouragement and inspiration.

Bill Hamilton and Ben Mason, who look after me at A.M. Heath, my literary agents, sorted out timescales, contracts and production arrangements, and Bill ran his experienced eye over the synopsis to help me shape it into a sensible narrative. An efficient and encouraging literary agency is a tremendous asset to any writer and I am grateful to Bill, Ben and all their colleagues for their ongoing professional support. I am similarly grateful to Jenny Finder and the library staff at Bradford University School of Management, who have been extremely helpful in tracing the many scientific and historical references I needed to consult.

Colin Wilson has been supportive since I first mentioned the project to him and showed him some early chapters. He read the book in early drafts and contributed many helpful suggestions, not to mention the Foreword. My thanks to him for his encouragement, and for allowing me to quote from his work. Tim Bentley, too, has read various drafts and made many helpful suggestions to improve clarity.

Kath Gourlay provided information about the carbon dating of the Kirkwall Scroll, allowed me to quote her work and cast a friendly but critical eye over the early drafts.

Brothers Josh Gourlay, Douglas Inglesent and David Wilkinson have all contributed many useful thoughts to my Masonic understanding, and my Brethren at the Lodge of Living Stones, No 4957, have been a continual source of support and inspiration as well as a sounding board for ideas.

Peter Waller at Lewis Masonic has been extremely efficient in sorting out production issues and facilitating editorial support. Roderick Brown, who edited most of the books in *The Hiram Key* series, has retired, and I wish him a long and happy retirement. However, before he took up full time gardening responsibilities he recommended an editorial successor, John Wheelwright. Roderick's choice was impeccable. John has proved to be a delight to work with, and has helped me clarify my sometimes tangled thoughts. Richard Lay also did a careful job of proof-reading.

The colour plates were created by Bro.s Martin and Trevor Jackson of www.tracingboards.com and I thank them for permission to use their artwork. I also thank the Brethren of Lodge Kirkwall Kilwinning for permission to reproduce the Kirkwall Scoll.

Finally I want to thank my wife and children for their ongoing support and encouragement – in particular, my daughter Delyth for turning the image of the Hiram Key into a wonderful piece of jewellery for me to wear, and my son Geraint for his computing support.

Contents

Foreword

I became aware of the work of Robert Lomas in May 1996, when my wife Joy and I were taken to visit Rosslyn Chapel. In the souvenir shop there I bought *The Hiram Key* by Christopher Knight and Robert Lomas, then only recently published, for Joy to read on the train. At this time I knew little about Freemasonry, except what I had read in a book called *The Brotherhood* written by a friend, Stephen Knight, which argued that Freemasonry was a kind of Old Boys' Network whose members were devoted to helping one another get good jobs. But then, Stephen (who was dead by then) had admitted that he knew very little of the history of Freemasonry. But he mentioned a tradition that Freemasonry had its roots in ancient Egypt, and another that the pre-Christian sect the Essenes were among its ancestors.

About a year later I began to research a book about the legend of Atlantis, and the great flood which Plato claimed engulfed the continent 'in a day and a night'. And since I recalled reading something about the Flood in *The Hiram Key*, I settled down to a more careful reading. I instantly became absorbed in Knight and Lomas's investigation into the history of Freemasonry. They argued that its origin could be traced back far beyond 1640, the year Stephen Knight said it began, first to the Scottish knight William St Clair, who had built Rosslyn in the fifteenth century, then to the Order of Knights Templar, founded after the first Crusade in Jerusalem and virtually wiped out on the orders of Philip the Fair of France in 1307, then further back still, to the Essenes, of which Jesus was almost certainly a member, and then to the Temple of King Solomon around 900 B.C. And before that, they argue, there is evidence that the legend of the murder of Hiram Abif, architect of the Temple, was based on a real event: the murder of the pharaoh Sequenenre during the reign of the 'Shepherd' (Hyksos) kings of Egypt in the seventeenth century B.C.. If they are correct, then the origins of Freemasonry can indeed be traced to ancient Egypt (and that extraordinary man Cagliostro, who called himself an Egyptian Freemason, is justified).

Why was I interested in this story? Because I was convinced that Plato's story of Atlantis (in the *Timaeus*) was based on a real event – an immense flood that occurred around 9500 B.C., possibly caused by a comet or asteroid that struck the earth. I was collaborating with a Canadian librarian named Rand Flem'Ath, who had studied legends of Native Canadians and North Americans that seemed to suggest that they were based on some tremendous real catastrophe in which 'the sky fell' and floods poured down, drowning most of the inhabitants of the earth.

The Hiram Key convinced me that Masonic legends may indeed date back to the Atlantis Flood. I also came to believe that those ancient traditions of Freemasonry were kept alive after the Roman destruction of the Essenes in the first century A.D., perhaps descending via the Merovingian kings of France to the Templars, then to William St Clair, the builder of Rosslyn, as well as to a secret order, known as the Priory of Sion, founded by Templars (as described in a seminal book, *The Holy Blood and the Holy Grail* and, even more recently, in Dan Brown's bestseller *The Da Vinci Code*).

As anyone who has read the latter will know, it claims that the Roman Catholic Church has always been deeply opposed to the Templars and Priory of Sion because they preserved the truth about the life of Jesus – and that truth has nothing in common with the Christianity of St Paul, in which Jesus died on the cross to save men from the consequences of Original Sin. The fact is, Lomas and Knight insist, that Jesus was a man, not a god, and the Roman Catholic Church is therefore built on a myth. (*The Hiram Key* even quotes Pope Leo X as saying 'It has served us well, this myth of Christ'. But then, some would say that Leo was himself a member of the Priory of Sion.) This could account for the immense and long-standing hostility of the Church to Freemasonry.

It is necessary to explain all this before moving on to the subject of the present book. (And I should add before I do so that Bob Lomas has grave doubts about the Priory of Sion, which I am sure he can explain better than I can.)

When Bob told me he was writing a book about the meaning of Masonic ritual, I felt relatively certain it would not interest me. Once again I was wrong, as I soon discovered when I read some of its earlier chapters.

I have written a great deal about religion since my second book *Religion and the Rebel*, published in 1957, in which I state my belief that St Paul's Christianity is his own invention and has nothing to do with the teachings of Jesus. (This point was made by Bernard Shaw in his brilliant preface to *Androcles and the Lion*.) But I have always been deeply interested in the experiences of the mystics, and in what one writer, R.M. Bucke, has called 'cosmic consciousness' (in his book of that title, written in the 1890s). Bucke had spent an evening with friends, reading and discussing such favourite poets as Wordsworth and Walt Whitman. As he went home in a carriage, he was startled by a red glow:

All at once, without warning of any kind, I found myself wrapped in a flame-coloured cloud. For an instant I thought of fire, an immense conflagration somewhere close by ... the next, I knew that the fire was

*within myself. Directly afterwards there came upon me a sense of
exultation, of immense joyousness, accompanied or immediately followed by
an intellectual illumination impossible to describe. Among other things ...
I saw that the universe is not composed of dead matter, but is, on the
contrary, a living Presence; I became conscious in myself of eternal life. It
was not a conviction that I would have eternal life, but a consciousness that
I possessed eternal life then; I saw that all men are immortal. ... The vision
lasted a few seconds and was gone.*

Bob begins this book by describing a similar experience he had
when driving through an electrical storm. His own glimpse of
'cosmic consciousness' convinced him that this is the true purpose of
the rituals of Freemasonry, and his scientific training has enabled him
to go into the brain physiology of such experiences. He finds
confirmation of his theory in *The Meaning of Masonry* by W.L.
Wilmshurst, and in Chapter Eleven of the present book he quotes
from my autobiography *Dreaming to Some Purpose* some of my own
experiences involving what the psychologist Abraham Maslow called
'peak experiences' – these moments in which the world ceases to
appear as mere solid and impenetrable reality, and is imbued with a
tremendous sense of meaning, or what G.K. Chesterton called 'absurd
good news'. This was the subject of my first book *The Outsider*
(1956), about those poets and artists of the nineteenth century who
experienced sudden visions of 'meaning' (like Van Gogh when he
painted *The Starry Night*), and when the vision has faded, find
themselves trapped in a world that leaves them feeling bored and
discouraged. I called such men 'Outsiders', because they felt alienated
from the everyday reality that most people seem to find so satisfying.
And my conclusion in that book was that the 'Outsiders' must learn

to overcome the sense of alienation and be prepared to take their place in society, which they must learn to change from within. For, as H.G. Wells says in *The History of Mr Polly:* 'If you don't like your life you can change it.'

In America, a remarkable man called Syd Banks – not a psychologist or an academic – was suddenly struck by a revelation: that nearly all human misery is caused by our own thoughts. As he spoke about this insight, he gathered an increasing number of followers, and had soon founded a new psychology. A New York psychiatrist named George Pransky, a dissatisfied and disgruntled Freudian, travelled to Salt Spring Island off the coast of Vancouver to attend one of Banks's weekend seminars, and was immediately struck by the fact that the people there seemed so healthy and wellbalanced, so much in control of their own lives. Pransky has gone on to become one of the foremost exponents of Banks's 'psychology of mind'.

This, it seems to me, is also one of the practical aims of Freemasonry – to teach people how to be in control of their own lives. *Turning the Hiram Key* makes an admirable starting point for this process, since it sets out to show how we can deepen our sense of meaning through a vision of the underlying reality – the reality that Wilmshurst discusses in *The Meaning of Masonry*.

Bob Lomas strikes me as very much the kind of person encountered by George Pransky on Salt Spring Island. He gives the impression of enormous energy and intellectual vitality – a man who is in control of his own life, and has the gift of being able to teach others to follow his example.

Colin Wilson

Prologue

Thunderbolts of the Gods

Thank You, St Barbara

Electric storms fascinate me. Lightning can captivate or kill, and the closer the thunderbolt, the more awesome its power.

On the afternoon of Thursday 17 May 2001 a lightning strike came so near me that my hair stood on end, my ears crackled and an ancient thunder god sparked to life in my mind. This close encounter with nature's raw power changed my life, but fortunately I survived to share what it taught me.

As a Freemason, I belong to an Order that is under the protection of St Barbara, who is said to divert lightning bolts away from the innocent. Before lightning conductors were discovered, operative masons caught on high steeples in bad weather prayed to her for aid. When I was threatened, though, I was far too engrossed by the rapid sequence of events to even consider petitioning her. But she must have realised I was a Freemason in distress and looked after me anyway. I have a romantic urge to thank her, not least because she symbolises a key feminine principle that has shaped the inner teachings of Freemasonry.

Let me explain what happened, and how it changed my view of the nature of consciousness and started me on a quest that would finally allow me to discover the spiritual secrets of Freemasonry.

I was driving up the road between Thornton and Queensbury in West Yorkshire, listening to the Steve Wright Show on Radio 2. This narrow rural road is the shortest route between my home and my university, and I drive it often, at all times of the day and night and in all weathers. But on this particular day the familiar views over open country seemed out of the ordinary. The natural light had become garish and strikingly unreal, and I felt I was experiencing a sensation that some modern artists try to arouse in those who look at their work. The technique – called *ostranenie*, or 'making strange' – is used to try to overcome the deadening effect of habit on our perception of familiar things. But on this day, on this road winding through a high, bleak part of West Yorkshire, no tricks of technique were needed to make the atmosphere feel strange.

One thing was obvious: there was a storm brewing. The sky was darkening, and I could sense a heavy feeling in the air. The landscape looked as if painted by Van Gogh on one of his bad days – the sort of day when the cypresses swirled too tightly and the crows massed together so closely that they eclipsed the sun. All the colours of the countryside seemed to have a much harsher edge than usual, and overhead the clouds had thickened to a dark, impenetrable dome. There was no other traffic in sight as I drove up the hill, and the green of the fields was hard-edged and backlit against the distant brightness of the horizon. The road ahead was now so dark that I was beginning to think about turning the car lights on. As I reached for the switch I felt the hairs on the back of my hand, and on my neck, start to rise. It was an eerie feeling: as if an imaginary 'something' was sitting in the back seat of the car staring at me. I imagined I'd picked up God as a hitch-hiker. I had to force myself not to turn and look 'what-ever-it-was' in the eye.

The whole experience was so unnerving that I pulled my Jeep over to the side of the road. I felt I could not go on driving with that supernatural presence in the back. But, as I pulled the car to the side of the road, I began to fear this brooding entity. I had to force myself to turn and face the source of the feeling. When I finally did, the seat was quite empty.

Then, as I looked back towards the centre of the impending electrical storm, I felt my mind expand to fill the cosmos. Time froze, and I felt a great peace and clarity. The stars moved in their courses within the spiral arm of the galaxy as it twirled slowly above me. I was enveloped by a flame-coloured cloud. For an instant I wondered if my Cherokee had caught fire, but then I realised that the light was inside my mind. It was a moment like sexual orgasm – without the normal physical effects. My mind felt as if it was exploding with the joy of a deep insight into the way the universe works. It was an instant of intense happiness.

I'm not certain how long that moment of ecstasy lasted, because I lost all sense of time. Then I was jolted abruptly back to frightening reality as the concept of time hit me right between the ears. A rapid sequence of events began that changed my entire perception of how life works – or, at least, of how I and everyone else with an electrically powered brain is able to understand it. It will take you far longer to read my account of what happened than it took me to live it: it was over in a matter of seconds.

It began with a strong 'zizzing' sound, which seemed to come from a source close to the light, well in front and to the left of the Jeep windscreen. The closest description I can offer is that it was like a cross between a hiss and a sizzle, and it increased in intensity and then died away within a single beat of my heart. As it was rising to its brief crescendo I saw a bright flash of light, which lit up the car from the direction of the field to the left of the road. Then the 'zizz' died away slightly before the light dimmed. As the light died I heard a sharp crack of electrical noise from the radio speakers.

I realised that the light was from a strike of forked lightning. Whenever I get the chance to watch lightning, I instinctively start counting seconds the moment I see a flash. 'One, *and* two, *and* three ...', I counted as this habit kicked in and I was jerked out of my timeless joy of awareness.* I had just reached three when the thunderclap hit my ears; this put the strike between 2,500 and 3,000 feet away, or just over half a mile. The sound of the thunder came from the same direction as the lightning.

I had heard three things. The 'zizzing' sound from the strike, the sound of the electromagnetic pulse hitting the radio and crackling the radio speaker, and the thunder which came from the same direction as the light pulse. I had never experienced this 'zizzing' noise before. I knew I was safe in the metal body of the car, so I waited and watched for further strikes. Two more were accompanied by 'zizzing' sounds, which appeared to come from almost the same direction as their light flashes. For all three strikes that I could 'hear', my count took under three seconds. Two or three further strikes were over a mile away.† I could not hear their 'zizzing' sounds, although the radio could: it clicked almost in synchronisation with the flashes.

---

*The counting uses the time gap between the lightning and the sound of the thunder to measure how far away the strike is: sound travels at 1,000 feet per second in still air, so every five secinds between lightning and thunder represents a mile's distance to the strike.
†Their counts were in excess of five seconds.

The first thing I did after my strange experience was to make careful notes about the times and my perception of the directions of the events, while the information was fresh in my mind. This account is reconstructed from the notes I wrote sitting by the roadside a few minutes after these events. But what does it all mean?

The sequence is clear. First I felt a period of ecstatic insight, in which I sensed my mind expand to become one with all creation; next I heard the 'zizzing', and this coincided with the pulse of light from the electrical discharge of the lightning; then I heard the electromagnetic impulse of the strike, via the radio speakers; and finally I heard the sound of the thunder, caused by the wavefront of displaced air reaching my ears. The interval between the 'zizzing' and the light pulse had been almost impossible to separate: it had felt as if I had heard electrons being dragged upwards from the Earth to neutralise the positively charged thunderclouds as the insulation of the air broke down. The perceived volume of the 'zizz' had increased in time with the intensity of the light, and I had not 'heard' the noise from the radio until the 'zizz' had finished.

There was ample time for me to react, and start to count, before the sound wave hit me, so whatever caused the 'zizz' travelled as fast as light. It had to be an electric field which directly stimulated my auditory nerve so that I interpreted it as a sound. The fact that I heard the 'zizzing' before I saw the light tells me it was caused by the collapse of the electric charge build-up on the hilltop – I must have been close to the centre of the charge build-up that caused the strike. As the atmosphere ionised during the lightning spark, this electric field rapidly drained away, which caused the voltage fall that I heard as a 'zizz'. The fact that the sound seemed to come from about 5° left of the direction of the light implied that my left auditory nerve had processed the signal marginally faster than my right, or the electric field had been delayed or attenuated as it passed through my head. I don't think there is much in my head to absorb and attenuate an electric wavefront, but the sheathing of the axon of the auditory nerve would offer a capacitive load to the fast-changing electric pulse. This could have caused a differential rise time between the two nerves, so creating the very slight time delay which my brain had interpreted as a slightly off-centre positioning.* It would also account for the way the volume of the 'sound' seemed to rise and fall.

The delay on the radio signal was easy to explain. The signal had to be decoded by the radio set and be transmitted to the loudspeaker, which then had to physically move the air to make the sound I heard in the normal way. I estimated it would take about 50 microseconds or so to do this. I calculated this by working out the rise time of the radio; the frequency response of the loudspeaker, and the time of travel of the air wave. This was long enough for the audio-processing part of my brain to detect the different sounds.

I could not detect the 'zizzing' effect when the strike was more than 6,000ft away. This convinced me that it was an effect of the intense electric field which accompanied the lightning strike. The fast-falling electric pulse would soon be attenuated by ground-wave absorption,

---

*Normally the auditory nerves in my head conduct electrical signals only when I am hit by a wave of sound. However, a strong electrical field will also trigger them in a different and strange way. The nerves connecting my left and right ears to my brain are about the same lenght, but they conduct electricity in one direction only, from dendrite to axon (or if you like from ear to brain). I judge the direction of a sound by 'hearing' the different times at which the same sound arrives in my brain from my two ears. When these two nerves are triggered by an *electric* field from a point off to the side of my head, then they conduct in opposite directions, so one pulse will be slowed down more than the other. The result of this time delay is that the 'zizzing' of the sound seems to come from somewhere about 5° away from the direction of the lightning flash. Believe me, it is a scary experience.

and so only when the strike was closer than about 5,000ft was I able to 'hear' it. This is the closest I have ever been to a lightning strike, and hence the first time I've noticed this effect.

The fact that I could 'hear' a light pulse brought home to me just how dependent my view of the outside world was on the way I interpret electrical impulses. I was suddenly aware that my whole consciousness, as I perceived it through my senses, was an illusion caused by the electrical pulses channelled into my brain. I had personal proof that external electric fields directly affect what I perceive. There is no way for me to decide which is a real sound, and what might be the electrical 'zizz' of a close lightning strike. I 'heard' the lightning three seconds before my ears were rattled by the thunder.

But what is perhaps most important for my quest to understand Freemasonry, is that I had just experienced 'cosmic consciousness'. This is a state of mind that the famous Masonic writer Walter Leslie Wilmshurst, whose work I was studying at the time, says is the purpose at the centre of Freemasonry. And that experience had been wonderful. I felt a warm glow of understanding and a deep pleasure in that knowledge. It was similar to, but stronger than, the afterglow I had occasionally experienced after working Masonic ritual. Attending a Masonic ceremony makes me feel good. So, was my experience on the road to Queensbury a clue to why I, and so many others, enjoy Freemasonry?

I now knew that the feeling that Wilmshurst called 'cosmic consciousness' could be caused by exposing my brain to an intense electrical field. Small wonder that the ancient Greeks met Zeus when he threw thunderbolts at them. Or that ancient Masons, working on high steeples in bad weather invoked the supernatural aid of St Barbara. I'd just experienced her sitting next to God in the back seat of my Jeep and diverting the thunderbolt to one side so that I lived to report the event.

V.S. Ramachandran, a brain scientist at the University of California, describes what I had just had as a God experience.

I've always suspected that the temporal lobes [of the human brain] are involved in religious experience. ... does this imply that our brains contain some sort of circuitry that is actually specialised for religious experience?[1]

I'd just been kicked into a weird level of activity by an intense electrical field. But Ramachandran is right. My brain fired a whole raft of spiritual circuits on a Yorkshire hilltop when the thunder god spat at me.

From reading Wilmshurst's published and private works, I knew he claimed that Freemasonry teaches a way of experiencing this ultimate state of mind without needing to be struck by a thunderbolt. Now, after my 'road to Queensbury' experience I knew what it was like, and I wanted to know more. So I decided to work through all the Masonic teaching about this syate of mind and see hoe Freemasonry thought it could bring it about. The obvious place to begin was Wilmshurst's unpublished notebooks.

The Masonic Path to Cosmic Consciousness

At the age of seventy Walter Wilmshurst was President of the Masonic Study Society and chaired his last meeting for it the day before he died. He was mourned as a mystical Mason. He describes a philosophic model of the human spirit and relates it to the teaching he found in the ritual of the Craft. It took him 33 years from his raising, as Freemasons call the ritual of becoming a Master Mason, before he felt his ideas on the spiritual aspects of Freemasonry were clear enough for him to write a book. And, even then, that book, *The Meaning of Masonry*, was not his final thought on the subject. He continued writing lectures to be delivered in Masonic lodges, reading and annotating the books in his library and keeping a journal of his reflections. It is from this range of sources that I put together a comprehensive summary of his ideas.

From the general direction and development of his thoughts, I became convinced that he had been collecting material to write a sequel to *The Meaning of Masonry* but died before he got around to drafting it. Trying to reconstruct this sequel, I spent many happy hours reading his notebooks, checking through his source volumes to read his marginal annotations and reviewing the lectures he presented to Masonic lodges. As a result of studying his writings I have come to the view that the world can only benefit from open and frank discussions on this subject of human belief and our interaction with the power that underpins the universe. Many people call this power God, scientists call it the Laws of Physics, and Freemasons use the term the Great Architect of the Universe. And Freemasonry, the second-largest and best-equipped spiritual organisation in the world, may well be the forum to foster this discussion. It has millions of members, thousands of temples and meeting rooms, and an infrastructure of Grand Lodges in most countries of the world. It is second in size only to the Roman Catholic Church as a worldwide spiritual movement.

However, there is a barrier to such discussion, and that is the standard explanation for the existence of Freemasonry. The United Grand Lodge of England asserts that its bizarre rituals are simply 'morality plays', borrowed from the initiation rites of guilds of working stonemasons by philosophic gentlemen for their own betterment. In my view this starting point is inherently silly, and any arguments derived from it are likely to be deeply flawed. I have found the rituals to work in a systematic psychological way to improve the minds and morals of those exposed to them.

Freemasonry is not a religion, but it is spiritual technique that is compatible with the belief systems of any religion as well as with the rational world view of science: to join, you must express a belief that there is order underpinning the behaviour of the universe. Its teachings can provide a focal point for many people who are not active in any particular faith – and for them it might be a replacement for religion. It provides spiritual values without a requirement to subscribe to an entire belief system. It is tolerant in a way that most religions are not, and its symbolic teaching allows a range of interpretation that embraces people of all beliefs. It allows them to take what they need from its system and, whilst doing so, to learn more about themselves and how to meet their spiritual needs.

It is my belief that Freemasonry is an ancient science that can drive human ambition and achievement. It can offer great insights that do not conflict with modern science. The path of Freemasonry is a way into the mystery of the inner self – whether you call it soul, spirit or state of consciousness.

This book describes my quest to understand this spiritual aspect of Freemasonry. Having found *The Hiram Key*, I wanted to know how to turn it and unlock the real spiritual secrets of the Craft. To do this I needed to understand how the message of the square and compass combines with the symbol of the centre to make darkness visible.

But this insight came much later. First I had to live the rituals, and so I will begin by describing exactly how they affected me as I worked them for the first time.

[1] Ramachandran & Blakeslee (1999), p. 175.

Part One

Let me Initiate you into the Mysteries of Freemasonry

The first Part of this book tells what happened when I first entered Freemasonry, how I felt during the process, and how it changed my perception of the Craft. But first a word about ritual - there are many local and national variations in the exact wording of Masonic ritual and when quoting the ritual I have drawn freely on this common heritage to quote sections which made the most impact on me.

One of Masonry's basic lessons is that to understand, you must experience. Now join me as I begin my first lesson in how to experience.

Chapter One

I Want to be Made a Mason

Setting Aside Worldly Things

At 6.45 pm on Wednesday 27 January 1988 I was standing in the ladies' toilet on the first floor of Eaglescliffe Masonic Hall. Next to me stood a man wearing a white lambskin apron and holding a sword, which he used to menace me.

'Get your clothes off ... and put your watch and rings in that tray.'

When a man threatens you with sword, it's sensible to take him seriously – and normally I am sensible. (Of course, you may think that nobody sensible would have got themselves into a fix like this, and perhaps you're right, but more of that later.) My immediate problem was to check that I hadn't misunderstood.

'Everything?' I asked. 'Is this some sort of ritual naked mugging?'

'No,' he said, his expression totally serious. 'You can keep your underpants on.'

'Thanks.'

As I pulled my trousers down, he produced what looked like a set of rough linen pyjamas.

'Put these on,' he ordered.

The light of the single bare light bulb sparkled from his sword as he pointed. I gulped but did as I was told.

This strange adventure began months earlier when I asked, 'What is the purpose of Freemasonry? Why do you enjoy it so much?'

My questions were met with counter-questions, my interest in joining the Order was tested, and, as I will explain, I was forced to decide if I was ready to think about the underlying nature of the world. Now, on the eve of my Initiation, I was being tested again. How far was I prepared to go to gain Masonic knowledge?

All the trappings of my social and academic status had been taken from me. I was left with my body, my intellect, a pair of underpants, a borrowed suit of rough white clothing and shoes that didn't fit. I also had my emotions: I felt ridiculous.

'Why do I need to wear such a strange get-up?' I ventured to ask the armed Mason who was supervising my preparation. His answer was blunt and unhelpful.

'This is how everybody comes in.'

Not until much later would I begin to understand what was done to me that night; at the time I felt confused, and even a little let down. I donned the rough linen pyjamas, then the swordsman opened my jacket to expose parts of my body and rolled up sleeves and trouser legs. I could see no rhyme or reason for his actions but he continued to fiddle with my flimsy rags until he was satisfied.

'Wait here,' he said, closing the door as he went out – as if I was likely to run out into the street and risk frostbite, or arrest for indecent exposure.

The muffled sound of hymn-singing drifted across the hallway. As a regular church organist I recognised the tune as '*Vienna*', but I couldn't make out the words.

The music was counterpointed by a sporadic rattle of crockery and pots coming from downstairs. The smell of boiling cabbage and cooking meat crept under the door. There I sat, stripped of my worldly possessions, wearing ill-fitting, borrowed clothes, serenaded by discordant hymn-singing, and with the aroma of roast beef to remind me how hungry I was.

The singing ended with a strange, disjointed chorus I did not recognise. It was followed by a flurry of knocking that seemed to echo round the ladies' convenience where I sat and pondered my fate.

Why did I get myself into this?

Do You Believe?

Well, to be honest, it was my girlfriend's fault.

'My mother's invited us to her Gentleman's Night at the Grosvenor Hotel,' she announced. 'Have you got a DJ?'

'Are we going to play records then?' I asked.

'Not a disc jockey, a dinner jacket,' she said. 'It's formal.'

'What's a Gentleman's Night?'

'It's a ceremonial dinner and dance organised by my mum's Masonic Lodge,' she said. 'The ladies invite men – normally gentlemen, but in your case she'll make an exception.'

'Your mother's a Freemason? A woman Freemason? I thought only men were Freemasons.'

'Well that shows just how little *you* know! She's been a Freemason for years. Anyway you'll enjoy it. Oh, and by the way you'll need a black tie.'

That is how I came into contact with Freemasonry, some forty years ago. That girlfriend became my wife, and when my mother-in-law died we inherited all her Masonic regalia and papers.

My first impression of Freemasonry was favourable. I enjoyed the ritual dining, in the plush surroundings of the Grosvenor Hotel, Chester. I enjoyed dressing up, wearing a white shirt, black tie and dinner jacket. And I enjoyed the archaic tradition of banging gavels and pounding on tables to call for silence. It felt solid, reliable and timeless. And the women involved took what they were doing seriously, displayed prodigious powers of memory and were at ease with themselves and each other.

Many years later I was living in a Yorkshire village. A male friend of mine joined the local lodge. My wife and I were invited to the Ladies' night, and we enjoyed the chance to resume going to formal dinner dances. I found again the traditional formality and ease of companionship that had impressed me at Gentlemen's Nights in Chester. Freemasonry seemed to be good social fun, and I was starting to get interested in it.

'What's it all about?' I asked my friend.

'The only way to find out is to join and experience it.'

So I asked to join Ryburn Lodge. I had taken my first step towards discovering just how peculiar a system Freemasonry is.

This peculiarity began to emerge when my friend, the late Bro. Mike, took me to one side as I prepared to give him my application form.

'Before you can hand that in, I need to talk to you about an important question. You'll have to come for an interview and answer it before we'll decide if you'll be allowed to join.'

'What's that?'

'When you come for interview you'll be asked if you believe in a supreme being.'

'Do you mean do I belong to a church?'

'No, that's not necessary,' he said. 'But you must accept that there is such a thing as a supreme being.'

'Can I think about my answer?'

By trade I am a scientist, and I found this question difficult to answer. It is ambiguous – with hindsight, I suspect deliberately so. I ended up doing considerable research before deciding how to answer, and I began by looking at the meanings of the words used.

According to the *Concise Oxford Dictionary*, 'being' is:

1. existence;
2. the nature or essence of;
3. a human being;
4. anything that exists or is imagined.

'Supreme' is defined as:

1. highest in authority;
2. greatest, most important;
3. involving death;
4. a rich cream sauce;
5. a dish in this sauce.

Often the term 'supreme being' is taken as a synonym for God. But the dictionary possibilities are wider. You could legitimately join if you believe in a deity who, though limited in power, is made of a rich cream sauce; this hypothetical supreme being might be called 'the custard god'. When I first saw this definition I wondered if this might be why Freemasonry is sometimes called 'the belly club' – certainly Hogarth's well-known series of Masonic etchings showing the Freemason with his distended belly still haunts many a festive board.

But a custard god is too weird for a scientist to accept, and anyway my wife keeps me on a diet. But, luckily, 'supreme being' can also mean the greatest nature or essence of existence that can be imagined; to me this is the 'Laws of Physics'.

This concept of supreme being was put forward in 1725, by Sir Isaac Newton in *Principia Mathematica*. He wrote:

> *The most beautiful system of the sun, planets, and comets, could only proceed from the counsel and dominion of an intelligent and powerful being. And if the fixed stars are the centres of like systems, these, being formed by the like wise counsel, must be all subject to the dominion of one; especially since the light of the fixed stars is of the same nature with the light of the sun, and from every system light passes into all the other systems; and lest the systems of fixed stars should, by their gravity, fall on each other, he hath placed those systems at immense distances from one another.*
>
> *This being governs all things, not as the soul of the world, but as Lord over all; and on account of his dominion he is wont to be called the Lord God or Universal Ruler, for God is a relative word, and has a respect to servants; and Deity is the dominion of God not over his own body, as those imagine who fancy God to be the soul of the world, but over servants. The Supreme Being is eternal, infinite, absolutely perfect, omnipotent and omniscient. ... We know him only by his most wise and excellent contrivances of things and final causes.* [1]

I found this is a powerful definition of supreme being. I showed it to Mike, who was going to propose me for membership of Ryburn Lodge, and asked him if it would be acceptable to Freemasonry. He read it through and looked me in the eye. His answer surprised me.

'What you believe is a matter for your conscience. It's not the concern of Freemasonry. We just want to know that you believe in something.'

He gave me some notes, which I later found to be a piece of ritual. They made clear how I might answer.

No man truly obeys the Masonic law who merely tolerates those whose religious opinions are opposed to his own. Every man's opinions are his own private property, and the rights of all men to maintain each his own are perfectly equal. Merely to tolerate, to bear with an opposing opinion, is to assume it to be heretical, and assert the right to persecute, if we would, and claim our toleration as a merit.

The Mason's creed goes further than that; no man, it holds, has any right, in any way, to interfere with the religious belief of another. It holds that each man is absolutely sovereign as to his own belief, and that belief is a matter absolutely foreign to all who do not entertain the same belief; and that if there were any right of persecution at all, it would in all cases be a mutual right, because one party has the same right as the other to sit as judge in his own case – and God is the only magistrate that can rightfully decide between them.

I was impressed with this creed of tolerance. As I read it I realised that this statement of Masonic belief requires only that the individual asking to join is seeking to understand his or her own place in the greater system of the universe.

The purpose of religions is to try and explain our place in the universe, and I accept that science has many features of a religion. In 1949 Albert Einstein wrote:

You will hardly find one among the profounder sort of scientific minds without a peculiar religious feeling of his own. But it is different from the religion of the naive man. For the latter, God is a being from whose care one hopes to benefit and whose punishment one fears; a sublimation of a feeling similar to that of a child for its father, a being to whom one stands to some extent in a personal relation, however deeply it may be tinged with awe. But the scientist is possessed by the sense of universal causation. The future, to him, is every whit as necessary and determined as the past. There is nothing divine about morality, it is a purely human affair. His religious feeling takes the form of a rapturous amazement at the harmony of natural law, which reveals an intelligence of such superiority that, compared with it, all the systematic thinking and acting of human beings is an utterly insignificant reflection. This feeling is the guiding principle of his life and work, in so far as he succeeds in keeping himself from the shackles of selfish desire. It is beyond question closely akin to that which has possessed the religious geniuses of all ages.[2]

If you are a scientist who is attracted by the fellowship and tolerant spirituality of the Craft, but are worried that you will be rejected because you are not a church-goer or a member of any particular religious faith, let me offer you a choice of definitions of 'supreme being' from two high priests of cosmological science. I find both of them deeply moving and inspiring, and fully identify with them; either will allow you to answer honestly the question which guards the entrance to Freemasonry.

Einstein: 'The harmony of natural law, which reveals an intelligence of such superiority that, compared with it, all the systematic thinking and acting of human beings is an utterly insignificant reflection.'

Newton: 'The most wise and excellent contrivance of things and final causes'.

Brother Mason, Martin Faulks, puts it like this:

The question about belief in a supreme being is asking if your knowledge of the universe has developed to a sufficient degree that you are able to understand that all things are one, all things are connected. There are many ways that one can come to this realisation/understanding without being a man of words. Our ancient Brethren were wise enough to avoid using the phrase 'Have you unified your understanding of the underlying workings of the universe?'. Unless you had come to this realisation by a strongly intellectual route you would never understand what was implied. Instead, since the dawn of time many have used the term god to relate their understanding of the wholeness of existence to the gestalt of life. The need to believe in a supreme being in Freemasonry is not due to the necessity to be fearful of the punishments of a god or indeed to have a holy book to live your life by. It is needed because you must be aware of the interrelated aspect of existence. You must know that you are part of existence, and to change yourself is to change existence. This is the route to true Masonic morality, when you realise that every being is one being. Pain to another is pain to you; if you cause pain to the world or to another animal you cause pain to yourself.

If I wanted to become a Freemason the first peculiar question I had to face up to was, did I believe that there was an order underlying the behaviour of the universe? Thinking my position through, I had no doubt. I could answer a truthful 'yes' to the admission question. And I did not have to compromise my scientific beliefs. This, then, is my definition of 'supreme being' – my scientist's creed if you like:

I believe in a number of immutable laws that apply throughout the whole of creation. These relate to the way matter behaves and are often called the Laws of Physics. They include such well-known relationships as the conservation of energy and mass and their interchangeability, the Heisenberg Uncertainty Principle, Fermi-Dirac statistics and the laws of thermodynamics. I believe that matter is made up of twelve fundamental particles, six quarks and six leptons. There are four forces, strong, weak, electromagnetic and gravitational. I also believe that forces are mediated by the exchange of particles. I accept the existence of twelve force-carrying particles and think there might also be a thirteenth, the graviton, but I'm not sure about that.

This world view is the standard model of physics. To accept it is to believe in a supreme order throughout the universe. Why there should be six varieties of quark and six varieties of lepton is not a matter of discussion. It is derived from experiments, and its acceptance leads to the type of universe which makes possible the evolution of an intelligent life form capable of asking 'Is there a supreme being within the structure of the universe?'

This supreme order gives me a comfortable world view. I expect DNA to be able to evolve, reproduce and give rise to living beings. I have no difficulty accepting that the twirly spirals of life mix and match like eels in a tub, to create our minds.

I was soon to find that Freemasonry teaches a deep truth about the way our minds work. But this can happen only in a universe where the interaction of fundamental particles follows known and reproducible paths. If the rules of interaction of atoms and molecules did not stay constant, our genes would not be able to reproduce the cells needed for our bodies to function.

Had I been asked to profess a belief that Jesus was a god, or that the Trinity made sense, I would have had to answer 'no' and would never have joined Freemasonry. In that case I would have missed out on a wonderful source of spiritual teaching and scientific inspiration. I suspect this may have happened to many potential recruits who would have benefited from joining the Craft, but who never found either Newton's or Einstein's definitions of the concept of supreme being.

A leading scientist of our generation adopts the metaphor of God (or supreme being) to explain his belief in the rule of order underlying the evolution of life. Stephen Hawking says:

> *If we discover a complete theory, it should in time be understandable in broad principle to everyone, not just a few scientists. Then we shall all, philosophers, scientists and just ordinary people be able to take part in the discussion of the question of why it is that we and the universe exist. If we find the answer to that, it would be the ultimate triumph of human reason – for then we would know the mind of God.* [3]

The first lesson that Freemasonry offers to the human spirit is to face up to your own perception of the purpose of the universe. Freemasonry makes its initiates experience things that are difficult, if not impossible, to put into words. It is a system of self-knowledge based in myth, allegory and symbolism – and in due course I would discover that it may even suggest an answer to the key question of modern science: 'Why does the universe go to the bother of existing?'

Over the ages, the Craft has evolved and refined its ritual forms to help its followers find answers to such questions. It may be that the absolute truth about ourselves cannot be expressed in language, and can only be revealed through symbols.

However, as I sat alone in the convenient room that is the ladies' lavatory adjacent to Ryburn Lodge I was about to discover that not only are the teachings of Freemasonry peculiar, so is its method of imparting its knowledge.

[1] Newton ([1725] 1934), p. 370.
[2] Einstein ([1949] 1956), p. 28.
[3] Hawking (1988), p. 175.

Chapter Two

Living the First Degree

Into Darkness

On that chilly winter night my lack of proper clothing was bringing me out in goose bumps. I looked down at my naked breast and could clearly see it shivering.

In the distance muffled conversations were audible; the sounds of different voices creeping under the closed door were overlaid with the rattle of cutlery coming up the stairs. I was alone, pondering the wisdom of seeking Masonic Initiation.

Whatever was going on, it was clear that I wasn't going to be told about it until it suited the Lodge. It felt like hours before anything happened, but was probably not more than twenty minutes.

Then there was a flurry of activity in the passageway. The door opened, and the man with the sword was back. This time he brought two apron-wearing mates with him, and they had ornate broom poles in their hands. Now what?

'Have you got him ready?' one of them asked the swordsman, who nodded.

The man with the pole looked at me and muttered to himself. 'Right ... arm, breast, knee, heel.'

'Pardon?' I said. He ignored me and spoke to the swordsman.

'He'll do. Black him out.'

The swordsman produced a black mask which he tied around my eyes, checking carefully to make sure that I couldn't see anything. Then he fumbled with the neck of my rough jacket until he was satisfied.

'He'll do.' I heard another voice say.

Somebody took my arm and guided me towards the door. I heard the voice of the man with the pole saying, 'Sound an alarm.'

First a knock and then a conversation between the swordsman and another voice followed. I heard myself described as 'Mr Robert Lomas, a poor traveller through a vale of darkness, who has been selected, submitted and sanctioned by an assembled lodge, and who now offers of his own volition to become part of the mysteries and privileges of Freemasonry'.

Mysteries and privileges? What might that mean? As the door closed I stood in the hallway, alone in my darkness. Then, as I felt a light touch on my arm to guide me forward, I found Einstein's words on mystery running through my mind.

The fairest thing we can experience is the mysterious. It is the fundamental emotion which stands at the cradle of true art and true science. He who knows it not and can no longer wonder, no longer feel amazement, is as good as dead, a snuffed-out candle. It was the experience of mystery — even if mixed with fear — that engendered religion. A knowledge of the existence of something we cannot penetrate, of the manifestations of the profoundest reason and the most radiant beauty, which are only accessible to our reason in their most elementary forms — it is this knowledge and this emotion that constitute the truly religious attitude.[1]

I was experiencing mystery in full. All the normal props of my daily existence had gone. I did not know what to expect and had no access to my normal visual ways of anticipation.

When I teach, I observe body language to help me decide how to respond to my students. I judge the effect of my words by the changing posture of their recipients — at least I do when I'm not blindfolded. But as I waited at the door of the Lodge I couldn't tell if the men with me were amused, disgusted or indifferent. The opportunities for making a fool of myself were multiplying by the second. Small wonder I could feel the excitement of adrenalin raising my state of awareness.

I forced myself to concentrate. The muffled voices behind the closed door stopped. The door creaked as it opened, and I felt the warm air from the room flowing outward across the hairs of my naked breast. I could feel my nipple tingling, reflecting the excitement of my mind as I sensed that the room held many people. My audience could see me, but I could only hear them. A slight shuffling suggested eyes turning in my direction. I felt vulnerable. I was being forced into a receptive state despite my inner resolve not to be cowed.

I felt a slight touch on my breast. It felt cold and prickly, like a spine or point. I stood still and waited. A new voice spoke from in front of me.

'Pass into this Lodge in the name of the Great Architect of the Universe'.

I sensed the owner of the voice step back. The two men who had come out to fetch me stood either side and, taking my elbows, guided me into the room. A voice came from the far end of the room. It sounded like one of the men who had interviewed me.

'You cannot become a Mason, unless you are free born and of mature age. I therefore ask, are you free by birth and of twenty-one years?'

I was prompted by the man holding my left elbow, who whispered, 'I am.'

I'm used to public speaking – I regularly address up to a couple of hundred students – but I found it hard to judge the impact my voice would make in these circumstances. I was surprised how much I need visual feedback to adjust my articulation.

With as firm a tone as I could manage I said, 'I am.'

It must have carried OK, because the distant voice spoke again.

'To order, Brethren.' A clattering and shuffling impinged from every side as the Brethren ordered themselves. Whatever they were doing, it was noisy.

'The blessing of the celestial regions will be called down on our proceedings. You will kneel to receive it.'

That sounded like a command. The increase in ambient noise suggested there was quite an audience for what I was doing. But what was I to kneel on? I had no way of seeing. Should I reach out with my hand to check?

While I hovered uncertainly the man on my left guided me down on to something which felt like a low cushion. I was prompted by his unseen hand until I was kneeling on both knees – one bare, one cased in rough linen. A different voice spoke from the far end of the room.

'Aid us, Supreme Ruler of the Universe, at this inaugural meeting, and ensure that this traveller towards the light of Freemasonry, who now kneels before us, may so consecrate his life to become a true and faithful member of our Order. Grant him such understanding of thy divine will that, aided by knowledge of our Masonic skill, he may the better be helped to discover the resplendence of true spiritual insight to the honour and glory of thy holy law.'

As he finished, a chorus of voices sounded out a strange response:

'So mote it be.'

There followed a series of questions which I was prompted to answer before I was allowed to stand up. By now my knees were beginning to feel the strain. I felt sure that the weave of the fabric of the cushion must be imprinted on the skin of my bare left knee. But I couldn't see it, and my arms were held by the men on either side of me. My feeling of vulnerability was increasing, as I'm sure it was intended to. I was being subjected to a steadily increasing crescendo of emotion to imprint on my mind the first clue about what Freemasonry teaches.

But that peak was still a long way off. First I had to stumble on in my personal darkness, searching for help to find light.

The voice from the far end of the room explained to the audience what I was about to do for their amusement.

'The Brethren stationed at the various points of the compass will take note that Mr Lomas is about to travel before them to demonstrate due cause that he is properly prepared to become a Mason. Brethren, be seated.'

The hand gripping my left elbow urged me to stand. I was turned to my left and led forward a few steps, stopped and rotated to my right.

'Step forward with your left foot first,' came a whisper in my ear. We did this twice more before my guide drew me to a stop.

'Spread out the fingers of your right hand,' he whispered. Taking hold of my arm he waved my hand so that it flapped against something givingly human. The object spoke.

'Who proceeds hither?' it said in a voice I recognised as Ken, my seconder. Now Ken is not over endowed with cranial hair, and as he spoke I imagined I must have been tapping his bald pate with my hand. No time to worry about that now, though. My guide was answering on my behalf – I was certainly being shown a culture of total dependency. What was he saying about me?

'Mr Robert Lomas, a poor traveller through a vale of darkness, who has been selected, submitted and sanctioned by an assembled lodge, and who now offers of his own volition to become part of the mysteries and privileges of Freemasonry.'

Ken spoke again. 'How does he aspire to achieve those privileges?'

(I felt as if I was having an audio out-of-body experience, listening as I was talked about in the third person.)

Again my guide answered, 'With the support of the Sacred Law and the accumulation of good reports.'

A gloved hand took mine and squeezed it reassuringly. Ken's voice said, 'Go forward, good report,' and the hand lifted mine over some source of heat before returning it to the guide.

Again we set off in stumbling squared laps round the room, stopping to turn a right angle at regular intervals until we reached some unseen destination.

Once more I performed the puppet-like taps, on what I felt was somebody's head, and once more I was introduced and handed on.

By now I was certain of one thing. I *was* a poor traveller in a state of darkness.

Moreover, being deprived of sight, I had little choice but to listen carefully. And a message was being hammered home by repetition.

But if I was travelling through the mystery of darkness, what privileges lay hidden in the light?

This time something different happened, I was not sent on my stumbling, fumbling way. The man, whose head I thought I had recently tapped, took me by the hand and led me forward, turning me round to face towards the voice at the far end of the room. He spoke for the benefit of my unseen audience.

'Brother Master. Let me introduce you to Mr Robert Lomas, a poor traveller through a vale of darkness, who has been selected, submitted and sanctioned by an assembled lodge, and who now offers of his own volition to become part of the mysteries and privileges of Freemasonry.'

There it was again: mysteries and privileges. By now I felt that just to see who was talking to me would feel like a privilege. Mysterious voices and an unseen audience, shifting and shuffling in the background, were making a dramatic point. How often would this assessment of my poor state of darkness be repeated to me?

But this time there was more, something new was added on the end of the well-worn introduction. The man holding my arm paused, either for breath or dramatic effect, before adding, 'For which ceremony he is now made ready.'

Made ready? Totally disorientated might be a closer description. Softened up by sensory deprivation. Deliberately stripped of all my normal social support mechanisms, my clothing, my wallet, my watch, my pocket PC, my mobile phone, my badges of rank. Forced to travel pointless paths, to stumble towards unknown destinations, having to trust guides I didn't know and be introduced to silent people who spoke only when I tapped them on the head – and then only to remind me of my poor state of darkness, as if I might not have noticed that I couldn't see them.

What was the purpose of this charade? Was I about to get some clue? The voice from the far end spoke. He was asking me questions.

I focused my only useful sense towards the far end of the room, hoping by more intense listening to understand something … anything.

'Mr Lomas. Do you seriously confirm, on your honour, that unmoved by improper inducements of outsiders, or against your own feelings and neither from monetary gain or any other unworthy motive, you freely confirm yourself as a traveller seeking the light of Freemasonry this evening?'

Nobody forced me to be here. I undressed myself and put this rough and ridiculous suit on, without the swordsman actually threatening me. I'd asked Mike if I could join, and then spent over three months deciding if I could give a truthful answer to what most people thought was a simple question.

In my academic job, being a Freemason might well be a disadvantage. It isn't cool, it isn't hip, it isn't trendy.

And are my motives unworthy? I'd been attracted by the easy sociability and a comradeship which seemed to underlie Masonry. Is that unworthy? I don't think so.

My answer is obvious.

'Yes.'

Wrong!

My answer provokes a bout of noisy shuffling among my unseen audience.

The man holding my elbow prompts me in a whisper, 'I do.'

Sounds like I'm getting married. He nudges me, so I repeat in a loud, lecturing type of voice, which I intend to project all round the room.

'I do.'

This is more satisfactory; the audience settles into quietness and disappears off my audio map.

More questions? The voice from the far end speaks again.

'Do you also confirm that you have been induced to seek those privileges from a good opinion of our Order, a desire for knowledge, and a deeply felt wish to make yourself more generally useful to humanity?'

I'd asked to join because I was curious. Here was an organisation which seemed to improve its members' peace of mind, something not common in my current calling of university lecturer. I'd seen how much my wife's mother had enjoyed her Masonry, and I'd felt a spiritual warmth at the social occasions I'd attended over the years. This gave me a favourable opinion of Freemasonry. Moreover, I had a desire for knowledge – that's a prerequisite for becoming a science PhD. And nobody goes into university lecturing for the money; you have to want to teach and research. But did this mean I wanted to be generally useful to humanity? Perhaps it did.

I knew the form. I didn't need prompting.

'I do,' I said in clear, ringing tones. I was proud of the resonant timbre of that reply and felt I was playing the unseen audience better. No shuffling and sub-vocal wittering this time. Was I learning something?

But there was more. The far-end orator hadn't finished his interrogation:

'Do you also pledge that, subduing anxiety on the one hand and audacity on the other, you will steadily persist through the journey of your Initiation, and that, if accepted, you will always act by the ancient usages and accepted customs of the Order?'

I hadn't experienced any anxiety yet. Uneasiness, a need to rethink, a query about how to respond? But was I tending towards audacious rashness in the way I was already attempting to adapt my tone of voice to try to appease the responses of my unseen audience? It felt like doing a radio interview down a telephone, where I couldn't see the interviewer's body language as I spoke. I certainly didn't intend to stop now.

I felt like the Duchess in *Alice In Wonderland*. Lewis Carroll was a Freemason – why else would his rabbit wear white gloves, and why else would he use a pseudonymous forename meaning, 'son of a Mason'? Perhaps it was during his Initiation he got the idea for practising how to believe in impossible things. The more I practised the easier it got.

Was this what I was supposed to be learning?

Would I abide by the ancient usages and accepted customs of the Order? If it led me towards spiritual warmth, why not?

'I do,' I replied.

My answer seemed satisfactory, although I couldn't help wondering what the Lodge would have done if I'd said no. I suspect it never happens, because there were no surprises. Now I saw how I'd been sounded out before I got to this stage.

But a ritual re-asking of key questions, while I was disorientated and off balance, made me think carefully about my answers.

Now what? Was I going to find out about these mysterious privileges?

Apparently not. I had to travel through further darkness first. The far voice instructed the keeper of my elbow to 'advance the traveller to the East in due form', whatever due form might be.

I soon found out. Once more I was led to my left, stopped and turned through a right angle before being walked forward. But this time I was swayed to and fro by my guides. I felt as if I was aboard a ship at sea as we rolled along together. At last we stopped, with me disorientated and off balance.

I was turned to my left. The room went quiet. A sense of anticipation built up in the slight rustling of my unseen audience.

The voice, now known as Brother Master, spoke.

'Mr Lomas. It is my responsibility to acquaint you with the

knowledge that Masonry is free and demands a perfect liberty of desire on the part of every traveller towards its central mysteries. It is built upon the virtuous precepts of ethical motive and moral excellence. It features many precious privileges to worthy men, and to worthy men only. Affiances of commitment are, however, required. But let me assure you that in those oaths there is nothing uncommensurate with your moral, civil or spiritual responsibilities.'

Brother Master coughed to clear his throat before continuing.

'Are you, consequently, willing to enter into a sober responsibility, founded firmly upon the principles I have already mentioned, to keep unimpaired the secrets of our Order?' He waited, expecting an answer. I instantly obliged.

'I do.'

The man holding my left elbow whispered to me: 'I am.' The unseen audience rustled and shuffled.

'I am,' I corrected myself. The rustling subsided.

Whatever other mysteries there are in Freemasonry, trying to second-guess the form of words the Lodge wants to hear when its Master asks a question is the most puzzling to my state of poor darkness. At least that's what I thought, until I experienced the oddest postural instruction I'd yet known.

I heard the words ... but what did they mean? Could I twist my body into such an odd position?

Unseen hands moved my body into the most unnatural posture I had ever adopted since I gave up courting in an Austin Healey Sprite. Goodness knows what strange species of endorphins were released into my brain as I struggled to keep my body still, using only the kinetic feedback of my stretched muscles to judge what was happening. My audience wasn't rustling any disapproval, so I must be doing it right. The book I was holding in this odd manner was bulky. It felt as if it was bound in embossed leather.

A slight shuffling, and a matching upward shift in the source of his voice, suggested to my useless eyes that Brother Master had risen to his feet. He must be after some sort of dramatic impact on the audience. I use gesture and movement to dramatise a point when lecturing, so no mystery there, but I was surprised at what he was about to dramatise.

He began simply, giving an order to the Lodge.

'Brethren, to order.' Then he spoke to me.

'Repeat your complete and full names in their entirety, and say after me I, Paul Powell in the presence of the Great Architect of the Universe, and of this worthful and venerable lodge of antient free and accepted Masons ...'

Paul Powell? Paul was managing director of a successful local engineering firm. He'd been on the panel which interviewed me before I was allowed to apply to join. My first impression of Paul was that he was used to having his orders obeyed.

He waited for me to repeat the sentence, which I did, substituting my name in place of his. As I finished he continued, 'Duly established, frequently held, gathered together, and decently devoted to the Sacred Law, do hereby and hereon, of my own free volition and intention ...' Once more he waited for me to repeat the words after him before continuing.

'Most solemnly promise, vow and swear that I will forever hele, keep, conceal and never reveal ...'

What does 'hele' mean? How binding can an oath be if it uses words I don't know the meaning of? Should I stop and ask for an explanation of the small print? Perhaps not; the context suggested 'hele' was a variation on 'hide'. It would only provoke more rustling, and I was getting fascinated by how many wordy triplets or quadruplets Paul would reel off before getting to the point. (I later checked 'hele' in the dictionary and found it to be a verb meaning to set in the ground and cover over. Eventually this would prove useful in helping me to understand what this ritual was trying to convey. But it didn't when I heard it this first time.)

While I was pondering, the relentless speech triplets continued, now adding a duplex timbre, an interior beat to the rhythm:

'... any piece or pieces, arcanum or arcana, enigma or enigmas of, or at all existing within this the First Degree in Freemasonry, usually known as the Entered Apprentice Degree ...'

I repeated the phrase, enjoying the rhythmic cadence as I rolled the words round my tongue. We must be getting near the end of this ritual.

My feet were really aching, and my elbow felt constricted. Dare I move to relieve my muscular tension? I felt sure it would provoke sharp intakes of breath, as well as shuffling, from my quiet yet critical audience, so I kept still and stayed cramped.

Onward orated Brother Master Paul, plumbing new pinnacles of peculiar patois:

'... to anyone in creation, unless it be to a genuine and legitimate Brother or Brethren, and not even unto him or them until after appropriate testing, rigorous scrutiny, and a complete belief, that he or they be deserving of that trust ...'

I duly repeated the qualifying small print of the obligation, amazed at the pedantry of its wording.

But there was more. My left arm felt as if it was turning into lead.

'... or in the assemblage of a lodge virtuous, consummate and uniform.'

Have we done? Is this the last over-wordy, over-engineered phrase I have to parrot? No. Brother Master had just got his second wind.

'I further seriously commit that I will not write those confidences, profile, sculpt, delineate, inscribe, or otherwise them record, or encourage or endure it to be so done by others, if in my power to prevent it, on anything static or fluid beneath the celestial sphere, whereby or whereon any missive, graphic symbol, or shape, or the least trace of a missive, graphic symbol, or shape, may become decipherable, or understandable to myself or any one in the world, so that our secret arts and hidden mysteries may inappropriately become known through my despicableness.'

If this didn't end soon I was going to have to move my left arm. Ever since I smashed the elbow in a horse-riding accident I've had trouble articulating my left wrist, and the position my arm was in, holding the book open at a right angle, was excruciating.

I forced myself to concentrate as Paul continued his relentless destruction of the Plain English Society's guidelines.

'These several points I solemnly swear to observe, without hedging, prevarication, or mental reserve of any devious nature, under no less a consequence, on the infringement of any of them, than that of having my throat rent asunder, my tongue forcibly removed and my worthless body buried on such a part of a beach where the tide doth ebb and flow ...'

Now this was sounding serious. A cramped elbow and aching legs were small beer in comparison.

I enjoy visiting the seaside as much as anyone, but having my throat rent asunder and my tongue extracted without anaesthetic before going paddling permanently, that sounded serious. If the Lodge decided to exact this penalty, it might smart more than a little. Was I ready for this?

Of course I was. The Health and Safety Inspectorate would never permit this archaic procedure to be used today. But what a wonderful way to focus my mind on the seriousness of the message. Surely this had to be the climax of the speechifying, though?

Oh no it wasn't.

'… or the more telling discipline of being denounced as an intentionally perjured liar, lacking all ethical value, and completely unsuitable to be accepted into this lodge, or any other warranted lodge, or society of men who revere honour and virtue above the trappings of rank and fortune. So help me, Great Architect, and keep me constant in this my major and most sober duty as an Entered Apprentice Freemason.'

Obviously they didn't intend to cut my throat if I accidentally let too much slip. But they were warning me that their tutting could get much worse than it had this evening.

Now would they let me straighten my aching legs and cramped arm?

I waited in darkness for permission to move. It didn't come.

I had been blindfolded for so long that even the multi-coloured after-images from my retina had long faded into pure blackness. How much longer was I going to have to stumble around in the dark? I heard a faint clanking, like small metal plates knocking together, as Brother Master fidgeted. (It sounded as if he was wearing armour. Surely not? Would I ever find out?)

He cleared his throat once more. I was surprised he hadn't stopped for a drink of water.

'To execute this, which as yet may be considered but a worthy pledge, a constraint upon your moral sense as a most sober obligation so long as you shall live, I command you to honour it once with the touch of your lips on the Volume of the Sacred Law.'

I wonder which particular volume of the sacred law they are using. My personal choice, and the one I would find most binding, would be a copy of *Principia Mathematica*. But I hadn't been consulted. The idea of a volume of the sacred law to underpin my individual concept of supreme being had not been mentioned before the ceremony.

The room went quiet while I hesitated. But I decided there was no point in fussing about detail now; the gesture was a symbolic statement of good intent. Whatever book the Lodge used, I knew which volume of the sacred law contained my truth.

I bowed my head towards the heavy book, smelling a mixture of leather and slightly musty paper as my lips approached it. I kissed the unknown book. My unseen audience drew a collective breath, loud to the sensitised hearing of my blind state.

Brother Master spoke again.

'Having travelled so far in conditions of darkness, what is now the preponderant desire of your spirit?'

Should I guess? My predominant wish was to straighten my legs and stretch. But the tenor of the question seemed to suggest a different answer.

I was learning to be cautious, so I waited for a prompt from the man standing at my left. He duly obliged, and I repeated, 'Light.'

I waited. I could feel a sense of anticipation building, there was rustle of movement about the room as though my hidden watchers were readying themselves for some expected event.

The voice of worshipful Paul rang out, reaching a dramatic crescendo.

'Let the boon of light be bestowed on the traveller.'

I heard a rhythmic creaking moving round the room in synchronised waves.

As the blindfold was ripped from my eyes a muffled clap sounded from the watchers. The light in the room was so bright on my fully dilated irises that I found it hard to focus. The single clap, performed by about forty white-gloved men had a surreal sound.

I blinked and screwed up my eyes, trying to focus. Before me, was that the lugubrious face of local businessman Paul Powell surrounded by a bright halo of light? He was wearing an elaborate uniform of blue and white. Behind him was some sort of ornate carved wooden chair with a triangular headrest. I was struggling to see any detail in the brightness of the light.

Was it over? Was I now a Mason?

Paul spoke again.

'You having been reinstated in the discernment of physical light, I am able to direct your attention to three major landmarks in the journey of Freemasonry, ...'

He pointed to an open Bible on the desk between us, 'namely the Volume of the Sacred Law, ... '

Next he pointed to what looked like a builder's set square and a set of dividers lying on the open book. '... the Square and the Compasses. ...'

He paused for a breath while I looked at the objects he called landmarks. I was hoping I would soon be able to stand up. But he had more to say about them before I was to be allowed to move.

'The Volume of the Sacred Law to regulate and guide our spiritual contemplation; the Square to modulate how we behave; and the Compasses to keep us within proper limits with all people.'

He took my hand and helped me to my feet.

'Rise, newly obligated Entered Apprentice Freemason.'

Rising was something I was glad to do. Thankfully, I stood up and stretched my legs. Kneeling with my feet in such a strained posture was neither a natural or comfortable position to maintain for any length of time.

But the enforced darkness and uncomfortable stance made sure that I paid attention during the ceremony.

Now for the first time I was to see the interior of a lodge in session.

A Great Light

For some twenty minutes I had been blindfolded and walked around an unseen obstacle course. Next I'd been cramped into a distorted foetal position for another quarter of an hour. Finally I had been blinded by the light of the lodge-room and disorientated by a great clapping noise as the hoodwink was ripped from my eyes.

In this state of impressionability I was shown a book, a builder's square and a set of dividers and told these were the three most important objects in Freemasonry. Were they the lights I had travelled round and round the Lodge's dark circumference, waymarked by its compass points, to discover? Only then was I allowed to stand up and stretch my cramped limbs.

There was a sudden movement as the be-aproned men standing round the sides of the room sat down, leaving me standing by the owner of the voice I had been calling Worshipful Master.

Now I could see that it was indeed Paul Powell.

He turned me round to face into the centre of the room.

On the floor was a black and white chequered carpet, looking like a giant chess board. It was lit from above by a bright light set within a high dome positioned in the ceiling of the room. Its light was partly shrouded by shining through a five-pointed star with a letter G at its centre.

As I faced the lodge-room Paul began to speak.

In my state of darkness I had wondered if the men doing the ceremony were reading from notes. Their speech seemed strangely formal, but now my eyes were open I could see they were quoting from memory. Paul continued his recitation, pointing to the requisite parts of the lodge-room as he spoke.

'Now your sight has been restored, I point out to you three lesser lights in Freemasonry, seen burning in the south, the west, and the east, symbolically representing the Sun, the Moon, and the Master of the Lodge: the sun to govern the day, the moon to oversee the night, and the Master to teach his Lodge.'

At each of the points he indicated an ornate chair with a small desk in front of it. The astronomical references in his speech showed the sun in the south (which would suggest meridian or noon point), the moon was in the west (so it was setting), while the Master was placed in the east at the point of sunrise. I could see now that during my blindfold travels I had been moved around the Lodge following the path of the sun: rising in the east, moving to the zenith in the south, setting in the west before traversing the nadir of the north to return to the brightness of the east. When my blindfold was removed I was looking east towards the Master, and, with my eyes fully dilated and sensitised by the long period of darkness, I had seen Worshipful Master Paul looking as bright as the rising sun. Was this intentional?

Paul interrupted my thoughts as he started to speak again.

'By your humble and forthright demeanour this evening, you have, symbolically escaped a great hazard, but there is another which awaits you until the latest period of your life. The danger you have escaped is that of impalement, for on your entrance into the Lodge, this dagger ...'

The man who had recently been holding my left elbow passed him a large shiny dagger, which Paul showed me with some relish. It looked as if it was kept sharp. But I was in no position to split hairs. Now I understood the prickling I felt against my nipple as I stood in the doorway to the Lodge. Having brandished the knife before my vulnerable and exposed chest Paul continued:

'... was presented to your naked breast, to symbolise that, had you recklessly sought to force yourself forward, you would have been the agent of your own demise by impalement; not so, however, the Brother who held it, he would only have stayed solid whilst carrying out his responsibility.'

Paul hadn't finished his litany of perils.

'But a more serious threat which would have awaited you at the latest period of your existence, is the physical penalty associated with the obligation of a Mason had you inappropriately revealed the mysteries of Masonry.'

He paused for dramatic effect, waiting until the silence became uncomfortable.

'That of having your throat rent asunder, your tongue forcibly removed and your worthless body buried on such a part of a beach where the tide doth ebb and flow.'

A quick vision of the tide coming in on my favourite beach flitted across my mind, whilst I pictured my bloodied corpse lapped by the water. This powerful image burned the next statement into my memory.

'The sacred promise you have entered into this evening will bind your conscience for as long as you shall live.'

Now I was a Mason ... for the rest of my life, it would seem.

But had I changed?

Everything Changes?

Was this all there was to Masonic Initiation? Where were the part or parts, secret or secrets, mystery or mysteries of this First Degree in Freemasonry? So far I'd been blindfolded, paraded about and then dazzled and deafened before being shown two sets of lights − and symbolic lights at that. Where were the secrets?

What had Paul called the main lights? The sacred laws, the square and compasses. The laws of physics underpin the interactions of all bodies, large and small, in the universe. The square is an instrument for measuring and testing right angles, the right angle being the key direction which separates vector interaction between physical dimensions. The compasses − or dividers as I knew them − are a measuring instrument for determining and replicating distances. If I were asked to state the three key principles of the physicist's craft, they would be the basic laws, the independence of the dimensions and the ability to measure accurately. So had I been given some deep secrets in poetic, rather than scientific, terms?

There had been some lesser lights as well. What were they? The zenith sun, the setting moon, and the Master of the Lodge, backlit by the radiance of dawn. The two brightest objects in the sky were being shown to me in dramatic settings, and the implication was that a man, backlit by the dawn, knew something about these objects and how they might affect me.

I had been taken round the Lodge tracing the apparent path of these objects around the points of the compass. I would have called the compasses dividers, so I wondered if the choice of word to describe them, compasses, was meant to make me reflect on the movement of the lights in the sky about the compass points of the world?

The purpose of Freemasonry was far from clear, but there did seem to be an underlying pattern to the information I was being given.

Would it continue?

Paul spoke again.

'You having now entered into the major cogent and sober commitment or responsibility of an Entered Apprentice Freemason. I am authorised to communicate to you that Masonry consists of several Degrees with peculiar secrets restricted to each. These secrets, however, are not bestowed upon travellers indiscriminately but according to merit and ability.'

What particular merit or ability did I need, though? When I'd tried to answer the questions in my own words I'd been tutted at. And the ritual didn't seem to involve much ability beyond a good memory, so how were the members of the Lodge going to assess my ability? I waited for Paul to tell me more.

'I shall now venture to confide in you the secrets peculiar to this Degree, but must first stipulate, for your general improvement, that all squares, levels and perpendiculars are dependable and indisputable signs by which to know a Brother.'

Paul came out from behind his desk. Roger, another of the men who had interviewed me, was sitting in the chair alongside him. He stood up, and took Paul's right hand. Paul came down from the chair holding on to Roger's hand while Roger shuffled passed him, keeping a tight grip on his hand, to sit in the vacant seat. Having seated Roger, Paul moved over to stand in front of me.

I stood at least four inches taller than Paul, who now stood looking up at me from the chequered carpet. He looked formal in his blue-and-white apron, light blue collar and dark suit. Now I could see what had caused the clanking noise. Hanging from the collar around his neck was a complex silver ornament made up of squares and triangles. It looked like a geometrical diagram of Pythagoras's theorem.

'You will therefore stand to me perfectly erect, with your feet in a form I will demonstrate to you.'

I stood up straight and looked at how Paul was standing. I took a deep breath and copied his difficult posture. No tutting from the massed observers around the sides of the room. I must have it right.

I felt awkward and off balance. This was similar to the way my feet had been arranged while I knelt for the ritual of the obligation. Now standing in this position felt even odder. My immovable feet wouldn't allow any relief either forwards or backwards. My feet were braced against each other, inhibiting the slight movements which I would normally use to keep me balanced. This way of standing felt unnatural and designed to promote tension in my legs. It was a posture I had to concentrate to maintain. Was this another ritual device to induce the release of stress hormones into my bloodstream and so modulate my brain?

I concentrated on what Paul was saying.

'That is called the first uniform step in Freemasonry, and it is in that position and that alone that the secrets of this Degree are expressed.'

Paul paused and looked up into my eyes.

'They consist of a sign, a token or grip, and a word.'

These three things, the United Grand Lodge of England confirms, are the secrets of the Degree. As I am obligated not to reveal them,

I will move on and relate what happened after they were given to me.

My first thought was, if those are the secrets, what a waste of time. A sign I can't make in public, a handshake that will convince people I'm trying to keep in touch with my feminine side and a word which every reader of the Bible knows. Some secrets! I had been told far deeper things when Paul pointed out the three great lights and the three lesser lights.

All the same, I have no wish to cause pollution on innocent tidal beaches, so I will not reveal these useless surface secrets. I was beginning to understand that the true secrets of Freemasonry cannot be given away, nor stolen nor impersonated. They have to be lived. As the author Gloria Steinem once said: 'Tell me, and I'll forget. Show me, and I may not remember. Involve me and I'll understand.'

The ritual of Freemasonry works by involving its students in a spiritual experience. When you do it, reflect on what you have done, and on what you felt while you were doing it … then you may begin to understand.

Let me now pick up the story of my Initiation a safe distance from any risk to my throat and tongue.

Suffice it to say that, having trained me in the ritual delivery of these three 'secrets', Paul told the man who had acted as my guide during the dark period to 'Convey Brother Lomas to the Junior Warden.'

Hmm … *Brother* Lomas now.

Once more I travelled round and round the lodge-room, moving from the sunrise of the Master's chair to the meridian of the Junior Warden, to the sunset of the Senior Warden before returning via the darkness of the northern horizon. But unlike the sun, I made square turns on each point of the compass.

During these travels I was tested in my ability to repeat the signs, tokens and grips by each of the seated Wardens. By the time I ended up facing Master Paul from the west end of the Lodge, I had practised the secret means of identification three times. When both Wardens were satisfied I could grip, stand and remember the word, I was ready for the next stage of the ceremony.

The Warden in the west stood up and took hold of my right hand. He was a small bird-like man with a rather squeaky voice and a pencil-thin moustache. I felt a little uncomfortable about the easy way in which a succession of grown men took hold of my hand and led me about; it made me feel childlike. Was the ritual *meant* to make me feel this way?

Bird-man nodded to Master Paul and spoke loudly, keeping a tight hold on my right hand – presumably to make sure I stood still.

'Brother Master. I introduce to you Brother Lomas on his Initiation for a token of your approbation.'

The guy with the pole, who'd guided me round in the dark, seemed to be fumbling behind the Warden's back. Was he passing him something? I concentrated on what Paul was saying.

'Brother Senior Warden. I will heed your introduction, and I authorise you to invest Brother Lomas with the distinguishing apron of an Entered Apprentice Freemason.'

The man Paul had addressed as senior warden now spoke to me.

'Brother Lomas. By command of the Worshipful Master, I invest you with the distinguishing apron of an Entered Apprentice Freemason.'

He whipped from behind his back a white leather pinny with two strips of fabric; these he wrapped around my waist and tied in a neat bow at the front. His action made me feel even more childlike: it was rather like having my mother tie my shoelaces. Having secured the laces, he lifted the triangular flap, standing it upwards like a pointed tongue before standing back. He looked me up and down and smiled before continuing.

'It is more ancient than the golden fleece or Roman eagle, more honourable than the star and garter or any other Order in existence. It is the badge of innocence and the bond of friendship, and I give it to you in the strongest terms of recommendation, ever to consider and wear it as such; and if you never disgrace this apron, it will never disgrace you.'

Were we talking about Jason's golden fleece or the medieval order of chivalry here? There's at least fifteen hundred years' difference in the impressiveness of the claims. But the Lodge left no opportunity for clarification. The ritual rolled on remorselessly with Paul picking up the oration.

'Brother Lomas. Allow me to add to the remarks already made by my Brother Senior Warden, that you are never to put on that apron and enter a lodge wherein there is any Brother with whom you are at variance, or against whom you entertain any feelings of animosity. In such case it is expected that you will invite him to retire in order that your differences may be amicably settled; which, if happily effected, you may then clothe yourselves, enter the lodge and work with that love and harmony which should at all times characterise Freemasons. If, unhappily, your differences be of such a nature as not to be so easily adjusted, it were better that either one, or both of you retire, rather than that the harmony of the lodge should be disturbed by your presence.'

This seemed to be good, homespun philosophy, even if phrased in archaic language: don't bring your quarrels into your hobby time, or you'll just upset everybody else and do yourself no good. Sensible but not earth-shattering. Why did I need to wear a pointed leather pinny to do it?

Paul was speaking again. Perhaps he might explain.

'Brother Senior Warden. You will now order the Junior Deacon to place Brother Lomas in the north-east corner of the Lodge where the address will be given by Brother Astore.'

Mike Astore had sponsored me to come into Freemasonry. Would he now tell me something which would help me understand what all these amateur dramatics were supposed to be doing to me? Senior Warden spoke.

'Brother Junior Deacon. By command of the Worshipful Master you will now place Brother Lomas in the north-east corner of the Lodge.'

The grey-haired man with the pole stepped forward and took my hand. Once more we set off, to the whispered command of 'left foot first', following the path of the sun around the compass points of the Lodge. Why the north-east compass point? This is where the sun rises on the longest day of the year. Was there some reason for this which would be explained when I arrived?

Junior Deacon stood alongside me holding his pole loosely upright in his left hand. Mike stood in front of me. His rimless glasses flashed in the lights from the roof of the temple as he nodded to himself. I winked at him, but he kept his face straight and serious. He seemed to be concentrating hard and composing himself. Only after he had finished would I realise he was focusing his memory for a long speech. Then he began.

'Brother Lomas. When beginning the work on all imposing and superior buildings, it is traditional to lay the first, or foundation stone, in the north-east corner of the building. You, being newly initiated into Freemasonry are placed in the north-east corner of the Lodge, symbolically to exemplify that stone, and, from the foundation laid this evening, may you raise a superstructure, perfect in all its parts, a living stone honourable to the builder.

'You stand, to all extrinsic semblances, an equitable and conscionable man, and an Entered Apprentice Freemason, and I give it to you, in the strongest terms of recommendation, ever to continue and act as such. Indeed I shall immediately proceed to put your principles in some measure to the test, by calling upon you to exercise that virtue which may be justly denominated the leading characteristic of a Freemason's heart, I mean, charity … '

I won't recount the whole long address. Having completed it, though, Mike smiled, stood back, turned to face Paul and gave a snappily executed penal sign. That sign seemed to be used like a military salute. Paul returned the salute and spoke to pole man.

'Brother Junior Deacon. You will now place Brother Lomas in the north where the working tools of an Entered Apprentice Freemason will be presented and explained by Brother Oldthwaite.'

Pole man – whom I would soon learn to call Deacon – took me round the Lodge once more, reminding me to salute the Master and Wardens using the special sign, until we stood about six feet to the left of where we had started. Why can we only move in a clockwise direction round the room? It's like playing a bizarre game of snakes and ladders.

Dennis Oldthwaite hauled himself out of his seat and trundled across the chess-board carpet to stand in front of me. Dennis was a red-faced, jolly man, whose family had farmed lands around the Ryburn valley since the compilation of the Domesday Book. He fitted into his dark suit like a badly wrapped side of beef. With a great sigh he bent over and picked something out of a wooden box which lay open on the floor. He stood up and faced me. His face split into an enormous grin, I had to grin back. His good humour was infectious as his broad Yorkshire voice boomed out.

'Brother Lomas. By command of the Worshipful Master ...' he nodded towards Paul to confirm who had told him to do this.

'... I now show you the tools worked by an Entered Apprentice Freemason which are the twenty-four-inch rule, ...' He handed me a two-foot folding metal gauge that he stretched out to its full length.

'... the common lump-hammer ...' He gave me a miniature round-headed hammer.

'... and the stone-cutter's blade.' Finally he handed me a broad metal chisel.

This felt rather like a children's game in which you have to try and hold lots of things without dropping them. Dare I pull out my pinny and hold them in that? Dennis boomed on.

'The twenty-four-inch rule is a tool used to measure the work. The common lump-hammer is used to knock off all knobs and excrescences and to bring matter into due form; whilst the stone-cutter's blade is to smooth the work ready for an expert workman.'

Once more that infectious grin spread across his face, as he watched me juggling the tools, trying to inspect them without dropping them. I'm sure if I had dropped them he would have roared with good-natured laughter.

He continued, 'But as we are not all operative, but free and accepted, or speculative Masons, we apply these tools to our ethics.'

What *did* he mean by applying the physical tools I held in my hands to the immaterial emotional responses I call my morals? This juxtaposition was so strange I listened attentively to what he said next.

'In this sense, the twenty-four-inch rule symbolises the twenty-four hours of the day; part of which is to be spent in prayer and praise to Almighty God; part in work and repast; and part in assisting a Brother in need.

'The common lump-hammer reminds us of our conscience, whereby we are enabled to suppress those recalcitrant passions which might otherwise force themselves upon our personality.'

He paused for dramatic effect, which he promptly undermined by smiling warmly at me.

'The stone-cutter's blade points out the advantages of education, by which we are helped to become useful members of a well and regularly organised society.'

He took the tools back from me and, bending down to return them to the box, dropped the hammer with a clatter. Standing up, he faced Paul once more and saluted, giving me a last encouraging grin before plodding ponderously back to his seat.

Was that it? Did I now know everything?

Apparently not, for Paul spoke again.

'This will be followed by the antient charge in the First Degree which will be given by Brother Tidewell.'

A dapper little man, compact enough to get lost in the depths of Dennis's bulky pockets, stood forward and saluted Paul. He turned to me and spoke in a precise, high-pitched voice, his face a model of concentration. And, as I was about to find out, he needed to concentrate to deliver what turned out to be the longest speech of my Initiation.

'Brother Lomas. As you have now passed through the ceremony of your Initiation, allow me to congratulate you on being admitted a member of our ancient and honourable society.

'Ancient, no doubt it is, as having endured from time immemorial; and honourable it must be admitted to be, because, by a spontaneous propensity, it conduces to make all those honourable who follow to its teachings closely.

'Indeed, no institution can boast a more solid foundation than that on which Freemasonry rests: the practice of social and moral virtue; and to so high an eminence has its credit been advanced that, in every age, monarchs themselves have become promoters of the art; have not thought it derogatory to their dignity to exchange the sceptre for the trowel; have patronised our mysteries and even joined in our assemblies. ...'

This simple homily continued for some time, complimenting me upon my reception into the Order and telling me about all sorts of rules and regulations I would be expected to comply with. Finally Ron Tidewell neared the end of his *tour de force* of recitation.

'From the very commendable attention which you appear to have given to this charge, I am led to hope that you will duly appreciate the excellence of Freemasonry, and imprint indelibly on your mind the sacred dictates of truth, of honour, and of virtue.'

He finished, and the seated members gave him a short burst of applause – he deserved it for the feat of memory he had just displayed. I wondered if he was a fan of amateur dramatics.

But what had that speech meant? It seemed to be full of basic ethical statements. But these were hardly secrets.

The most notable feature to impress me that evening was that I had been made to stand in the north-east corner, on the line of the sunrise on the longest day to listen to it. This is the day with the most hours of light. Had that midsummer's day been real, rather than symbolic, it felt as if the length of Ron Tidewell's speech would have used most of the daylight.

The ceremony seemed to be almost over. Paul spoke again.

'You are now free to withdraw in order to be reunited with your personal effects, and on your return to the Lodge something further will be communicated to you. But if you are perfectly comfortable, you may take your seat in the Lodge.'

I took the hint and sat down in my borrowed pyjamas.

What else was I going to be told, and would it help me understand the ceremony?

I listened carefully as Paul explained.

'Brother Lomas, there are certain test questions and answers in this Degree, and for your instruction, and the benefit of the Brethren, generally, those questions will be put by Brother Astore to Brother Nansen who will give the necessary answers.'

Mike stood up and faced a curly-haired man who sat at a table in the north-east part of the Lodge. The guy, whom I later knew as Gerry, stood and faced him. Mike began.

'Where were you first prepared to be made a Mason?'

So began a game of verbal ping-pong which I little realised I would soon know intimately. One key question stands out in my memory.

'When were you made a Mason?' Mike asked.

'When the sun was at its meridian.'

What was that Gerry had just said? It was dark outside. The sun had certainly not just passed the meridian; it had long since passed the yard-arm, and even the horizon. Who was he trying to kid?

Mike ploughed on with his questions.

'As in this country Freemasons' lodges are usually held and travellers initiated in the evening, how do you reconcile that which at first sight, appears a paradox?'

Yes indeed, how are you going to get out of this? Gerry didn't seem fazed.

'The sun being a fixed body, and the earth continually revolving around the same, on its own axis, and Freemasonry being a universal science, diffused throughout the whole of the inhabited globe, it necessarily follows that the sun must always be at its meridian with respect to Freemasonry.'

Gerry had just outlined Galileo's heresy in its full glory. My cold, questioning scientist's heart warmed to Freemasonry at that moment.

When Mike and Gerry had completed the long liturgy of questions they turned to face Paul, saluted him and then returned to their seats. Paul now had a shock for me.

'Those are the test questions and answers in this Degree, which, together with the obligation you have taken this evening, you are expected to commit to memory, before you can be passed to a higher Degree. Your proposer, seconder, or any other Brother in the Lodge will be pleased to give you any assistance you may require.'

What? Be serious, Paul! Me memorise all that medieval claptrap before I can go any further? It'll take months, if I can be bothered.

But memorise it I did – and much more than I would have believed possible at that point.

I had been made a Mason. But I was not much wiser. Afterwards I spoke to Mike, my proposer.

'What was that all about?'

'It'll get clearer when you've done your other Degrees?'

'Are you sure?'

'Wait and see,' he replied, peering at me over the top of his glasses and trying to look enigmatic.

I did, but it would be many years before I would begin to understand what I could learn from this experience.

[1] Einstein ([1949] 1956), p. 5.

Chapter Three

Tracing the First Board

Let's Go Visiting

The week after my Initiation into Ryburn Lodge, my friend Mike, the guy who had proposed me into Freemasonry, rang me up and said, 'How do you fancy coming to visit Rokeby Lodge? They're doing the First-Degree Tracing-board.'

'What's the First-Degree Tracing-board and how do they do it?' I asked. It sounded like some sinuous sort of sand dance. Could I watch or would I be expected to take part?

'It's a piece of ritual which explains the meaning of the Tracing-board.'

'Great! Now share with me ... What's a Tracing-board?'

'Do you remember something which looked like a painting, on a wooden board, in front of the Master's pedestal?'

'Not really,' I answered. I had been so disorientated by the continual movement and the bombardment of question and answer, I couldn't really remember a lot about the contents of the lodge-room.

'Just before we closed the Lodge, Walter came forward and turned it to the wall. After we'd put out the officers' candles,' Mike added. Now I remembered something.

'A picture of the sky with three pillars standing on a chess board?'

'That's about it. So do you want to come and find out more?'

'I haven't got a pinny.'

It's called an apron, and the Tyler at Rokeby will fix you up with one,' he said. 'What time shall I pick you up?'

So I went on my first Masonic visit and got the first clue as to what Masonic Initiation might be trying to do.

A Different Temple

Rokeby Lodge met in Blackwall Masonic Rooms in Halifax. Mike led the way in. He was carrying a smart rectangular leather case, which I assumed held his apron. I'd stuffed my newly purchased white gloves into the pocket of the black suit I was wearing. Under my smart dark jacket I had a white shirt and a plain black tie.

'You look like you're going to a funeral,' my wife had said, when I appeared, dressed to go.

There were a number of men, also in dark suits, white shirts and black ties, milling about in the cloakroom, all in the process of putting on their aprons and gloves. Mike took me to up to meet a jolly-looking red-faced guy.

'Meet Frank,' he said. 'Frank's the Tyler., He'll fix you up with an apprentice apron.'

'I'm sure we've got a good one here,' said Frank, rummaging in a cupboard. He turned round and handed me a white leather apron, with cotton-strand laces. Mike helped me tie it around my waist and set the pointed flap upwards.

'Why do I have to wear the flap upwards?' I asked.

'It's to show that you're a new Apprentice, and it also displays all five points of the apron.'

'Why should five points matter?'

'You'll find out in good time,' Mike told me.

'I've never been in a lodge as it's being opened,' I said. 'I won't know what to do.'

'I'll sit next to you and show you,' Mike promised.

I felt odd sitting among all these men dressed for a funeral and uniformed in white gloves and blue-and-white aprons. I was the only one there wearing a pure white apron, which made me feel even odder, and, to add to my discomfort, nobody else had the peak of their apron turned up. I felt that everyone was looking at me ... but they all seemed friendly and welcoming.

We seated ourselves in the lodge-room – the temple as Mike told me to call it. When everyone was ready the Lodge was opened.

The Master stood up and asked us all to assist him in singing the opening hymn. Mike discreetly passed me a printed sheet; on it were the words of a Masonic hymn.

There was an organ in the corner of the temple, and it struck up a tune I recognised: *Vienna*. I had a quick flashback to waiting semi-naked in the Ladies at Ryburn Lodge, ready to be initiated. Was this what I'd heard through the two doors? Everybody else seemed to know the words by heart. I had to use the hymn sheet, but held it low so it wasn't obvious I was cribbing the words. This wasn't a conscious decision on my part, but I was already starting to accept the Masonic principle that if something's worth knowing it's worth learning by heart.

When we finished singing, the Master unconsciously straightened his black tie before starting an obviously memorised ritual instruction.

'Brother Masons. You will help me to form this Lodge.'

He turned to a dark-haired man seated halfway along the left-hand side of the Lodge.

'Brother Jackson what is the initial concern of all Masons?'

'To make sure our meeting is well guarded Brother Randall.'

Seemingly satisfied with this answer, the Master told Brother Jackson to make sure the Lodge was well guarded. Apparently this was not a job that the guy seated in the fancy chair in the south could do himself. He quickly passed the buck to another weedy little chap who stood by the doorway self-consciously clutching a dagger. He didn't look as if he knew how to use it.

'Brother Yates, make sure we are well guarded.'

Brother Yates knocked on the door with the hilt of his dagger and somebody outside the Lodge knocked back. Now the result of this test, although completely obvious to all concerned, was passed back up the chain of command – the guy by the door telling the guy in the comfy chair, 'We are well guarded,' and the seated guy passing on the information to the Master, just in case he hadn't been paying attention.

The Master now turned to another long-faced man, also sitting in a comfy chair, directly opposite him. He seemed to be checking that the guy was paying attention, unless he'd forgotten where he was up to.

He spoke. 'Brother Susman. What do we do next?'

This guy was on the ball, though. He answered quickly, 'Confirm that all here are Brethren.'

His memory suitably jogged, the Master turned to the rest of us.

'You will all give the secret sign of this degree.'

Everybody did but me. I wondered if I could hear the beginnings of a muffled tutting beginning in the far reaches of the room, or if it was just my fevered imagination thinking of a trip to the beach.

Mike whispered to me, 'Give the sign you were shown last week.'

I did, as quickly as I could, and the incipient tutting subsided. I breathed a sigh of relief. My throat was safe for a while longer.

It appeared, from my point of view, that whoever wrote the Freemasonic ritual, thought that the Master and his wardens were likely to be forgetful. They seemed to keep asking each other what to do next – but nobody was tutting, so this must be par for the course.

The Master spoke again to the man in the posh chair to his left.

'Brother Junior Warden, how many key functionaries are there in this Lodge?'

I looked round and wondered how to spot a key functionary. Did they wear special collars, or carry poles? Perhaps they sat in comfy chairs? Mike nudged me to pay attention.

The Warden knew the answer.

'Three,' he said, without hesitation and then named them. 'The Master, a Junior and a Senior Warden.'

The Master looked at the Junior Warden. 'And how many supporting functionaries are there?'

This Warden was just as quick to respond, but his answer had a familiar ring.

'There are also three,' he said, 'beside the External Guard. These are the Elder and Younger Deacons and the Internal Guard.'

So everybody now knew how many officials were needed to make up a lodge: three folk who sat in posh chairs, two guys with poles and two others with swords guarding each side of a locked door. Seven in total. An interesting choice– seven is traditionally a number used to represent perfection and completeness.

What was the purpose of this ritual? It seemed to be taking an audit of the roles each member of the Lodge was playing. Did they do this every time they got together? And, if they did, why? As these thoughts tumbled through my mind I realised the listing of functions wasn't yet over.

The Master continued, 'Brother Junior Warden. Please explain the function of the External Guard.'

'He stands outside the Lodge, holding a drawn sword, to protect the Brethren from the incursions of cowans* and other eavesdroppers whilst making sure that Candidates are well prepared to become Brothers among us.'

The Master now turned to the weedy little man holding the dagger, who was still guarding the door and spoke to him.

'Brother Internal Guard, what is the duty for which you stand at the portal of the Lodge?'

'I will allow true and tested Masons to enter, prevent candidates from rushing forward, and carry out the instructions of the Junior Warden.'

So it had been this functionary who'd held his dagger to my chest when I entered Ryburn Lodge in my state of darkness. The drawn-out opening was beginning to tell me something about the functions of each role; perhaps that was its purpose. But would it help me understand what Freemasonry was trying to teach?

The Master spoke again, this time to one of the pole-carriers, a portly gentleman wearing a dark blue suit under his apron.

---

*I later the consulted the *Shorter Oxford Dictionary* and found this word means:, 'a dry-stone-waller; or a person who does a mason's work without having been apprenticed to the trade', or 'a person who is not a Freemason'.

'Younger Deacon, what is your duty in this Lodge?'

The reply was immediate. 'I stand beside the Senior Warden, always ready to carry his instructions to the Junior Warden and ensure that they are carried out.'

Is this supposed to be serious? The Junior Warden was no more than three metres away and could hardly avoid hearing any instructions that might be passed on. Why was a messenger needed to carry instructions over such a short distance? Was there some deeper symbolic meaning to these roles? I couldn't see it then, and it would be many years before I came to understand this symbolism. My initial confusion deepened when the Master asked the other pole-man to explain himself.

'I stand beside the Worshipful Master and carry his orders to the Senior Warden and wait there to meet with the Younger Deacon.'

This was hierarchy gone mad. The Senior Warden and the Master both had messengers to talk to people in the same room, while the Junior Warden had a two-man army to defend the door of the Lodge. Weird, or what?

I nudged Mike. 'Do they really need messengers?'

'Ssh,' he said. 'It isn't over yet.'

He was right; the Master spoke again, this time to the Junior Warden.

'Why are you placed in the southern region of the Lodge?'

'I celebrate the sun at high twelve. I announce transitions from work to leisure, so that a profitable balance may be struck by the Brethren.'

Now the Master spoke to the man in the posh chair directly opposite him.

'Why are you seated in the west?'

During my Initiation I had been told these grandly seated men represented the sun, the moon and the Master of the Lodge. Would this ritual opening of a lodge confirm my impression? I listened carefully to the answer this Warden gave.

'I align with the sun as it sets. As the light fades in the west to show the day is over, so do I sit in the west to conclude the business of the Lodge when the Master commands it.'

The ritual was clearly intended to remind its members of the role each player took in the set-up of the Lodge. It had begun by naming each functionary, and then the Master had moved around the individuals, getting them to outline the purpose of their job. But there was an inconsistency between the statement of the Senior Warden and what I had been told the previous week. I had been told he represented the moon, but he had just said that he showed where the sun set. Was there some subtle symbolic difference between the setting moon and the setting sun, or were they both just symbols of the darkness of night?

The Master turned to the man sitting next to him.

'Brother Immediate Past Master. Will you please explain why I am seated in the East?'

Surely he could remember something as basic as this! Is the ritual intending to make a point here? The man drew himself up to his full five feet six inches and gave a snappy Masonic salute before answering.

'The Master is seated in the East, where the sun comes up, that he may shine upon the Lodge whilst engaging and informing his Brethren in the art of Freemasonry.'

I whispered to Mike, 'Do you go through all the rigmarole every time you meet? Or are you showing off because I'm new?'

He sounded slightly irritated, as though I'd been speaking in church during prayers, as he whispered back, 'This is how we always open a lodge. Now hush.' He settled his glasses firmly on his nose to indicate he was concentrating.

The Master turned to face the centre of the lodge-room.

'My Brothers. At this moment our Lodge is complete, but before it can be fully opened we have a further matter to consider. Let us contemplate for a moment the importance of the divine order in supporting our labours. Without the security provided by the sacred law of the Great Architect of the Universe, we would know no benefit from our efforts, know no peace and never achieve harmony. Let the great blessings of the Sacred Law rest on our Lodge.'

The members, standing round the room all responded. 'So mote it be.'

The Master lifted his arms towards the roof and, holding them aloft, announced, 'Brethren. In the name of the great architect of the universe, I open this Lodge for the practice of Masonry in the First Degree.'

The Master knocked with his gavel as he finished his pronouncement. Many others round the room echoed the knocks, till at last the man standing outside the room beat on the closed door.

The Lodge was finally open.

For the next few minutes nothing very exciting happened. It was just like any formal business meeting, apart from the funny clothes and pinnies. They read and approved minutes, took reports from treasurers and almoners … all the usual stuff. Is this one of the secrets of Freemasonry: it holds formal business meetings in fancy dress? No wonder they wouldn't talk until I had been sworn to secrecy. Who wants to join a society for holding business meetings in frilly pinnies?

'When are we going to hear about this Tracing-board?' I asked Mike as the deacons bustled round the room with the minute book, waiting while the Master and Wardens signed it.

He passed me a leaflet. 'There,' he said. 'It's the next item on the summons.'

I looked, and there was an agenda. He was right. The next item was 'The First Degree Tracing-board'.

I looked at the Tracing-board, where it stood in front of the Master's desk. Three pillars rising from a cluttered chess board stood out against a brightly coloured sky filled with sun, moon and stars. Nice, but what did it mean?

Tracing the Board

The two Deacons went forward and took the Tracing-board, laying it flat in the centre of the Lodge. They managed to walk completely round the Lodge in a clockwise direction to do the job. The chap giving the talk stood next to it, holding a pointer in his white-gloved hands to trace out the shapes as he spoke. Tall and distinguished-looking, with an almost military bearing, he had a shock of white hair that seemed to defy gravity and surrounded his head like a halo.

He began to speak in the well-rounded tones of middle-class Yorkshire – not the farmer-speak of the local villages but the more educated accent of a local worthy. I later found he worked for our local building society. His delivery fitted the sonorous opening words of the talk quite nicely.

'The practices and traditions among Freemasons have always maintained a close kinship with those of the ancient Egyptians. Their adepts, being loath to reveal their secrets to the vision of the uncouth, framed the essence of their teachings and sacred guidance within symbols and tokens, which were revealed to their chief priests and worthy acolytes only, who were obligated by sober declarations to shield their meaning.'

This sounded very formal for a lecture. He was delivering it just as if he was reading it, but hadn't got any notes.

'The discipline of Pythagoras was established on an analogous rationale, in the same way as many other systems of more modern vintage. But Masonry is not just the oldest but also the most noble order that subsists, as none of the symbols or graphic devices revealed within it does other than engender precepts of righteousness and honour within the minds of all its true followers.'

I tapped Mike on the arm. 'Is this a ritual speech?'

'Of course it is,' he whispered back. 'He's memorised it. Now shut up, watch and listen.'

'Allow me initially to observe that the shape of the Lodge, is a regular parallelepiped which stretches from east to west and from north to south. It is as deep as the centre of our world and reaches even to the heights of the celestial sphere. The lodges of our Order are symbolically so immense to illustrate the comprehensiveness of our art, that a Mason's benevolence should meet no limits except those of discretion.'

As he spoke, he used his pointer to show the direction symbols of the compass, which were marked around the outer edges of the Board. The edges of the Board were formed from a series of blue and red triangles. There were what looked like tassels at the four corners. The Board was a rectangle, and the long axis ran from east to west, with east at the top.

The story continued.

'The Lodge is said to be erected on sacred earth, for the reason that the initial Lodge was sanctified by virtue of three august gifts offered there, which drew down heavenly approval. Number one was the quick submission of Abram to the volition of the Supreme Being by proffering Isaac, his first-born, as a forfeit to be destroyed by fire, when it gratified the Most High to depute a more accordant substitute in his place. Number two was the righteous supplications and interjections of King David, which propitiated the anger of the Most High and quelled a plague which rampaged amidst his subjects, caused by his unwittingly calling a census against divine instruction. Number three was the vast number of blessings, sacrifices, burnt offerings and expensive oblations which King Solomon of Israel gave at the topping off, sanctification and commitment of the Jerusalem Temple to the Most High. These three then did, since have and ever will, dedicate the foundation of Freemasonry to the sublime.'

He again used his pointer to indicate the longer axis.

'Our Lodge is placed along the sunrise line of the vernal equinox, due east and west. Not only Mason's Lodges but all sacred sites of worship should be placed on this holy alignment. We have three Masonic reasons for this sacred positioning. Firstly, at this sacred season, the Sun, a visible manifestation of the Most High, ascends from the eastern horizon and sinks below the western sea. Secondly, our Royal Art began in the east and afterwards spread its beneficial potency to the west. Thirdly, there is a last grand reason, concerning the appearance of the Bright Morning Star in the pre-dawn sky, of which you will learn more as you progress through our ancient system.'

He now pointed in turn to each of the three pillars which were painted on the board.

'Our Lodge is founded on these great pillars, three in number.' As he pointed to each pillar he named it:

'They are called Wisdom, Strength and Beauty: Wisdom to excogitate, Strength to sustain, and Beauty to embellish; Wisdom to guide our actions, Strength to carry us through our difficulties, and Beauty to grace the spirit.'

So far this guy had not hesitated in his delivery. It was an impressive feat of memory. He pointed to the space contained within the pillars, saying, 'The Universe is a temple to the influence of the Sacred Law, in which we all express belief. Wisdom, Strength, and Beauty are paths to approach understanding of the hidden order of the world. Wisdom is sempiternal, Strength is a mighty force, and Beauty shines through the whole of nature in balance and proportion.'

His pointer floated over the sun, moon and stars shown in the sky above the pillars.

'The heavens stretch above our Lodge as a canopy; the earth endures beneath our feet; the stars crown our world with beauty, power and glory. The movements of the Sun and Moon carry messages of order and stability, affirming by their actions the power of the sacred law. The three pillars underpinning all Mason's Lodges are symbols of this sacred law; and can be personified in the models of Solomon, King of Israel, Hiram, King of Tyre, and Hiram Abif: Solomon, for his Wisdom in conceiving, building, and devoting the Temple at Jerusalem to divine service; Hiram, King of Tyre, for his Strength exemplified by men, material and workmanship; and Hiram Abif, for his consummate skill in beautifying and adorning the Temple.'

Each of the pillars, painted on the board, was carved in a different style. He pointed to each one in turn as he described it.

'There are no orders in architecture known by the names of

Wisdom, Strength, and Beauty, so we celebrate Masonic virtues using the names Doric, Ionic and Corinthian.'

He paused for breath and looked up at the roof of the lodge-room. It was painted a deep blue and on it were painted bright stars. He continued, 'The roof of a Masonic lodge is a celestial covering of sublime colour, even as the open sky.'

He pointed back to the Tracing-board, indicating a ladder which rested on a cubical altar and stretched upwards towards a bright star in the east.

'The means by which a Mason anticipates reaching an understanding of the heavens is by the assistance of a ladder, called in the Bible Jacob's ladder. This stairway is made up of many roundels, which represent mental virtues, but there are three cardinal steps; these are Faith, Hope and Charity. Faith in the underlying fabric of the Sacred Law, Hope that we may ascend to knowledge of the centre of sacred knowledge, and Charity that we may live in amity with mankind. This ladder reaches to the domain of the stars but is founded on the statement of the Sacred Law. Because of the message of divine order contained in the Volume of the Sacred Law, we are shown how to use its teachings to find the series of steps which will take us to the centre of sacred knowledge. Our acceptance of underlying order fortifies our expectation of understanding the promise contained in the Sacred Law., This expectation makes us capable of raising our understanding of the centre of sacred knowledge, and this in turn informs our worldly attitude and brings us to peaceful co-existence with our fellow men. Emblematically we have ascended to a celestial plain symbolically depicted by seven stars, which is also a reminder of the number of Brethren who make a lodge perfect and make new Masons.'

The opening ritual had named seven functionaries without whom a lodge could not be opened. Here, in the story of the Tracing-board, was a clue that said these seven Masons were associated with the appearance of stars in the sky. The Sun on the Tracing-board was placed in the north-east quarter, where I had stood to be told about the foundations of Freemasonry. The sun rising in the north-east said that this Tracing-board represented the summer solstice. This day is one of the most important in the solar calendar, and it kept being alluded to in the symbolism of the ritual, but nobody and no part of the ritual had mentioned the longest day.

I listened as the lecture progressed to a description of the furniture of a perfect lodge.

'A Mason's lodge contains ornaments, furniture and jewels. The ornaments are the chequered flooring, the Bright Morning Star and the enlozenged border. The chequered flooring is the beautiful pavement of the lodge, the Bright Morning Star shines forth the beauty of the centre, and the enlozenged border marks the boundary of the black and white pavement.'

He pointed out the black and white chequerboard flooring of the Lodge, which was reproduced in the Tracing-board.

'The chequered flooring may well be called a beautiful flooring, by reason of its being multi-coloured and divided into squares. This points out the variety of cognitions which embellish and bedeck the cosmos, both living and lifeless.'

He pointed to the bright star in the east of the board.

'The Bright Morning Star, or beautiful light at the centre, makes us think of the Sun, which shines upon the earth, and by its genial potency distributes grace to humankind.'

This did not make sense. The sun was shown rising in the north-east, and the star above the altar was rising due east. Its symbol was not that of the sun, but of a bright morning star. I put the puzzle to one side and listened as he continued, pointing to the triangulated border of the Tracing-board.

'The enlozenged border refers us to the wandering stars or planets, which in their complex movements create a beautiful boundary around that great notable, the Sun, as the other does round that of a Mason's lodge.'

He pointed towards the Master's chair and pedestal.

'The furniture of the Lodge are the Volume of the Sacred Law, the Compasses and Square. The Sacred Law guides our understanding. We test our candidates to Freemasonry by their understanding of supreme being symbolically contained in this volume. The Compasses and Square, when brought together, modulate our actions and lives. The Volume of the Sacred Law contains the rules which govern the cosmos, the Compasses belong to the Master in particular, and the Square to the whole Craft.'

He pointed to a series of objects scattered between the pillars on the black and white ground of the Tracing-board.

'The jewels to be found in the Lodge are three mobile and three fixed. The mobile jewels are the Plumb Rule, the Square and the Level. Our operative brethren use the level to check horizontals and lay flat elevations; the square to set right angles truly; and the plumb rule to fix uprights in a vertical manner. We speculative Masons use these tools as moral emblems, the Plumb Rule demonstrating upright behaviour, the Square, moral rectitude and the Level, equality. We call them mobile jewels because each year they move into the care of the officer-holders. The Master holds the Square, the Elder Warden the Level, and the Younger Warden the Plumb Rule.'

He stood back and indicated two stone blocks which stood on

either side of the Tracing-board on the floor of the Lodge, one rough-finished, the other smooth-worked.

'Our fixed jewels are also three in number, being the Tracing-board, the rough-hewn ashlar and the worked or perfect cube. The Tracing-board is where the master of the craft expounds designs for the guidance of the workers. The rough-hewn ashlar is the stone die on which the Entered Apprentice perfects his skill. The perfect cube is used by a Master of the Craft as a standard to prove his square, level and vertical. These jewels are fixed within the body of the Lodge for the Brethren to reflect upon.

'Just as a Master of the Craft uses the Tracing-board to work out physical designs to enable the workers to turn the drawings into living buildings, so the Volume of the Sacred Law is the spiritual Tracing-board of the Great Architect of the Universe, where are laid down the working drawings which explain the natural processes of the eternal, celestial realms. The rough-hewn ashlar is a rock taken from the earth, crude in form, ready to be shaped by the tools of the apprentice worker into an imperfect cube. It symbolises the human mind in an immature and uneducated state, rough and unpolished. Only by the civilising influence of education and the discipline of focused study does the unripened mind become prepared for a more responsible role in society. The perfect cube is a standard by which working tools may be tested and the state of improvement of rough-hewn ashlars be assessed. It is a standard fit to calibrate the square and compasses of the Master of the Craft. It is emblematic of the mature and educated mind, a state which we can only hope to attain by applying the Masonry's lessons of spiritual development to our rough-hewn minds.'

This was a new thought. Does Freemasonry see itself as a science for forming the human mind? The stones are symbols of a mind before and after education. But how was Freemasonry going to educate me? The lecturer was about to give me another clue, though I wouldn't begin to understand it for many years yet.

He continued, 'In a correctly established lodge can be found a point within a circle round which a Mason cannot err. This circle is bounded between North and South by two grand parallel lines, the one representing Moses, the other King Solomon. On the upper part of this circle rests the Volume of the Sacred Law, supporting Jacob's ladder, the top of which reaches to the heavens, and were we to become as conversant with the laws contained within this volume as both those parallels exemplify, they will lead us to a greater understanding of the purpose of the cosmos.'

The lecturer pointed to this symbol, drawn out on the altar, which supported an open book and the square and compasses. He added more detail.

'In going round this circle, we must of necessity touch on both those parallel lines, likewise on the Volume of the Sacred Law; and while a Mason keeps himself thus circumscribed, he cannot err.'

This description of the bounded circle and the glory of light at the centre would become an important key to unlocking the ancient secrets of Masonic teaching. But when I first heard this lecture it meant little to me. The lecturer took his pointer and indicated other items lying on the ground of the Tracing-board. He described them thus.

'This metal tool, which clasps and grips the stone, assists our operative brethren to lift large masses with relative ease. The Masonic name for this tool is a Lewis, and the symbolic import of the name is strength. The term Lewis or Lewisa means the son or daughter of a Mason, duty bound to carry on the work of the parents and forebears when they become too weak to continue the work, for which they are privileged to be made Masons before any incomers.'

This comment, almost an aside, suggested that Masonry did in some way think of itself as an hereditary duty – an idea that I would later investigate in great detail in other books. But, when I heard it for the first time, what most amazed me was not the idea itself but the speaker's prodigious memory. He'd been speaking for about twenty minutes without any sort of prompt and without provoking any tutting. I wondered if these feats of memory were commonplace among Masons.

He continued, 'Placed at the four extreme corners of the Lodge are four tassels, meant to remind us of the four cardinal virtues – namely Temperance, Fortitude, Prudence, and Justice – the whole of which, tradition informs us, were constantly practised by a great majority of our ancient Brethren. The distinguishing characteristics of a good Freemason are Virtue, Honour and Mercy, and even if these be banished from all other societies, may they ever be found in a Mason's breast.'

He turned and gave a snappy salute to the Master. The Master saluted him back and the room erupted into spontaneous applause.

'He's good, isn't he?' Mike said.

'I suppose so,' I said. 'I've never heard a better rendition of it.' This was, of course, perfectly true, because the whole lecture was totally new to me. But Mike took my comment at face value.

'You probably won't,' he said. 'Usually it's shared between half a dozen people. That was a really good delivery.'

But I was disappointed to find that was the end of the discussion. I wondered if we were going to talk about the content of the lecture, reflect on possible meanings and have the opportunity to ask questions. In the university environment I was used to, a lecture would be followed by a seminar, to develop the ideas, and then a tutorial to enable learners to practise these new skills and hone them to a higher level of perfection. This didn't happen. We ritually closed the meeting, had a meal, drank toasts to each other and lots of other people I'd never heard of, then wished each other a safe journey home.

In the car, travelling back, I asked Mike about the meaning of the lecture.

'It seemed to be a mixture of astronomical references, a homily on the importance of basic laws to understanding the universe and a message about the importance of education.'

'I suppose you could describe it that way,' he agreed.

'But how do they fit together? And what does it have to do with the oddball secrets I was given?'

'You'll have to wait until you pass your Second Degree,' Mike said. 'Let's practise the questions. ... Where were you first prepared to be made a Mason?'

So instead of discussing the meaning of the First Degree and its symbolic Tracing-board, we practised the test questions I would need to get into the Second Degree. This was frustrating at the time, but a few weeks later I was glad Mike had taken the trouble to teach me well.

Chapter Four

The Spiral of the Second Degree

The Art of Memorie

My wife was beginning to suspect I was going a little odd. For the past month and a half I'd spent all my spare time mumbling to myself and showing increasing signs of incipient desperation. The last Wednesday in March was fast approaching. Soon my ability to memorise would be put to public test.

'Are you alright?' she asked.

'Yes, why shouldn't I be?'

'Well, you've taken to talking to yourself.'

'I'm memorising something secret,' I said, trying to sound mysterious and suppressing the slight tingling in my throat as I thought about the penalty of talking about what I was doing.

'Is it your test questions and obligation?'

'How did you know?'

'My mother used to get me to test her on her ritual. Do you want me to test you?'

Now I was confused. I was pledged to protect secrets but it seemed these are quite well-known secrets.

'I'm not sure.'

'Stop being so silly,' she said. 'It's much easier to learn if you say it out loud and have somebody else check you're doing it right. I'll fetch my mother's old ritual book.'

She soon returned carrying a small blue book which she opened at a well-thumbed page. 'Where did you first become aware you needed to become a Mason?'

Without hesitating I replied, 'In my centre.'

So I made my first stumbling steps in the 'antient art of memorie', as the oldest Masonic charges call the skill I was learning. Rote leaning of large chunks of text is something rarely practised in modern education, but studies of the brains of London taxi drivers learning what they call 'the Knowledge' has shown that they grow many new neural connections. My brain was also growing new neural links, hard as it seemed to appreciate that while it was happening. All the same, none of this rationalising made me any less nervous as I prepared to put myself to my first Masonic test.

A Passing Ceremony

By now I was getting into the routine of Masonic meetings. I was waiting in my dark suit, white shirt and black tie when Mike picked me up. I was now quite confident about what to do as the Lodge was opened. I knew when to stand, when to sit and when to make gestures, and each time I used them they seemed less weird.

'Are you all ready?' Mike asked as we walked into the crowded temple.

'Yes,' I said, with far more confidence than I felt.

Paul Powell, dressed in his Master's regalia, was already sitting the East. Once the lodge had been formally opened they were ready to test me. Paul looked across and winked at me before knocking his gavel on his desk. As the knocking was repeated around the room he cleared his throat.

'Brethren, our next business is to pass Brother Lomas.' He looked round the room. 'Brother Deacons, please attend to the Aspirant.'

The two pole-carriers stood up and saluted Brother Paul before formally marching round the Lodge to stand one each side of me, facing the pedestal where the Brother Master always sat. Paul looked towards me and said, 'Brother Lomas, do you aspire this evening to be move up to the next spiritual level of Masonry, to that of the Second Degree?

I was learning how these things work, and so I waited for one of my pole-bearing escorts to prompt me before replying. 'I do.'

'Before you can be permitted to so move, you must prove your Masonic ability in the former degree.

'I shall thus ask you to venture and rehearse the requisite test questions, which I will put to you.'

So now the testing time was upon me. For the last week I'd been word-perfect each of the numerous times I'd tried. Could I do it as well for real?

Paul began. 'Where did you first become aware you needed to become a Mason?'

Each question prompted me for an answer, and the answer keyed in the words of the next question. Paul could have taken any question he liked and the answer would have come just as easily to me, as would the words of the subsequent question. This was actually fun. I was enjoying the rhythm of the ritual, until at last Paul said,. 'How do you show these qualities to others?'

'By formal signals, stylised movements and a well-trained sense of timing.'

So far so good, but I wasn't home and dry yet. That had been a simple introduction to memorising, because after each chunk of ritual I was prompted by a response. Now I was about to face a harder test of my memory. Paul smiled at me encouragingly.

'Please repeat in full the words of the solemn pledge of an Apprentice Freemason.'

I took a deep breath, focused my mind and began.

'I, Robert Lomas, in the presence of the Great Architect of the Universe, and of this worthful and venerable Lodge of antient free and accepted Masons. Duly established, frequently held, gathered together, and decently devoted to the sacred law, do hereby and hereon, of my own free volition and intention. Most solemnly promise, vow and swear that I will forever hele, keep, conceal and never reveal. Any piece or pieces, arcanum or arcana, enigma or enigmas of, or at all existing within this the First Degree in Freemasonry, usually known as the Entered Apprentice Degree. ...'

On and on went I went, each word keying in the next as the sequence flowed from my lips. Finally I realised I had reached the final sentence. And there had been no outbreaks of tutting from the watching experts, so I must have been doing OK.

'... So help me, Great Architect, and keep me constant in this my major and most sober duty as an Entered Apprentice Freemason.'

I could feel the tension draining from me as I finished. I'd done it – and it hadn't been anything like as difficult as I'd imagined. I flashed a quick smile at Paul, and he winked back before saying, 'Brother Lomas. Do you also pledge, on your honour as a man and your faithfulness as a Mason, that you will steadily persist through the hidden pathways of nature and science to pass to the level of the Second Degree?'

I waited for the Deacon's prompt, before replying, 'I do.'

'Do you likewise gravely accept to hide that which I am about to make known to you, with the same rigorous circumspection as you did the mysteries of the former degree?'

I responded, and he went on:

'On that basis I entrust you with a test of merit to help you find the path from the First to the Second Level of Freemasonry.'

My escorts, one on each side, led me from the west of the Lodge to the Master's pedestal in the East. There Paul took my white gloved hand in his.

'The test of merit consists of a pass grip and word.' He then demonstrated the grip to me, before continuing, 'You must be particularly careful not to forget this word as, without it, you will be unable to gain admission into a lodge at a superior level.'

Paul smiled at me. 'You will now retire in order to be guided to the level of the Second Degree.'

The Deacons grabbed my elbows and took me out of the lodge-room. My old mate with the sword (whom I now knew as Winston) was waiting with my tattered pyjamas, and this time I knew the drill. When he came back I had the trouser leg ready rolled and shirt folded back.

Winston looked at me and grinned. 'Good try, Bob. But no coconut.'

He then rearranged my skimpy white clothing to reveal different parts of my anatomy.

'A different peep-show?' I asked.

'Wait until you've done all the degrees, then you'll understand.' he answered. 'They're about ready for you. You all set?'

I nodded and he took me out into the corridor where the two Deacons were waiting, poles at the ready. Crossing to the Lodge door, he knocked. After a few moments the door opened, and the interior guard came out and asked, 'Who seeks guidance?'

Winston, his sword held high, answered for me. 'Brother Lomas, who has been properly apprenticed to the Craft of Masonry and now proceeds of his own free will and volition to meekly petition to be enlifted to the level of the Second Degree, having proved himself ready in open Lodge.'

'How does he hope to obtain this enliftment?'

'By the guidance of the Grand Geometrician of the Cosmos, the potent help of the Square and the benefit of a passing grip and word.'

David, the Inner Guard, looked at me. 'Give me that passing grip and word.'

I gave them, exactly as I had been shown by the Master. He made no comment, but he didn't tut at me either.

'Halt, whilst I report to the Master of the Lodge,' he said, closing the door behind him.

I could hear muffled voices coming through the closed door. Winston shuffled from foot to foot and aimlessly waved his sword about as he waited. Finally the door opened and David gestured me and my two escorts into the temple.

I was taken into the temple and positioned in front of the Senior Warden, facing the Master. The kneeling stool I had first used at my Initiation had reappeared, and I was positioned in front of it while Paul, the Master, spoke to me.

'Let the Aspirant, kneel whilst the benediction of the celestial realms is called down to enlighten what we are about to do.'

My escorts nudged me into a kneeling position. Meanwhile the Master knocked with his gavel on the desk, and around the room lots of others did the same. As the cacophony of knocks died away he spoke again.

'Brethren, to order.' Turning to his left he nodded to Stan, one of the older Past Masters, 'Brother Chaplain.'

Stan rose to his feet and positioned himself behind a small dais. He shuffled some papers, straightened his glasses and spoke in a high-pitched, elderly voice.

'We make humble, earnest petition for guidance, O Grand Geometrician of the Cosmos, on behalf of our Lodge of fellows and the aspirant who kneels before us. Grant that the good work, begun in studies of the liberal arts, may be continued to lead to understanding of the glory of thy works and evermore be fixed in us by strict observance of the precepts of the Sacred Law.'

The Lodge members all seemed to agree with this prayer for the improvement of my education, chorusing. 'So mote it be.' Such concern for my intellectual improvement was encouraging.

Now what? Paul, the Master, spoke:

'Let the Aspirant rise.'

I stood up.

'The Brethren in all points of the compass will please observe that Brother Lomas will now perambulate before them to demonstrate that he is an aspirant for enlistment made properly ready to be transposed to the Degree of a Fellow of the Craft. Brethren, be seated.'

Once more I was led around the Lodge, stopping at various officers' chairs to make sure that I hadn't forgotten the signs, postures or words of the First Degree and that I really did know the passing grip and word. When all the formal checking was complete I ended up with Simon, the Senior Warden, holding my hand. He gave it a friendly squeeze as he turned me towards the Master in the East and speaking on my behalf.

'Brother Master. Allow me to acquaint you with Brother Lomas, who has been properly apprenticed to the Craft of Masonry and now proceeds of his own free will and volition to meekly petition to be enlifted to the level of the Second Degree, having proved himself ready in open Lodge.'

Paul replied, 'Brother Senior Warden. I look to your instauration and ask you to instruct the Senior Deacon to progress the Aspirant to the East by the traditional steps.'

So I was going to be shown another set of steps. But this time I had my eyes open and was ready. Simon passed on Paul's instructions to Syd, the Deacon who held my right arm.

'Brother Elder Deacon.' Syd promptly saluted with a First-Degree sign. 'At the request of Brother Master, will you now advance Brother Lomas to the Pedestal using the traditional steps, there to make his serious pledge?'

A steady pressure on my right arm pushed me towards the north-west corner of the Lodge. Syd spoke to me with the flat, comfortable vowels of someone who had once lived in Manchester.

'Brother Lomas. The way of proceeding from west to east in this degree is by a series of steps, some emblematical of ascending a spiral path, the rest bold ones. I will demonstrate the method to you so that you may then reproduce my exemplar.'

He then showed me how to walk from west to east. The other Deacon then nudged me to copy these strange steps. Suppressing a giggle I copied the steps, lifting my feet high as if wearing a pair of invisible swimming flippers. I must have managed to look silly enough because there wasn't any tutting from the assembled Brethren.

The other Deacon now followed me along this weird pathway that only we could see. Finally all three of us stood in the East, in front of the Master's pedestal, where we waited quietly for him to speak.

'The wisdom of Masonry keeps the knowledge of each degree separate, so that only well-prepared aspirants may obtain their knowledge. So another grave pledge is required of you. It is similar in many ways to the one you made as an Apprentice. Are you ready to take it, as you should?'

I waited to be prompted before answering. By now I was enough of a Mason not to try and guess what odd form of words would be needed. The prompt came quietly from Syd, and I duly repeated it.

'I am.'

Just as at my Initiation, I was told to kneel in a strange and contorted posture and to support a book. This time, not being blindfolded, I could see it was the Bible from the main pedestal which I was holding, in the shape of a right angle.

Once my escorts were satisfied that I was in the correctly uncomfortable position, I was led, phrase by phrase, through another sacred pledge.

'I, Robert Lomas, before the Grand Geometrician of the Cosmos, and this worthful and venerable Lodge of antient free and accepted Fellows of the Craft of Masonry, duly established, frequently held, gathered together, and decently devoted to the Sacred Law, do hereby and hereon, of my own free volition and intention ...'

The pledge rolled on, very similar to the First-Degree pledge until we got to the penalties. These were interestingly different.

'These several points I solemnly swear to observe, without hedging, prevarication, or mental reserve of any devious nature, under no less a consequence on the infringement of any of them, than that of having my chest cavity ripped open, my pulsing heart rent from hence and cast upon the surface of the earth as offal for the ravenous beasts of the field and fowls of the air.'

Now I quite like birds, but I'm not sure I like them enough to volunteer to feed them in that fashion. It gave a quite new dimension to the RSPB campaign to feed your garden birds in cold weather.

'So help me the Grand Geometrician of the Cosmos and keep me steadfast and firm in this my second great and worthy pledge of a newly uplifted Fellow of the Craft.'

Was this another great chunk of rambling ritual that I would have to memorise before I was allowed to learn the real secrets of Freemasonry? Last time the words were reinforced with actions. Would this ritual follow the same pattern? I waited for Paul to continue.

'To execute this, which as yet may be considered but a worthy pledge, a constraint upon your moral sense as a most sober obligation so long as you shall live, I command you to honour it twice with the touch of your lips on the Volume of the Sacred Law.'

I did as I was told. If this ritual kept following the same pattern as the Initiation, then I should now get some sort of explanation. Would it make any more sense than the last time? As expected, Paul began his explanation.

'Brother Fellow of the Craft. You will observe that at the spiritual level of a Fellowcraft Lodge a single point of the compass has been revealed to you. When you were but an Apprentice both points were concealed from your sight. At this level the other point is still concealed, showing you have further to travel before you achieve the full understanding that Masonry can offer you. Stand proud, newly articled Fellow of the Craft.'

He looked around the Lodge. 'Brethren, be seated.'

Well that wasn't much of a secret. I was privileged to see another point of the compass. Was that it? No Paul was obviously preparing himself to deliver some more ritual.

'Now you have united yourself with our Lodge of Fellows of the Craft, I will share with you the singular secrets of this level of Masonry.'

He got out of his chair, performing a complex hand-holding changeover as the Past Master took the chair. Then he came down on the black and white floor to stand in front of me. Here we go again – am I going to have to stand in another of those incredibly awkward poses, with my feet in such a position that I feel I'm just about to fall over?

'You will, therefore, stand before me in the posture you learned at your Initiation. Step forward as an Apprentice.'

Yes, I was!

'Give me a First-Degree salute,' Paul whispered. I did. He then told me how to place my feet in yet another strange posture before he was ready to tell me the secrets of the degree. But I won't mention them to you – I have no wish to have my chest cavity ripped open, my pulsing heart rent from thence and cast upon the surface of the earth as offal for the ravenous beasts of the field and fowls of the air.

Don't feel deprived, though. A few odd ways of standing, yet another wacky handshake and a password to go with it are not going to help anybody understand what these rituals are all about. Trust me, you are missing nothing significant, I'm just telling you about the important stuff and sparing you tedium and boredom. I think this is something which should be done more often; it could encourage and maintain the interest of new Masons.

Once Paul finished telling me the formal secrets he sent me off on another ritual circling of the Lodge. First I set off to the south, where I met the Junior Warden, who made sure I knew the formal secrets. Then I went round the circle of the compass points again before stopping at the Senior Warden in the west. He tested me in the formal giving and receiving of the secrets before standing me in the west and turning me to face the Master in the East and delivering a formal introduction.

'Brother Master. I introduce to you Brother Lomas, who aspires to ascend from the rank of Apprentice to become a Fellow of our Craft. On behalf of our Lodge will you recognise and promote his aspiration?'

Paul replied, 'Brother Senior Warden. On behalf of our Lodge I depute you to invest Brother Lomas with the characteristic apron of a Fellow of our Craft.'

This time I was ready when the Senior Warden whipped a new apron from behind his back. It was similar to my Apprentice apron but with the addition of two blue rosettes. He held the new one in front of me while the Deacon loosed the ties of the symbol of my apprenticeship. As my new pinny was tied in place the Senior Warden said to me.

'Brother Lomas. At the request of the Worshipful Master, I invest you with the characteristic apron of a Fellow of our Craft, and the words said to you when you first donned a Masonic apron should echo in your memory now.' He saluted Paul with what I now recognised as the Second-Degree sign. Paul looked straight at me and took a deep breath.

'Brother Lomas. Now you wear that apron, you are recognised as a Fellow of our Craft. As such, the liberal arts and sciences should be the focus of your Masonic study. Such education will help you better discharge your duty as a Mason and make you better enabled to move towards an understanding of the wonderful works of the Most High.' He paused to let this injunction sink in before turning to the Senior Warden.

'Brother Senior Warden, please ask Brother Elder Deacon to stand

Brother Lomas in the South-East Corner of the Lodge.'

So I was to be placed in the South-East Corner for the next part of the ceremony. This is the direction from which the sun rises on the shortest day of the year, at the winter solstice. The Deacons took me via the northern side of the Lodge, past the Master's chair in the East, to the South-East Corner. As I stood there Mike left his seat and made his way clockwise around the Lodge to stand in front of me. He pushed his glasses to the end of his nose, peered at me over them and smiled. Then he began a formal speech.

'Brother Lomas. When you were transformed into a Masonic Apprentice, you stood in the North-East Corner of the Lodge, marking the rising of the Sun on the day of most light. Now, as an aspirant to greater knowledge of yourself, you mark the rising of the Sun at the time of winter darkness. As the beautiful floor of the Lodge is made of light and dark squares, so is the progress of the year made up of days of light and days of darkness. As you learn to enjoy light, so you must learn to withstand darkness; in this way you mark the progress you have made in our Craft.

'When you stood at the point of high summer you were likened to the foundation stone of a great temple. You were encouraged to become aware of your ethical and moral nature, exposed as it was to the light of high summer. Now, as you stand at the point of greatest winter darkness, look around and above you to see the more hidden mysteries of nature and science. They will be your next great area of study, to develop your rational nature.'

Mike nodded to me and then turned and saluted the Master, before continuing in a clockwise direction around the Lodge until he regained his seat. Meanwhile Master Paul had something else in store for me. He spoke to my escort.

'Brother Elder Deacon, will you please escort Brother Lomas to the north, where Brother Gibblin will reveal, present and interpret the Working Tools which Freemasonry offers to aid our Aspirant in this task?'

Arthur Gibblin, a retired Army engineer, always spoke with clipped military diction. I was taken round the Lodge to stand in the north, then Arthur marched round from his seat near the western door until he stood before the southern seat of the Junior Warden. He saluted the Master crisply. This time I noticed that the tool box was back on the edge of the black and white carpet. Arthur bent down to take some silvery objects out of it, then turned to face me.

'Brother Lomas. These are the tools which a Fellow of the Craft uses to improve his rational nature and study the more hidden mysteries of nature and science. They are the Square, the Level, and the Plumb Rule.'

He handed me a right-angled measure to hold before continuing.

'The Square is an instrument employed in the construction of fine buildings to ensure that all its corners form right angles. This helps turn raw building material into graceful temples.'

Now he passed me a T-shaped tool with a pendulum-type weight hanging from it. I added it to my collection and listened while he described it to me.

'The Level is to test surface orientation and verify the horizontal.'

Next he handed me a plumb-bob attached to a frame, saying, 'The Plumb Rule is to test and align uprights when securing them on a firm basis.'

Now I held three builder's tools. I looked down at them while Arthur continued with his ritual.

'But as we are not all operative, but free, accepted, or speculative Masons, we apply these tools to our minds and ethics.

'In this manner, the Square teaches us a sense of right and wrong, the Level that all people are of equal worth, and the Plumb Rule justice and upright action in life, so that by square strides, level gaits, virtuous and upstanding aims, we hope to move up to those celestial regions from which all order proceeds.'

He saluted the Master and then reached over to take the tools back from me, replacing them in the blue-velvet-lined box at his feet before marching away round the Lodge back to his seat.

As Arthur sat down Colin Brown, a rotund and jovial used-car dealer, stood up and set off round the Lodge until he stood in front of me. He nodded to the Master and, receiving a nod of assent, looked at me where I stood between my two escorts. Colin was an excitable Geordie, but he was obviously trying hard to speak slowly and clearly tonight, as I could follow most of what he said.

'Brother Lomas. Having aspired to the Second Degree of our Masonic Art we compliment you on your increase in Masonic awareness. As a Fellow, you already know the responsibilities of a Mason, and we do not need to remind you of the importance of continuing to practise them, as your experience as an Apprentice has demonstrated their value to your development.'

So I was being reminded to keep paying attention to the value of education in making me less emotional. But was there anything new coming up?

'Your demeanour as an Apprentice identified you as worthy of Masonic advancement, and in your new persona we anticipate that you will not only respect the principles of our Order but will purposely continue to develop your Masonic skill. The mastery of the

Liberal Arts, which so refine and develop the mind, is seriously commended to your meditations, especially the Science of Geometry, which is truly the basis of our Masonic Craft.'

The Liberal Arts? I quickly ran through them in my mind. Grammar, Rhetoric, Logic, Arithmetic, Geometry and Music. No, that's only six; what's the other one? I glanced at the temple roof and saw the patterns of stars there. That was it! Astronomy. But Colin was moving on, so I paid attention.

'The gravity of our ritual demands an earnest demeanour if you are to benefit from our regular assemblies; you are now a custodian of our ancient usages and customs which we urge you to keep as sacred and inviolable, and inspire others by your example, to learn from their application. The laws and ordinances of our Order you are urged to keep inviolate. You should not belittle or enhance the imperfections of your Brethren, but appraise with frankness, reprove with fellowship and disapprove of with clemency. Now you are a Fellow, you are encouraged to proffer your feelings and impressions on those fields of study which will be discussed in our lectures under the guidance of an experienced Master, who will secure the boundaries against violation.'

I had lots of thoughts on astronomy. Was I really going to get the chance to have open discussion about the naked singularity at the hidden centre of a black hole? I looked at Colin and decided I'd have to soft-pedal the maths.

'By this route you may improve your cerebral skill, develop yourself to become a more useful member of society, and strive to understand that which is good and great. You are punctually to accept and abide by all regular signs and summonses given and received. You are to promote diligence and reinforce worthiness; supply the wants and relieve the necessities of humanity to the utmost of your power and ability; and live in harmony with society, neither wronging or accepting wrongs which it is within your power to set right. Your interests are a part of the entirety of creation, and you should learn your place in this Order.'

He grinned at me, and the warmth of his delivery showed why he was such a good used-car salesman.

'Such is your way as a Craftsman, and you are bound by the most sacred ties to observe your new duties.'

As Colin finished he saluted the Master, set off round the Lodge, past where I was standing, and made his way back to his seat. Now Paul nodded to my escorts, who turned me to my left and led me right around the Lodge until I was standing two feet from where I had started, in front of the Master's pedestal. I wondered why we had to use such a long way round to go sideways. I decided not to ask at that point; it would surely cause an outbreak of tutting and might even make me a candidate for bird-feeding.

Paul looked at me and said, 'That concludes the ceremony to make you a Fellow of the Craft, and you may now withdraw, if you wish, to be restored to your personal comfort, but on your return to our company we have something further to impart to you.'

I knew better than to withdraw. My jacket was passed through to me and I sat down in the Lodge, waiting to see what other little treat of memory work was still in store for me — after the last ceremony I didn't expect to get away without homework. Paul turned to look at me. Here it comes …

'Brother Lomas. As before, there are test questions and answers in this degree which must be committed to memory. For your education, and to refresh the minds of the Brethren generally, Brother Junior Warden will put those questions to Brother Inner Guard, who will answer.'

I took a deep breath as I listened carefully to what I would soon know intimately.

The Junior Warden began. 'How were you equipped to be uplifted to the level of Fellow?

'In a somewhat similar manner to the First Degree, but I was not deprived of light and I had alternate areas of my body exposed.'

The questions went on and on. And I was going to have to remember them all. This time a different question stood out to reveal a new aspect of Masonry. This is the exchange which struck me as important as I listened.

'What are the singular aims of your study in this degree?'

'The hidden mysteries of nature and science.'

The litany of question and answer seemed to go on for ever, and the thought of having to memorise it all was getting a little worrying. At last it ended.

The Inner Guard gave the last answer I would need to memorise.

'The former to establish, the latter in strength, and, when brought together, stability; for the sacred law of the Most High says, "In strength will I establish my law, in this mine house, that it shall stand fast for ever".'

While the Lodge was closed in the Second Degree and lowered to the First-Degree level I sat and tried to recall as much of the test questions and answers as I could. Very little had stuck so far, but I did have an impression of what the Second Degree was about. It seemed to be about using scientific method to understand the hidden workings of the cosmos – an area of mental effort I was more than happy with. This degree seemed to mark some progress towards an understanding which had not yet become clear. But what was clear was that I was being encouraged to expand my mind by following appropriate intellectual and meditational exercises, all of which seemed to be preparing me for something more.

In the car, on the way home from the meeting, I asked Mike what the ritual of the spiral steps was trying to teach me.

'From what I've been told, there are three entrances to the Middle Chamber of the Masonic Temple, the place where you will discover Truth.' Mike said. 'These are the Gate Beautiful, the Gate of Works and the Gate of Knowledge.'

'But what do those mean?' I asked.

'Well, the Gate Beautiful is entered by devoting yourself to all that is good and beautiful. It means developing your aesthetic faculties. The Gate of Works is entered by carrying out good works and altruistic service and sacrifice for the good of society.'

'And what about the Gate of Knowledge?'

'That is the intellectual path, which you enter through enlightened mental application.'

'But how does this fit in with the idea of the spiral path?' I persisted.

'It's telling you that the cosmic law of the grand geometrician operates spirally.'

'And what might that mean?'

'The Second Degree shows you that motion and progress is not found by moving in straight lines, but by circling and approaching a truth which is invisible to us while we are searching for it,' he answered. 'The winding staircase is a symbolic representation of your personal path to the spiritual heights of awareness. In order to move upwards you must repeatedly practise rituals as you circle closer and closer to the centre of knowledge.'

'I'm not sure that makes a lot of sense to me,' I said.

'You wait until you've done your Third. Then it'll all be clear.' Mike stopped his car outside my door and I climbed out.

He was wrong! It took another eighteen years of study, and the research for five books, before I began to understand it. I hope reading this book will shorten that process for you.

Chapter Five

Another Tracing-board

Passing the Pillars

I was a Fellowcraft Freemason, and this meant I was allowed to wear a fancier pinny. It was still basically white, but with two pretty blue rosettes to jazz it up a bit. Now I cut a fine figure of a Mason in Lodge. But there's no such thing as a free festive board, and with the new finery came a new mission.

I was to make the liberal arts and sciences the focus of my Masonic study to help me better understand 'the wonderful works of the Most High'.

An uplifting thought, but how was I to set about it?

I was learning a little more about the peculiar ways of acquiring Masonic knowledge. I kept learning new words – for example I now knew that my ceremony of welcome into the Second Degree was called 'my passing'. I'd also noticed that, as the Lodge was lowered from the Second Level back to the First, a different picture board had been displayed in front of the Master's desk; this must have been revealed while the Lodge was open in the Second Degree. Was there a lecture for this new Tracing-board? As the Second-Degree Lodge was closed, the new picture had been covered by the now familiar Tracing-board of the First Degree. I'd had only a brief glimpse of it, and, if I'm honest, I'd been too worried about hearing the next test of memory I was about to be set to bother studying it. All I could recall was a vague impression of a drawing of a large building with a black-and-white chequered floor and a spiral staircase leading off it.

'Where do I find out about that new Tracing-board?' I asked Mike, as we drove together to the practice Lodge the following week.

'I think one of the lodges over at Lightcliffe is giving it in a couple of weeks' time,' he replied. 'I'll fix it for us to visit.'

That's how, two weeks later, I came to be looking for a parking space outside Lightcliffe Masonic Hall. The building had originally been built as a fire station, and from the road it still sported the large garage doors that had once concealed the fire engines of the local brigade. We entered by a side door and went upstairs. It didn't look like a fire station any longer – not unless it had been modelled on that of King Solomon's personal fire-protection unit. The temple was wood-panelled; above was a blue, star-strewn dome of a ceiling that hidden uplighters made to look like a summer evening sky. I pulled my gaze down to the floor, which was not a carpet but an inlaid chequerboard floor. As I stood in the doorway I felt a towering presence beside me. Turning, I saw the base of a great pillar, matched by an equally grand column on the other side of the doorway. Tilting my head back I marvelled at the carved network patterns, the rows of pomegranates, the lilies and the globes towering over me.

'Wow!' I said.

Allen, the Brother who was giving the Second-Degree Tracing-board, was a friend of Mike's, and I was soon introduced to the Lodge, welcomed and kitted out with a borrowed Fellowcraft's pinny. Allen had been in the Royal Navy in his youth, and still sported a full set of whiskers; later he'd taught science at secondary level for years, and his voice boomed out with the assured self-confidence of a senior teacher.

'You and Mike can sit in the north,' he said, ushering us into the temple. 'We'll be starting soon.'

Between the Two Pillars

This temple was the most impressive I'd so far seen. Its oak panelling, domed ceiling and marble black and white-tiled floor perfectly complemented the massive entrance pillars. The officers' chairs and pedestals were built into the wood-panelled walls of the room and were as magnificently carved as the entrance pillars. Some local worthies must have spent a 'bit o' brass' on the place. Looking back, I could see above the door a pair of double-interlaced equilateral triangles set in a curved arch. In the centre of this arch was a keystone that looked like a tapered plug set into the top of the curve. I was impressed. Here was symbolism on a grand scale.

I sat down next to Mike and watched the officers parade and take their seats. By now I was an old hand at going through the motions of opening the Lodge in the First Degree. But, as they worked through the minutes of previous meetings, I realised that to give the Second-Degree Tracing-board the Lodge would have to be opened in the Second Degree. I'd never even seen a lodge being opened in the Second Degree, let alone taken part in it. I felt a distinct twinge in my breastbone, just above my heart.

'I don't know the ritual for opening in the Second,' I whispered to Mike. 'Do I need to worry about the birds?'

'Just copy what I do,' he whispered back, 'You'll be OK. They all know you were only passed a week or so ago.'

'So they won't all jump on me and tear me to bits, then?'

'Probably not,' Mike grinned. 'Not unless you make a *total* pig's ear of the sign.'

'Thanks, you've really cheered me up!'

At that moment the Master knocked, and the sound was echoed around the room.

He spoke. 'Brethren. Please join with me to raise the level of this Lodge to the Second Degree.'

We all stood up and waited.

'Brother Junior Warden, what is our first duty as Masons?'

The Warden replied. 'To see that the Brethren are guarded from outside influences, Brother Master.'

The formality continued, with the chain of command being carefully followed.

First the Master said, 'Please check that we are well guarded', and then the Warden repeated the instruction to the Inner Guard. For reasons that would not become clear until much later, even Second-Degree masons pretend they can't hear the Master's voice directly but have to receive their instructions through a well-defined command structure. Once the guard had made sure the guy standing outside with the drawn sword had not been swamped by rampant cowans, an assurance was passed back up the chain of command.

Reassured that we were not about to be overrun by profane seekers after our secrets, the Master conferred with the Senior Warden sitting at the opposite end of the room.

'Brother Senior Warden, what do we do next?'

As I was coming to expect, this Warden also had an answer ready.

'Confirm that all here are Brethren, Brother Master.'

Once more I felt my heart twitching. Any moment now I'd have to try and give a snappy Second-Degree sign.

The Master spoke. 'Brethren, you will all give the secret sign of the First Degree.'

This was easy. I'd practised this sign quite a few times now and I was getting quite slick with it. It must have been reasonable, because nobody challenged me. My tongue was safe.

The Master spoke again. 'Brother Junior Warden, are you a Fellow of our Craft?'

That seemed a very formal question, as, from what Mike had told me, the Master chooses his junior officers. Either he had forgotten to check, or this was being done to remind the Lodge. This seemed to be a pattern with Masonic ritual.

'I am, Brother Master. Test me and authenticate me.'

'How would you be authenticated?'

'By the Square.'

'Explain the Square.'

'The Square is an angle of 90 degrees or the perfect quadrant of a circle.'

The Master was satisfied by this answer, but now he was about to set a test for me. My heart gave another little twitch of gruesome anticipation, as I realised what was coming.

'Now I have authenticated you to the satisfaction of the Brethren. Will you now authenticate the rest of the Brethren as Fellows of our Craft?'

Now I would have to try to remember the sign I'd been taught to give during the ceremony of my passing. The Junior Warden of a strange lodge was about to find out just how little I could remember about the teaching of my Second Degree. I took a deep breath.

'Brethren. Following the instruction of Brother Master you will show yourselves Fellows of our Craft by posture and sign.'

Well, I knew how to stand, and I had a rough idea of how to make the sign. I watched Mike carefully. He did each part of the sign slowly, waiting for me to copy his movements before continuing. We were the last to finish proving ourselves, and I got the distinct feeling that nobody was watching me too closely in case they made me nervous. Was it good enough? The Junior Warden was now looking me in the eye and seemed about to speak.

'The Brethren now having authenticated themselves as Fellows of our Craft, I also confirm the mystic sign.' He gave a much slicker rendition of the sign I'd clumsily copied from Mike, then winked at me.

The Master also gave a practised sign before moving on to speak to the Brethren, who were now all standing at attention.

'So, Brethren, our Lodge being prepared to ascend to the next level, let us take a moment to be aware of the influence of the Grand Geometrician of the Cosmos, that the celestial rays of the heavens may cast their genial effect upon us, so we may traverse safely the paths of virtue and science.'

He raised his arms in a dramatic gesture before continuing.

'Brethren. In the name of the Grand Geometrician of the Cosmos, I raise the level this Lodge to practise Masonry in the Second Degree.'

I joined in the chorus of 'So mote it be,' while everybody with a gavel banged it as loudly as possible.

For the first time I'd got through the opening of a Fellowcraft Lodge. Now I could sit down and relax while all the mysteries of the Second Degree were explained to me.

The Second-Degree Board

Allen cut a splendid figure in his Masonic regalia. 'Age and wisdom' – so he told me later in the bar – had bleached his full set of naval whiskers to a brilliant white. He looked like a blue-and-white Masonic Father Christmas as he stood in the centre of the Lodge. The two Deacons ceremonially carried the wooden Tracing-board from its normal place in front of the Master's desk to the centre of the Lodge and laid it on the floor. Allen had a long white pointer in his hand, ready to indicate areas of interest on the symbolic image now spread out before him.

He waited for the rustling of relaxation to quieten before speaking.

'Brethren ... the Tracing-board of the Second Degree tells us what reward we will receive for the Masonic work we have done as an Apprentice, as we travel the spiritual path to the Middle Chamber.'

He looked directly at me before carrying on.

'The Masonic work set for an Entered Apprentice is to develop the rational mind and bring the intellect into balance with the irrational urges of the flesh. The Tracing-board is a symbolic representation of the path to this reward, explained in terms of the myth of building a temple.'

The Tracing-board showed what looked like the entrance hall to a splendid building. There were various figures, a spiral stairway and a corridor disappearing to into a darkly mysterious inner chamber. Was this supposed to be Solomon's Temple?

Allen continued, 'The Masonic story says that Hiram, King of Tyre, was the civil engineer responsible for building the first Jewish Temple in Jerusalem, and he supplied many craftsmen for this historic endeavour. The client with the vision to commission such a great enterprise was Solomon, King of Israel, and he was responsible for paying the wages of the workforce. The symbolism tells us Hiram of Tyre set the standard of workmanship required, and Solomon decided the actual rewards for work done. As you work, so shall you be rewarded.'

Straightforward enough, so far. This lecture sounded almost like a discourse on contractual good practice. Much less esoteric than the First Degree.

'We are told that in those days the artificers were of two grades, Apprentices and Fellows. The Apprentices were given a weekly portion of corn, wine and oil, to feed them while they learned their craft; the Fellows were paid with metal tokens and had to present themselves in the Middle Chamber of the building site, to be paid in person by Hiram Abif, the supervising architect, a widow's son from the tribe of Naphtali.'

So there were two grades, and I was in the group who were supposed to be presenting themselves for payment. I'd acted out the charade of stepping round an invisible spiral staircase and felt rather silly doing it. Would it make more sense when I'd heard the full story?

'Our reward is to be found in the darkness of the Middle Chamber, which the Tracing-board shows us is approached from the East by passing between two great free-standing pillars.'

Allen pointed first to the pillar at the right hand of the doorway of the Lodge and then down to the Tracing-board.

'The southern pillar is called Boaz, after Boaz the great-grandfather of David, King of Israel. This name is connected with strength, and our Masonic tradition says of the southern pillar that "in it was strength".'

He then pointed to the other pillar, first the real pillar in the Lodge and then to the depiction on the Tracing-board.

'The northern pillar is called Jachin, after Jachin the High Priest of Jerusalem, who counselled King Solomon during the consecration of the Jerusalem Temple. Masonic tradition connects this name with stability, and it says of the northern pillar "its purpose was to establish".'

He swept his pointer in an arc to describe the key-stoned arch above the Lodge door.

'The two pillars combine to create harmony and stability; for the sacred law of the Most High says "In strength will I establish my law in this mine house that it will stand fast forever".'

Allen moved over to stand between the two pillars in the Lodge doorway. They towered over him. He paused and looked upward.

'Each pillar is seventeen and one half cubits in height, with a perimeter of twelve and one half cubits and a diameter of four cubits. They are cast as hollow structures, so their empty centres can be filled as a repository of Masonic wisdom.'

He pointed out the features of each pillar as he continued, 'Atop each pillar is an ornate chapiter*, five cubits tall. Each chapiter is adorned with tasselled, lozenge-shaped nets. This is an ancient symbol of fertility and spiritual life, known to the initiates of the inner secrets since time immemorial. Two rows of pomegranates, one hundred in each row, border the network; the profuse seeds of the pomegranate also symbolise birth and the gift of life. Topping each chapiter is a circle of lilies, a traditional symbol of new life, and all these symbols of life enclose the empty centre of the pillar.'

---

*The Capital, or decorative upper part of a pillar.

Returning to the centre of the Lodge he pointed down to one of the pillars graphically displayed on the Tracing-board.

'The southern pillar is placed in the region where the Sun rises on the darkest day of the year, and is topped with a globe of the world. It symbolises the darkness which swathes the material world.'

Moving his pointer to indicate the other pillar, he continued, 'The northern pillar is placed in the region where the Sun rises on the day of most light and is topped with a globe of the heavens. This symbolises the illumination and harmony of the sacred law, which can only be found by seeking knowledge of the centre, on which the globes rest.'

As he spoke, I realised that I had played the part of each of these pillars. As an Initiate I'd been placed where the sun rises at the summer solstice, but to become a Fellowcraft I was placed on the sunrise line of the winter solstice. The theme of the seasonal movement of the sun seemed to play an important role in the ritual. And as a Fellowcraft I was encouraged to study astronomy. I realised Allen was speaking again.

'When Hiram the architect completed these pillars he set them facing due east, so that the light of the rising Sun at the vernal equinox would illuminate both equally, thus ensuring a level sharing of enlightenment. Over each globe he cast a further lozenge net, indicating that fertile life is diffused throughout the cosmos, both in the world and the heavens.'

This was the first clear mention of the east–west line which seemed to be the main axis of the Lodge. Was I going to learn something about it? I focused my attention.

'These pillars remind the Craftsmen that, as an Apprentice, the Craft guides them from the darkness of the world to place them at the point of greatest light to show them where they might aspire to travel. When they become Fellows they are placed back at the point of greatest darkness, to show them it is their duty to carry light back into the world.'

This seemed to be clarification of my ritual placement in the first two ceremonies. I waited to see what would come next. Allen pointed to the Tracing-board, to two figures standing between the pillars.

'After passing between these great symbols of harmony the Fellow came to a guard, standing by an ear of corn, the symbol of the builders of civilisation. The farming of corn produced an economic surplus which freed some of the population from food production and allowed them to develop the skills of building.'

Allen paused, took a deep breath and looked slowly round the room before continuing.

'Here the Fellows were asked to prove themselves by means of a pass grip and a password. The word represents abundance of crops, shown symbolically in the Tracing-board as an ear of corn growing alongside a source of water. The word reminds us that our freedom to build rests on the labours of farmers, and by our work we must prove ourselves worthy of being freed of the daily toil of food production in order to build a great temple to the benefit of all.'

I remembered reading a paper about the domestication of corn, which pointed out that the most abundant corn strains would not reproduce naturally, and therefore needed to be harvested and replanted. Corn really is the key to civilisation. If we had continued to wander about hunting and gathering, then we would not have learnt how to build. This was an interesting idea.

Allen continued, 'This guard tests that we are properly prepared to proceed on into the perils within the building, leaving behind the light of the rising Sun to journey towards the darkness now visible in the Middle Chamber.'

What risk could there be in pretending to climb a non-existent spiral stairway? Was this just dramatic hyperbole or did it have some more subtle meaning? I paid attention to Allen, hoping to learn more.

'Beyond this guard is a black and white lozenge-covered pavement, reminding us that the web of light and life is intimately intertwined with, and a part of, a balancing web of darkness and death. We must expect to walk in both darkness and light to reach the spiral stairway leading upwards to the Middle Chamber, where the wages of our Masonic industry will be paid.'

This symbolism seemed to be talking about the ups and downs of living, for better, for worse, the good times and the bad. Did it have a deeper message?

'The spiral, another ancient symbol, older even than the lozenge net, symbolises the cycle of seasonal life combined with movement forwards. An early Masonic catechism tells us that circular staircases are passages which wind among the walls and point out the hidden knowledge which becomes known only to those who ascend to celestial things.'

The reference to celestial things echoed what had been said in the First-Degree Tracing-board lecture. Was I about to be told something more?

'The spiral also reminds us that a ritual may need to be repeated many times before progress can be made towards the level of the Middle Chamber, where we receive our reward and share in the hidden knowledge of the centre.'

Now that was something I could relate to. Practice is necessary for most things. Dewey, the American educational theorist, had talked about the spiral path of learning – how we move from unconscious incompetence to conscious incompetence, then continue via conscious competence until, with enough repetition, we finally achieve unconscious competence and wonder what all the fuss was about. I stopped reflecting on the nature of learning and paid attention to the on-going lecture.

'The steps we take on the spiral path are three, five, then seven or more. These remind us that three leaders are needed to guide a lodge, five to make it whole, and the spiritual message of Masonry is clear for any seven or more who would give heed to it.'

Allen cleared his throat, first pointing slowly to the Master, then to each of the Wardens in turn.

'Masonic legend says that three principals guide a lodge, because during the building of the first Jewish Temple in Jerusalem there were three key leaders: Hiram, King of Tyre, the engineer and builder who provided skilled workers and converted raw materials into a beautiful temple: Hiram Abif, the architect and supervisor who drew the designs and oversaw their fabrication; and Solomon, King of Israel, who had the vision to create a temple and paid the wages of the craftsmen who constructed it. But if we look a little deeper, the symbolism will remind us that to create our own temple we need a vision to believe it can be created, we need to convert our raw materials to beautiful worked stones, but we also need a detailed design to follow if we are to achieve a perfect structure.'

He pointed to the two Deacons whilst continuing.

'The five, who make a lodge whole, are said to symbolise the five noble orders of architecture being the Tuscan, Doric, Ionic, Corinthian and Composite, each representing different combinations of strength, soundness and beauty which we will experience as we move through the light and shadow of our path towards the Middle Chamber.'

Then, in a great sweeping gesture, he indicated all the assembled Brethren.

'Masonic myth says the seven or more who make a lodge perfect alludes to the seven years and upwards taken to build and dedicate the Temple at Jerusalem to the Most High. But this number can also refer to the seven liberal arts and sciences, which are Grammar, Rhetoric, Logic, Arithmetic, Geometry, Music and Astronomy. And should we choose to look at the personal meaning of the seven, it tells us that by devotion to the liberal arts of education and learning, our mind may become exalted above surface appearance to ascend gently and gradually by the spiral path to levels of widened consciousness and understanding.'

Allen began to trace out the steps of the degree, proceeding from west to east. As he moved slowly forwards he explained his steps.

'As we spiral round the rising centre of the stairway we are lifted to the higher level of the Middle Chamber where we find a pavement of black and white squares and another guarded door. We must cross this more geometrically perfect square pavement, but even as we strive for square behaviour we cannot avoid meeting both darkness and light as we travel towards the Middle Chamber.'

He stopped and cowered back, as if confronted by an armed guard.

'As we approach the entrance to the Middle Chamber a guard challenges us to demonstrate that our knowledge of Masonry extends to the level of a Fellow before allowing us to enter the Middle Chamber, warning us that only those who are morally equipped and emotionally stable should venture into the darkness of the Middle Chamber. Those who are not yet qualified are denied access.'

Allen held out his hand and slowly rotated, holding his open palm out to each direction of the Lodge in turn.

'Once inside, we receive the payment due for our work – no more, no less. This assessment comes from our own mind, and so can never be challenged.'

He closed his hand and made the Masonic sign of fidelity.

'In the centre of his heart, each fellow knows how much work has been undertaken.'

He stopped turning and pointed upwards to the roof of the temple, where there was a brightly lit five-pointed star in the roof space.

'The ritual records that the more aware Brethren observe that within the centre of the Middle Chamber is a profound symbol, the letter 'G' shining from the centre of a blazing star.

'This symbol we display in the centre of our lodges and know it as "the Glory". It symbolises the Grand Geometrician of the Cosmos, to whose sacred laws we must all submit, and most cheerfully accept.'

Allen turned, saluted the Master, bowed to the Lodge and walked clockwise around to the Lodge back to his seat.

What's a Tracing-board?

In the car, driving back home after the meeting, I asked Mike where the idea of the Tracing-board had come from.

'The idea of the Tracing-board,' he said, 'is really to help a Mason reflect on the quickening of consciousness that Freemasonry is trying to encourage.'

'Do you mean it's a visual way of teaching how the symbols relate to each other?'

'Not quite,' he said. 'I think that Freemasonry is a serious spiritual system. As you saw with the First-Degree Tracing-board, it starts by explaining that a human is made up of three parts. An elementary, emotional personality, a mental or intellectual nature and a spiritual self which is part of the glory of the Centre.'

'But how does this relate to the Tracing-boards?' I asked.

'In times past, the Tracing-boards were diagrams drawn personally by each Brother to symbolise this spiritual journey. Before a ceremony the board of the degree would be drawn with chalk on the floor, and the candidate would walk the path through the symbols, as Allen walked the steps tonight whilst explaining them. The diagram would be explained to the candidate as an intrinsic part of the ceremony, and, to impress it on the mind, the candidate would have to clean it from the floor with a mop and bucket, before re-dressing in worldly finery. This was to teach both humility and secrecy.'

'Sounds pretty humiliating,' I commented.

'Not really. It reminded you that nobody can avoid collective responsibility, and that each, from the lowest to the highest, should take a turn at all the important tasks of society,' Mike said. 'Still that's long gone. Some Brother got the idea the diagrams could be drawn on a floorcloth and rolled out for the meeting. Then the job became helping to roll up and store the floorcloth.'

'That sounds less hassle,' I said.

'Yes, but it took away the need to develop drawing skills, which have always been important to operative masons. But it did keep the tradition of letting the Candidate walk the steps over the symbols of the floorcloth. We lost that when picture-boards replaced floorcloths. That's why I like the way Allen does it. Walking the path round the Lodge, and laying the board on the floor at the centre of the Lodge.'

'So what do you think I should reflect on about this Second-Degree Board?' I asked.

'You need to realise that the Tracing-board lecture you have just seen shows you as midway on your journey to Masonic knowledge. You need to learn the lessons of the degree, to develop your understanding of the hidden mysteries of nature and science to perform the work well enough to be worthy of your wages. But this is still a stage on your spiritual journey to a fuller light which lies at the centre but which is not yet visible to you.'

'So, in the meantime, what do I do?' I asked.

'Learn your questions,' Mike said. 'You'll soon be tested on them. Now, how were you equipped to be uplifted to the level of Fellow?'

'In a somewhat similar manner to the First Degree, but I was not deprived of light and I had alternate areas of my body exposed,' I responded, hoping to make myself ready for the Third Degree. For all my careful preparation, though, the reality of the Third-Degree ritual would surprise me, and even shock me.

Chapter Six

A Matter of Death and Life

Riding the Goat

'Are you ready for this?' Mike asked as we walked through the porch-way of Ryburn Lodge a few months later. It was the evening of my Raising, as he kept calling the ritual of the Third Degree that I was at last to undergo. 'You've remembered? Sober, clean underpants?'

'Of course,' I said. 'Is it tonight I really get to ride the goat?'

'You've been listening to Denis, haven't you?'

'That's a secret,' I grinned.

'Well, David had the cattle trailer behind his Land-Rover when he arrived,' Mike countered.

'I hope it's a nanny goat.'

'Of course, it's a nanny goat. You aren't thinking you might have to take part in an unnatural act are you?' Mike laughed. 'Want a last run through the questions? How were you equipped to be uplifted to the level of Fellow?'

Soon afterwards these answers were still running through my mind while I sat in the north side of the Lodge

giving my signs to prove myself a Fellow of the Craft as the Lodge was opened to the level of the Second Degree.

Paul, the Master in the chair, announced the next business: to reincarnate Bro. Lomas. I stood up ready, as Paul spoke to the Deacons.

'Brother Deacons, please escort our Novitiate to the west.'

One more I stood in the west of the Lodge facing the Master's pedestal, running quickly through the test questions in my mind as I waited. Paul interrupted my revision.

'Brother Lomas. Are you mentally, emotionally and spiritually prepared this evening to be transposed to the Third Degree?'

I didn't need prompting to answer. 'I am.'

'Before you can be effectively transposed to the sublime level of Craft Masonry, we must be sure that you have developed sufficient skill in the former degrees. Will you therefore be prepared to be tested with the requisite questions?'

Here it comes. Could I remember them all? I'd soon know.

'How were you equipped to be uplifted to the level of Fellow?'

'In a somewhat similar manner to the First Degree, but I was not deprived of light, and I had alternate areas of my body exposed.' So far so good.

'What symbol marked your entry?'

So it went on, and I found the answers flowed automatically as I heard the next question. ... Finally, Paul said:

'What do these names mean?' That's the last question. I've done it! *And* without provoking any obvious tutting!

'The former to establish, the latter in strength, and, when brought together, stability; for the Most High stated, "In strength will I establish my laws, in this mine house, that it shall stand fast for ever".'

Paul smiled at me, and I could hear the rush of air as the Brethren watching stopped holding their collective breath. Now came the hard part. Paul was going to ask me to repeat the full obligation. No prompts for this memory test.

'Please repeat the pledge you made when you became a Fellow.'

I took a deep breath and began.

'I, Robert Lomas, before the Grand Geometrician of the Cosmos, and in the presence of this worthful and venerable Lodge of antient free and accepted Fellows of the Craft of Masonry. Duly established, frequently held, gathered together, and decently devoted to the sacred law, do hereby and hereon, of my own free volition and intention. Most solemnly promise, vow and swear that I will forever hele, keep, conceal and never reveal ...'

On and on through the tortuous language of the obligation I continued. It was easier this time, much easier than the First Degree. I found that each phrase keyed in the next, just as the questions had keyed the answers into my memory. I was beginning to enjoy working the ritual.

'So help me the Grand Geometrician of the Cosmos and keep me steadfast and firm in this my second great and worthy pledge of a newly uplifted Fellow of the Craft.'

I'd done it. No hesitation, no deviation, not even any repetition. I could memorise ritual. The Brethren gave me a brief round of glove-muffled applause. Paul was smiling at me. Then his face went solemn as he continued with his own ritual recitation.

'Brother Lomas. Do you also pledge, on your honour as a man and your faithfulness as a Fellow of the Craft, that you will steadily persist along the dark spiral pathways of your inner self to ascend to the sublime level of the Third Degree?'

'I do.' There was a mention of that spiral again.

'Do you likewise gravely accept to hide that which I am about to make known to you, with the same rigorous circumspection as you did the mysteries of the lower degrees?'

I knew the routine now.

'I do,' I answered confidently.

'On that basis I entrust you with a test of merit to assist you in finding a path towards the mystery at the centre of Freemasonry.' Paul then went on to tell me a password, and show me yet another odd grip.

'This is called the passing grip, leading from the Second to the Third Degree in Freemasonry.' He took my hand and made sure I knew how to give the grip correctly. Then he told me a word, which my obligation does not allow me share with you. But Paul warned me:

'You must be particularly careful not to forget this word, as, without it, you will be unable to gain admission into a lodge in a superior degree. You will now retire in order to be prepared to be raised to the Third Degree.'

Winston, the Tyler, was waiting for me.

'Get 'em off lad.' he said. 'You know the routine by now.'

I *was* quite used to the procedure. Winston prepared me, making sure all the right bits of my anatomy were on public display, and then the Deacons came out to inspect his handiwork. They approved, and we all stood line abreast behind Winston, who knocked on the closed door of the temple.

'Hang on,' said Syd, the Senior Deacon. 'We've still got the outside lights on.' Winston turned the hall light off, and we stood in darkness waiting for the Inner Guard to open the door. When he did I began to realise that this degree might be different from everything which had gone before.

Facing My Inner Darkness

Outside the Lodge the unlit hall was black and dark. As the door opened, light flooded out of the Lodge.

Graham, the Inner Guard, spoke out of the backlit brilliance: 'Who seeks enlightenment?'

Winston replied, 'Brother Lomas, who has been properly apprenticed to the Craft of Masonry, has been duly enlifted to the level of a Fellow of that Craft and now proceeds of his own free will and volition to meekly petition for enlightenment within the sublime degree of a Master Mason, having proved himself ready in open Lodge.'

'How does he hope to obtain this enlightenment?'

'By insight of the Most High, the potent support of the compass and square and the knowledge of a passing grip and word.'

I felt a hand touching mine. 'Give me that passing grip and word.' I gave the grip and pronounced the word I had been given just a few minutes before. I must have got it near enough because Graham said, 'Halt, Brother, whilst I report to the worshipful Master.' Then he closed the door.

After a few minutes the door opened again but this time the interior of the Lodge was dark and threatening. My escorting Deacons led me forward while Graham held the twin points of a well-spread pair of compasses to my naked chest. As I fell the prick of the cold steel points he said, 'Enter this Lodge of Master Masons within the scope of the compass.'

As my eyes adjusted to the deep gloom I realised that the temple was not in complete darkness. In the East there was a faint glimmer of light. As I looked more closely I saw that it was the Master's candle, which had been shielded so that no direct light from it shone into the Lodge. The reflector directed the flickering candle glow on to the eastern wall of temple, making it look like the pre-dawn sky on a moonless night.

The Deacons led me into the western side of the Lodge, so that I looked towards the faceless black shadow that I knew must be Paul, the Master of the Lodge. He spoke, and his voice confirmed his identity.

'Let the Novitiate kneel whilst the light of the celestial realms is called down to illuminate what we are about to do.' Paul knocked with his gavel, and the knocking was echoed around the room. 'Brethren, to order. Brother Chaplain. ...'

The voice of Stan, the chaplain, came out of the darkness.

'Oh Most High Custodian of the Sacred Law, whose dependable edicts ensure the regularity of the cosmos, we are simple novices in the ramifications of that law, seeking by contemplation to draw nearer to a greater understanding of thy underlying truth. Help us to educate our Brother, kneeling here, to aspire to enlightenment. May this Lodge unite to share its tranquillity of mind with this seeker after truth. We offer our support on the most awesome journey any mortal being can undertake, through the dark depths of spiritual night to the brightness of the eternal stars.'

As he finished the whole Lodge spoke in chorus, saying, 'So mote it be.'

Paul's voice spoke again.

'Let the Novitiate rise. The Brethren in all points of the compass will please observe that Brother Lomas will now perambulate before them to demonstrate that he is a novitiate for enlightenment made properly ready to be conducted towards the sublime knowledge of a Master Mason. Brethren, be seated.'

Syd, the Senior Deacon, took hold of my arm, and whispered in my ear, 'Left foot first. Square the Lodge,' before leading me off on the well-known pilgrimage of the outer circumference of the temple.

As we went round and round we occasionally stopped at the chairs of the Wardens, so that they could test that I knew all the right grips and passwords of the earlier degrees as well as the keys to the present one.

I ended up standing in front of Roy, the Senior Warden. He had just tested my knowledge of the passing word and grip and made sure I knew exactly what it meant. Now he stepped out from behind his desk, took my hand and turned me to face the faintly lit East. He spoke to Paul.

'Brother Master. Allow me to acquaint you with Brother Lomas, who was properly apprenticed to the Craft of Masonry, has been duly enlifted to the level of a Fellow of that Craft and now proceeds of his own free will and volition to meekly petition for enlightenment within the sublime degree of a Master Mason, having proved himself ready in open Lodge.'

'Brother Senior Warden, I look to your presentation and ask you to instruct the Senior Deacon to progress the Aspirant to the East by the traditional steps.'

Senior Warden Roy told Senior Deacon Syd what he had to do, and Syd took my arm and led me to the north-west corner of the Lodge. There he let go of me and moved to stand in front of me. By now my eyes had adjusted to the low, flickering light from the shaded candle in the East, and I could see Syd as a dark mass against the black-and-white squares of the Lodge flooring as he spoke.

'Brother Lomas. The manner of progressing from west to east in this degree is by seven or more paces. I will demonstrate the method to you. Observe and copy.'

Reg, the Junior Deacon, helped me copy the strange series of steps, so that I ended up standing between the two Deacons in front of the altar, which held the volume of the sacred law. Being so much closer to the tiny flame, I could see the book lay open. Paul was standing on the far side of the pedestal. Now he spoke to me.

'The wisdom of Masonry keeps the knowledge of each degree separate, so that only well-prepared novitiates may obtain knowledge. A further grave pledge is required of you. It is similar in many ways to the one you made as a Fellow. Are you ready to take it, as you should?'

Syd prompted me: 'I am.' I repeated the words, and Paul continued.

'It is but just to warn you that a more severe test of your strength of mind and faithfulness now opens before you. Are you prepared to meet it as you should?'

Again Syd prompted me. 'I am' I repeated.

Paul continued, 'Then you will kneel and place both hands on the Volume of the Sacred Law,'

Lawrence, the immediate Past Master – who I now noticed was sitting in the Master's chair – knocked with the Master's gavel, and the sound was copied around the darkened temple. As the sound of the knocking died away Paul's voice sounded out, giving a command.

'Brethren, to order.'

There was sudden movement round the temple, as all the members pulled themselves to their feet. Then quiet descended in the darkness, and Paul spoke again.

'Say your complete name in full, and repeat after me.'

I repeated after him saying, 'I Robert Lomas, before the Most High Exemplar of the Sacred Law, and of this worthful and venerable Lodge of antient free and accepted Masters of the Craft of Masonry. Duly established, frequently held, gathered together, and decently devoted to the sacred law, do hereby and hereon, of my own free volition and intention. Most solemnly promise, vow and swear that I will forever hele, keep, conceal, and never reveal ...'.

And so I became an obligated Master Mason. On and on went this new pledge, which by now I knew I would be expected to memorise by the next meeting. It contained far more detail than previous ones, and a particular part caught my attention.

'... I also soberly affirm that from this moment forward I will take the mystical union of the Compass and Square to be the focus of my Masonic meditation and insight ...' I wondered what that might mean, but the momentum of the ritual carried me on, committing me to things I didn't yet understand.

'I will defend and maintain the Five Points of Fellowship, in enactment as well as in concept; that my grip given to a Brother Master will be a certain assurance of companionship, that my steps shall track through perils and risks, to join with his in forming a file of reciprocal protection and reinforcement; that, whilst meditating on the Sacred Law, I will not forget the deprivation and privations of my fellow humans and dispose my centre to alleviate their needs and assuage hardship, so far as may be done without damage to myself or family.'

What were the Five Points of Fellowship? Whatever they might be – I made a mental note to ask Mike about them later – I was committed to defend and upholding them. But the commitments went on and on, until at last I found myself repeating:

'These several points I solemnly swear to observe, under no less a consequence than that of having my body split in four, burnt to ashes, and those ashes scattered before the four cardinal compass points of the world, so that no trace or remnant of so vile a wretch may longer be found among men, particularly Master Masons.'

This was the most serious consequence so far. There would be nothing of me left to smart if this one ever got carried out. I silently thanked the Health and Safety Executive for its benevolent influence.

'So help me the Most High Exemplar of the Sacred Law and keep me steadfast and firm in this my third great and worthy commitment of a newly pledged Master Mason.'

Now I had made the formal pledge of a Master Mason, the ritual obviously freed Paul to explain part of the degree to me. Interested as I was, I didn't want the speech to take too long, though. I was still kneeling in one of the highly uncomfortable postures that Freemasonry seemed to specialise in, and was hoping I could avoid making a spectacle of myself by hopping around the Lodge in an agony of cramp.

'Allow me, once more, to point out the emplacement of the Compasses and Square. When you were but an Apprentice both points were concealed from your sight. Then as a Fellow of our Craft, one point was revealed, showing you had further to travel before you could achieve the full understanding that Masonry can offer. Now you are about to enter the sublime condition of a Master Mason, the full scope of the compasses are revealed to you, in order that your spirit may encompass the mystery of the centre.'

Finally he allowed me to stand and stretch my cramped legs. He also allowed the standing Brethren to sit down. Then he began a lengthy speech which focused my attention on the progress I had already made within Masonry.

'Now you have pledged your fidelity to this Lodge of Master Masons, you have the right to require us to guide your spirit on that final and most extraordinary journey by which you may hope to experience the sublime delight of the centre. But first allow me to remind you of the work you have already accomplished, so you may reflect and understand the purpose of our Craft.'

There again was the reference to this mystery at the centre. Was this the objective I was moving towards? Perhaps the ritual might help me make sense of the earlier degrees?

'You joined our Order in a state of darkness and spiritual poverty. You were allowed to bring nothing into the Lodge but your own spirit, stripped to a state of naked indigence. As an Apprentice Freemason you were told there was a spiritual light at the centre, and how to prepare your spirit to perceive it. You were shown how to use the working tools of an Apprentice to equip you to develop a rational mind and bring your intellect into balance with the irrational urges of the flesh. To aid you in this, you were equipped with postures, a Lodge structure to focus your thinking, and a set of symbols and spiritual tools. Only when you had balanced your rational mind against your bodily urges, learned how to use posture and symbolism, and gained proficiency in the use of spiritual tools, were you ready to move on the Second Degree.'

So the purpose of the First Degree was to help me bring the emotional drives of my body under the rational control of my intellect. This is a key feature of education and made sense of the working tools of that degree. But had I really managed to bring my emotions under the control of my intellect? I rather doubted whether I had gained much proficiency in staying placid.

Paul continued, 'When you passed the test of merit which lifted you to the spiritual level of a Fellow of our Craft, you were exhorted to develop your intellect and to study the more hidden ways of nature and science in order to better understand the rule of the Sacred Law and to begin to contemplate the mind of the Grand Geometrician of the Cosmos. The Second Degree helps you to balance your intellect and your emotions, so that you learned how to recognise truth and discriminate between irrational urges of the flesh and the truth of the spirit. You were given further postures, tools and symbols to help you strengthen your rational mind and learn to handle your emotions, so that you were prepared for the discovery of the blazing star of truth, which was as yet only visible as darkness at the centre. Here you met the spiral symbol which can teach you how to approach the centre. The postures affect your body and feed back hormonal responses into your rational mind, so helping you learn how to subdue emotion. But before you can proceed to the Third Degree you must prepare yourself to let go of your ego and self-regard.'

I had found the intellectual challenges of the Second Degree far more interesting than the urging towards dry emotional control which had formed the message of the First Degree. But I could see now why the spiral was such a useful symbol if I wanted to bring my emotions and intellect into balance. I would need to practise. But what was the purpose of such a task? What would it do for me? I listened as Paul explained further.

'Now your mind has been shaped by morality and logic, creation has a further noble and functional insight to offer the prepared mind and body: the knowledge of yourself. As you ponder, anticipate your own demise, when you must face the final challenge of personal extinction.'

Was this the core of the Masonic secret – a cure for existentialist angst? Did I have any existentialist angst to cure? I wasn't sure. I certainly had a strong curiosity about extinction, though. As a scientist I could hardly expect to be immortal, but, if anything, I inclined towards the Woody Allen school of existentialism: I wasn't really afraid of dying, I just didn't want to be there when it happened.

Was Freemasonry going to help with this?

Paul continued, 'This, my dear Brother, is the singular aim of this sublime degree of Freemasonry. It invites you to meditate upon this sombre subject and seeks to show you that, to the true Mason, death has no horror which matches that of being false and dishonourable. The great myths of Freemasonry record a magnificent illustration of the undaunted fidelity and inopportune murder of our historical Grand Master, Hiram Abif, who was killed just before the conclusion of the construction of the Jerusalem Temple, of which you should be well aware he was the supervising architect.'

I really had little idea of who Hiram Abif was. The only mention I had ever heard of his name was in the Second-Degree Tracing-board, where I had been told that he administered the wages of Fellowcrafts in the Middle Chamber of the part-finished Temple of Jerusalem. Paul seemed to nearing the end of his explanation.

'This is the way in which Hiram the Architect met his death,' he said, and then turned to my escorts. 'Brother Wardens.'

The Darkness of High Noon

My escorts drew me back, through the encircling gloom of the temple, towards the centre. Meanwhile the two Wardens, each holding some sort of architectural tool came and stood alongside Paul. Once everybody stopped moving about I was standing in line with Paul, who stood directly in front of the Master's place in the East.

My First Degree had been conferred in the North-East, where the sun rises on the day of greatest light. My Second Degree was awarded in the South-East, where the sun rises on the day of greatest darkness. Was it deliberate that my Third Degree was about to be given while I stood in the East, where the sun rises at the vernal equinox? It is the one day when light and dark are in perfect balance.

The Master and his Wardens formed a menacing line of black out-lines against the flickering reflected candle glimmer. Paul spoke in a solemn and dramatic voice.

'During the construction of the Jerusalem Temple the secrets of the Centre were known to only three: Hiram, King of Tyre, the civil engineer responsible for building the first Jewish Temple in Jerusalem; Solomon, King of Israel, the client with the vision to commission such a great enterprise; and Hiram Abif, the supervising architect. A group of Fellows of the Craft, fifteen in number, were appointed as overseers, but were not given the secrets of the Centre. Feeling that, as responsible overseers, they should be entitled to these secrets, they decided they would attempt to extort them from the three Masters.

'As the sun set, on the day before they had agreed to execute their plot, they met. Twelve individuals thought better of their plan, but three more of a stubborn and depraved nature resolved to continue with the villainous project. Hiram the architect was known to pay homage to the Most High at the hour of High Twelve when the sun stood at its southern zenith, the day's light was brightest, and a man's shadow was at its lowest ebb.'

Paul paused, while a slow tolling bell rang out twelve echoing tones. The lonely sound reverberated through the darkness of the temple. As the sound died away Paul picked up the story.

'In furtherance of their malign intent they stood at the East, West and South gates of the unfinished temple, knowing full well that Master Hiram was inside the structure at this sacred moment of the day.

'When Master Hiram had completed his venerations he went towards the Southern gate, where the light was brightest. This gate was known as "The Gate Beautiful", representing all that is good and beauteous and love-worthy.

'There he was set upon by the first assailant, who had taken as a weapon the symbol we use to represent moral uprightness, the plumb rule. The miscreant called for Master Hiram to reveal the secrets of the centre, threatening to use the force of moral uprightness to destroy him if he should refuse. Being aware that the reprobate was not yet fit to experience the knowledge of the centre, Master Hiram refused to reveal it.

'This answer not proving satisfactory, the aggressor struck our Master a savage stroke to his right temple, forcing him to fall to the ground on his opposite knee.'

As I was listening to this enthralling adventure story I suddenly realised that it was more than a gripping yarn. The Junior Warden raised his hands. Against the flickering backdrop I could see the shape of a plumb rule as he brought it down towards my head. The story came alive for me at that moment. How should I respond to such an attack? My will told me to protect myself, but the ritual situation told me this was only symbolic, and I should submit to it. At that moment I felt the confusion and indecision of how to respond in a life-threatening situation. As I hesitated, I felt a light blow to my right temple, and simultaneously my escorts made sure that I slid down on to my left knee. I felt as dazed as Hiram must have done. What should I do? Before I could decide, Paul continued. The ritual story-telling took over again, and I was drawn back into the unfolding story.

'Although slightly dazed, Master Hiram rose to his feet and hurried towards the darkness of the Western gate, known as "The Gate of Works", which represents selfless activity and sacrifice.'

I was lifted to my feet by the Deacons, and the threatening figure of the Junior Warden stood back.

'There he was accosted by a second assailant, who had seized the strength of equality, and adopted as a weapon its symbol, the level.'

The figure to the left of the Master was raising an architect's level above his head and stepping towards me. Again I felt the surge of adrenalin which told me I was being threatened and should prepare to respond. I began to lift my left arm in a blocking movement, but I was held by the Deacons as the level descended towards my left temple. Paul's voice continued its impassive unfolding of this ancient myth.

'Once again our Master was ordered to reveal the secret of the centre, under threat of death – but, well knowing that equality alone did not qualify the attacker to understand the secrets, he refused to reveal them. The miscreant struck Master Hiram a fierce blow to his left temple, forcing him to fall on the opposite knee.'

Once again the Deacons forced me down, this time on to my right knee. As I acted out the role of the mistreated Hiram, my bodily responses provided an emotional background script as I experienced the feelings of a man under attack. But I was not given time to reflect. The Deacons once again pulled me to my feet, as the looming presence of the Senior Warden withdrew into the surrounding gloom. Like a solid stream of reality, Paul's narration continued its unperturbed flow.

'Realising there was but one chance of getting away from these material forces, Master Hiram stumbled eastwards, hoping to escape from the demands of The Insidious by the East gate, known as "The Gate of Wisdom".'

What was Paul doing now? He was raising what looked likely a heavy stone-setting hammer above his head. His dark shape personified threat. Even though I knew this was only ritual, as he moved towards me I felt an instinctive fear of death move deep within me. But, even as he menaced me, Paul's unemotional voice continued to unfold the dreadful myth.

'There he was faced with a third assailant, armed with the temporal force of a heavy stone hammer. Once more the secret of the centre was demanded, but Master Hiram did not acknowledge that temporal force should be sufficient qualification to allow an unsuitable candidate to extort the secret, and so he refused.'

At this point Paul brought the hammer down towards my head. I flinched and closed my eyes in anticipation as I felt the heavy maul touch the centre of my forehead. The steady force of the contact pushed me backwards. As I started to overbalance I tried to flail out my arms to regain balance, but they were restrained by two Deacons who stopped me struggling. Paul hadn't finished the story.

'The attacker struck Master Hiram a ferocious blow to the centre of his forehead, which killed him instantly. This, my Brother, is how Hiram the Architect died to guard the knowledge of the centre.'

I felt myself being lowered backwards towards the black-and-white chequered floor of the Lodge. Above me, barely visible in the gloom, I could just make out the outline of the unlit Glory, high in the dark recesses of the temple roof. The Deacons were arranging my arms as if I were a corpse. I lay still and let them. Meanwhile Paul's voice continued.

'To conceal their crime, the three assailants buried Master Hiram in a shallow grave.'

The Deacons had covered my prone body with a fine linen sheet. In the gloom of the Lodge the cloth looked either grey or white; I couldn't tell. As I lay, still as death, shrouded in a grave cloth, all I could see was the dim shape of the five-pointed star surrounding the letter G, high above me in the roof of the temple. Another voice spoke from somewhere off to my right.

'Master Masons of Ryburn Lodge, assemble round the grave of our Brother here laid low.'

I could hear shuffling and movement as the Brethren of my Lodge stood around me. As I looked upwards from the centre of this ring of silhouettes, I seemed to be watching my own funeral. Paul spoke to my assembled Brothers.

'Brethren, in this ritual, our fallen Brother has symbolised one of the most illustrious Brothers in the ancient tales of Freemasonry, that is Hiram the Architect, who chose to die rather than fail to be true to the sacred knowledge of the centre which he held in trust. We hope Hiram's fidelity has made an enduring impression, not only on our own Brother's mind, but on your minds too.'

His voice dropped as he spoke an aside.

'Brother Junior Warden. You will now attempt to resurrect this symbol of Master Hiram, using the grip which represents the knowledge of an Apprentice Freemason.'

I saw a dark shape looming, blocking out what little light there was. How come, if I'd been buried in an unmarked, shallow grave, they were now all standing round me? The story seemed disconnected. Obviously, for the ritual to have a suitable climax my body needed to be found, but the whole question of its discovery had been neatly glossed over. I stopped worrying about narrative consistency and played my limp and tacit part in the developing tension.

The cloth was pulled back, and a gloved hand took mine. It pulled at me with a weak First-Degree grip, which slid off my hand and up my fingers. My hand was laid gently back across my chest, and the cover replaced. I lay back and contemplated the dark Glory above me.

I heard the voice of the Junior Warden saying, 'Brother Master, the knowledge gripped by an Apprentice is not enough to resurrect our Brother.'

The organist then struck up the Dead March and the Brethren surrounding my grave marched in solemn procession around my supine form. The impact was awesome, and seemed to last for ever, but finally the dirge stopped and the Brethren stood to attention above me. Paul spoke again.

'Brother Senior Warden. You will now attempt to resurrect this symbol of Master Hiram, using the grip which represents the knowledge of a Fellow of the Craft.'

Once more the winding sheet was unwrapped, my limp hand drawn out, and this time a weak Second-Degree grip slipped from my hand. Once more my arm was replaced under its shroud. I heard the voice of the Senior Warden.

'Brother Master, the knowledge gripped by a Fellow is not enough to resurrect our Brother.'

Again the organ sounded a dirge, and the Brethren marched in procession around the centre where I lay. When the music stopped Master Paul spoke again.

'Brother Wardens. You have applied the combined knowledge of an Apprentice and a Fellow, yet have failed to resurrect our fallen Brother. But Masonry offers a third technique, that of elevating him on the Five Points of brotherly society. With you to offer your support, I will now try this method.'

For a third time the shroud was rolled back and my limp hand taken by a Brother. But this grip was different. With the two wardens taking my weight I was hinged upwards into Paul's close embrace. I realised afterwards that his body touched mine at five points, the five points of fellowship which I had committed myself to defending and upholding.

Paul held me in this intimate five-pointed embrace while he whispered to me.

'In this way, my dear Brother, has each and every Master Mason been resurrected from a symbolic death, to rejoin with the fellow spiritual pilgrims.'

Paul let me go and stood back from me. Over his shoulder I could see a bright five-pointed star glowing brightly on the eastern wall of the Lodge. I gazed, fascinated, at the star, which seemed to hover above the Master's chair, and in the surrounding darkness cast a bright narrow beam of light towards the west. Paul spoke again.

'Allow me to point out to you that the light from the centre is darkness made visible; only by penetrating the gloom and despair which hangs over our future prospects can we pierce the veil of darkness which swamps the human mind. Yet the gleaming flash of light, rising in the east, allows you to see that you now stand on the edge of the tomb from which you have symbolically risen, and which, when this fugacious fancy of life is stilled once more, will once more take you into its cold embrace.'

As I looked back at the white shroud covering the Lodge floor, the faint ray from the rising star illuminated a skull placed above a pair of crossed thigh bones. In the faint light of the star they looked real. Paul let me gaze for a long moment before speaking.

'Let those symbols of morbidity, which the rising of the Morning Star has illuminated for you, help you to reflect on your ineluctable fate and direct your thoughts towards the most valuable of all studies, the knowledge of yourself.'

He turned me round to face the light of the star once more, before continuing.

'Be mindful to carry through your assigned endeavours while the light of the Sun remains. Within your fragile person there is a critical and spiritual principle which inspires a sacred inspiration. The knowledge of the Sacred Law will enable you to rise above chaos and fear, and lift your eyes to that bright Morning Star whose rising brings peace and tranquillity to the aware members of the human race.'

Paul faced the body of the Lodge.

'Brethren, resume your seats,' he said. The lights of the Lodge were turned back on, and, like rabbits startled by car headlights on a quiet road, the Brethren bustled back to their seats.

Now what? I had not yet been given the grips and passwords which had accompanied each of the earlier degrees. I was not to be disappointed.

The Final Secrets?

The Deacons placed me back in the north-west corner, opposite Master Paul who stood facing me in the south-west corner.

I waited for Paul to instruct me to step forward. I knew how to cope with these odd steps; I was even learning how to keep my balance while being told this series of rather banal secrets. Whatever Paul was going to tell me in the next part of the ritual couldn't possibly match what I had just been shown. I'd been shown just how insignificant my self-awareness was as a part of the great scheme of the universe. I'd been shown how life would continue after my death, and the implication of this knowledge was that there is more to life than self-perception. But what was it? The Bright Morning Star, rising at the vernal equinox, shining into the grave which held my mortal remains carried a deep symbolic message. Was it intended to show me that the world would not stop when I did? That the earth would still turn on its axis, the sun would still move with the seasons, and the bright planets would rise, lifting the darkness of the pre-dawn sky? Was this the mystery of the centre, or was I about to learn more? Did the message of the spiral mean this would be a ritual I would have to practise many times before I understood its full meaning?

Paul's voice pulled me back to the reality of the Lodge.

'Now that you have experienced the knowledge of your transient reality, I will proceed to pass on to you the peculiar secrets of the Third Degree.'

What, no balancing in awkward positions, so that my leg muscles struggled to keep me upright?

'You will, therefore, stand to me as at your Initiation, and then advance to me as a Fellow of the Craft,' Paul said.

Yet another gruelling posture. I hoped the secrets were worth suffering for.

Now, unless you are already a Mason, you are just going to have to take my word for it that the secrets that Paul told me were pretty boring. A meaningless word that sounded as if it was corrupted ancient Egyptian − a matter I discussed in detail in *The Hiram Key*[1] − and a few more grips and odd ways of standing. There are three reasons I do not intend to reveal these 'secrets'. Firstly, apart from the possible ancient Egyptian translation of the 'Mason Word', they are supremely uninteresting and, secondly, because if I do, then I leave myself open to having my body split apart, burnt to ashes, and those ashes scattered before the four cardinal compass points of the world, so that no trace or remnant of so vile a wretch may any longer be found anywhere. Alright, I know United Grand Lodge of England has officially forbidden the current use of this penalty and certainly most modern Masons would hesitate before carrying out this penalty, but there may be the odd one out there who would love the chance to see what I'm made of – so why risk it? But leaving aside the unlikely enactment of these ritual and colorful medieval punishments, my third reason is that these are not the real secrets of Freemasonry.

Anyway, once I had been tested by all the officers of the Lodge in the giving and taking of the new grips, postures and passwords, I finally ended up holding hands with the Senior Warden and standing facing Master Paul. The Warden had just dressed me in a pretty new Master Mason's pinny, saying to me, 'I now adorn you with the characteristic apron of a Master Mason, and the comments made at your two previous investments are just as valid at this.'

The Master added his comments to those of the Warden.

'Brother Lomas. Permit me to extend the comments of my Brother Warden. The apron which now adorns your person not only shows your position as a Master Mason but also serves as a prompt for you to recall the critical responsibilities which you have vouched to observe. This badge shows your rank within the Craft, but also entails a duty to show charity and provide teaching to the Brethren at lower spiritual levels.'

Paul turned to the Deacons.

'Brother Deacons, please conduct Brother Lomas to the centre of the temple, where Brother Astore will show and elucidate the working tools of a Master of the Craft.'

Was I finally reaching the centre? But what did it mean? I would be placed directly under the blazing Glory, which had been only dimly visible as I had lain ritually dead beneath it, just a few minutes earlier.

The Deacons led me forward until I stood directly in the centre of the Lodge. Mike had moved round to stand to the east of me, directly in front of the Master's place. He smiled at me and reached down into the tool box, which had once again appeared on the edge of the carpet. 'Brother Lomas. At the request of Brother Master, I will now demonstrate and interpret the working tools of a Master of the Craft, which are the Centre Marker, the Scriber and the Dividers.'

Mike handed me what looked like a peg and a pointer, connected by cord.

'The Centre Marker is a tool which employs a line fixed at a centre to draw out a perimeter about a selected point and is used for marking out the foundations of a building.'

Next he handed me what looked like a simple pencil.

'The Scriber, in the hands of a skilled draughtsman, is used to draw out a plan of the building to guide the work of the craftsmen.'

Finally he handed me a pair of compasses.

'The Dividers enable the Master Mason to determine the plan with truth and exactness in all its comparative dimensions and components.

'But we are not workers in stone but free and accepted Masons. So we apply these tools to the shaping of our spirits.'

Mike looked down at the tools which I held in my hands before continuing.

'So the Centre Marker makes us aware of what a firm foundation to reality is to be found by placing the Rule of the Sacred Law at the centre of our awareness.'

He reached out and took back the centre marker.

'The Scriber reminds us that all our thoughts, words and actions form a part of the greater actions of the cosmos, and we must be ready to justify our actions through life.'

I was ready, and handed him the scriber so he could continue.

'The Dividers show us the limits of good and evil, and enable us to judge our place within this great scheme, that we may act to the greater benefit of humankind.'

He reached for the compasses, and I gave them to him. He now held up the full set of tools.

'These, then, are our working tools, and they teach us to live and act, according to the precepts of the Sacred Law, so that when we shall be summoned from this sublunary abode, we may ascend to that Grand Lodge above, where the world's Great Architect lives and reigns for ever.'

He replaced the tools in the box at his feet, turned to Paul and gave the Third-Degree salute that I had just been shown, then made his way in a clockwise direction round the Lodge and back to his seat.

Paul now spoke.

'Brother Terence Ezran will now deliver the Third-Degree charge.'

Terry had a shiny bald head, a bushy white moustache and an infectious laugh. He was an accountant by trade, but said that he tried not to be too boring. He grinned at me as he made his way round the Lodge to stand in front of me.

'Brother Lomas. Your fervour for the society of Freemasonry, the advancement you have made in this noble art, and your compliance to our rules and customs, have made you a focus of our favour and esteem. Now that you are a Master of our Craft, you are instructed to rectify the mistakes and misunderstanding of Brethren and Fellows, and help protect them from infringements of dedication ...'

This extremely long speech about my new duties and responsibilities went on for some time, but did not really add any further information to help me understand this new degree. Finally it concluded:

'... By worthy demeanour, you will persuade the world that merit has allowed you access to our privileges, and that our favours have not been undeservedly bestowed on you.'

Terry beamed at me, obviously proud of his unhesitating delivery of a long piece of ritual. He saluted Paul and set off clockwise around the Lodge, back to his seat. Now I could relax. There were no more degrees to take, so the monthly test of memory didn't need to worry me, or so I thought.

Just as I thought it was safe to begin learning the art of forgetting, Paul sprang a ritual surprise on me.

'Brother Lomas, that concludes the ceremony of your Raising. If you wish you may retire to be restored to your personal comfort, and on your return something further will be communicated to you,' he winked at me. 'But if you are perfectly comfortable you may take your seat in the Lodge'

I took the hint and, accompanied by my two familiar Deacons, I made my way back to my seat in a clockwise direction.

As I sat down Paul announced: 'Brother Lomas. There are certain test questions and answers in this degree which it is advisable you should commit to memory.'

'For your instruction, and for the benefit of the Brethren generally, my Brother Junior Warden will put those questions to the Inner Guard, who will supply the necessary answers.'

So there was more to learn. In fact, I was to find out there was a *lot* more to learn, but these test questions and answers were to be my next task. I listened as the series began.

'How were you made ready to be raised to the spiritual level of the Third Degree?'

The sequence went on, until one particular exchange struck me as important, for reasons I could not at the time explain to myself.

'On your entrance into the Lodge did you observe anything different in this degree?'

'I did. All was dark, save a glimmering light in the east.'

'To what does that darkness allude?'

'To the darkness of death.'

There was a pattern in these rituals which might be important. In the First Degree I was in darkness and the Lodge was in light, in the Second Degree I was in light and so was the Lodge, but in the Third Degree I was in light while the Lodge was in darkness. Was there a message in this sequence that I did not yet understand? Now I had the secrets of a Master Mason, and yet I did not seem to know much more than I had when I first entered the Lodge with my eyes tightly bound. There were hints of a profound teaching, and I had sensed deep emotions being stirred by the rituals. I felt this ritual to be deeply satisfying in a way I found hard to put into words. Its form had been unexpected and startling, but it made me feel good. It seemed to be meeting a spiritual need I had not quite realised was lurking in the hidden depths of my subconscious: not until this ritual stirred a secret longing to understand a purpose for life. But what was it I had learned?

The biggest clue was in the words spoken to me as I stood on the equinoctial line of perfect balance looking into the darkness of death, with the bright Morning Star rising in the East:

'Direct your thoughts towards the most valuable of all studies, the knowledge of yourself.'

But there was one last formal Masonic lesson I could now expect. The lecture of the third Tracing-board – and a very grim board it had appeared to be during the few moments I had seen it revealed. Soon I hoped to be told the ritual meaning of this image, in open lodge.

[1] Lomas & Knight (1996), p. 143.

Chapter Seven

Tracing the Great Leveller

A Third Board

What are we doing next month?' I asked Mike, soon after my Third.

'I think we might persuade Gordon to do the Third-Degree Tracing-board,' he replied.

'That would be good,' I said. For, to be honest, I was having a great deal of trouble understanding the Third Degree and felt that I really wanted to learn more.

'Well, Gordon keeps saying he'd like to do it, and, with you just having done your Third, it seems a good time.'

Gordon was a retired businessman in his late seventies and a Past Master of the Lodge. He had a gruff Yorkshire voice, was always smartly dressed in a suit and tie, and walked with a stick.

'There are three of you who've done their Thirds in the last six months,' Mike went on, 'so we might have a question–and–answer session after Gordon's done the board.'

'Sounds good to me.'

And so there I was, on the last Friday of the month, standing next to Mike and singing the opening hymn as the Lodge was opened in the First Degree. This was old hat for me now; I knew exactly what to do, how to stand and when to respond. Strange that less than a year ago, when I first visited Blackwall Masonic Rooms, this ritual had seemed frightening and complicated.

Once the boring business of the minutes of the previous meeting were out of the way, Paul, the Master in the East, announced that the next item would be Brother Earnshaw, who would give the lecture of the Third-Degree Tracing-board. He then opened the Lodge in the Second Degree. Once again the ritual was comfortable, the postures felt natural, and I felt at ease in the Lodge. Then Paul prepared to open the Lodge in a higher degree, so we would be at the correct Masonic level to listen to the tracing-board lecture.

'Copy me,' Mike said, realising this was my first time for a Third-Degree opening. 'Nobody will bother if you don't get it quite right, at least not this time.'

Once the Lodge was safely open in the Third Degree, the Tracing-board was laid in the centre of the Lodge, and Gordon stood over it. He didn't have a pointer, but he held his silver-headed walking stick in his right hand, supporting himself as he got ready to start. Once he had composed himself he looked directly at me.

The Traditional History

'During the ritual of your Raising, that part of our traditional history which mentioned the death of our Master Hiram Abif, and what effect that melancholy event had on King Solomon, was left incomplete. In this lecture the story is told in full.'

He took a deep breath and composed his face into a solemn look.

'A loss so significant as that of the key craftsman could not fail to be widely and seriously noticed. No drawings or instructions, which had been supplied on a regular basis to the different classes of workmen, were forthcoming. This was the first sign that some major misfortune had occurred to our Master. The Overseers, Menatschin or Prefects as they were known, authorised a number of the most distinguished members to inform King Solomon of the complete chaos which the disappearance of Hiram had caused, and to tell him that they feared that some deadly mishap must have caused his abrupt and mystifying failure to appear.'

Gordon lifted his free hand and cupped his ear, a gesture I had seen him use in the bar, when the background noise was high.

'When King Solomon heard this report he instantly called a full congregation of the workmen throughout the Temple workings. It was found that three overseers could not be found. Also twelve Menatschin, who had originally taken part in the secret plan to extract the secret, came before the King and made a willing admission of all they knew, down to the time when they withdrew from the conspiracy.'

Gordon drew himself up and looked around the Lodge.

'King Solomon, being afraid for the well-being of his key craftsman, selected fifteen dependable Fellows of the Craft, and ordered them to thoroughly search for the physical body of Master Hiram, to ascertain if he were still living, or if he had been killed in the effort to wring from him the inner knowledge of his enlightened situation.

'King Solomon set a day when they should return to Jerusalem, and these honest Fellowcrafts set up three Lodges, and each Lodge set out from a different gate of the Temple; they spent many days in futile investigation. The Lodge which departed through the Gate Beautiful … ,' Gordon pointed with his stick towards the south of the Lodge, where sat the Junior Warden who had struck me with the plumb rule when I had played the role of Hiram. '… returned without making any discoveries of significance.

'The second Lodge, which left through the Gate of Works, had better luck.' He pointed towards the west, where the Senior Warden sat at his desk holding the level he had aimed at my head.

'After undergoing the considerable hardship and physical privations, as the day's light faded one of the Brethren lay on some rough ground. To help him get up he grasped a sprig which was growing nearby, but found that it was not rooted, merely pushed into the earth. He looked more closely and found the ground had been dug. He called his Brethren, and together they re-dug the disturbed earth and discovered the mortal remains of our Master Hiram interred in an unseemly way.'

Gordon pointed downwards the Tracing-board, indicating the grave with the faint outline of a body within it.

'They reburied him with deference and veneration. To mark the place they hele-ed in a twig of acacia at the top of the temporary tomb.' Gordon pointed to the sprig of flowering acacia on the western side of the Tracing-board.

'Then they hurried back to King Solomon to apprise him of the dreadful situation. When King Solomon received this sad news he was overcome with sorrow, but once he regained his emotional composure, he instructed the Brethren to go back and recover Master Hiram in order to place his remains in a sepulchre worthy of his status and degree of knowledge. He also told them that by the unexpected demise of Master Hiram the secrets of a Master Mason had been lost. Solomon therefore told them to be extremely scrupulous to watch for any cursory signs, tokens or words which might be used whilst carrying out this final distressing service of esteem for erstwhile worthiness.'

'The Brethren expedited the instruction, and, when opening the grave once more, one Brother saw some of his Brethren covering their eyes, as if affected by the frightfulness of the awful and atrocious vision … ,' Gordon gave the sign of horror which I had been taught the previous month, 'whilst others, seeing the grisly injury which stood out on his brow, struck their own foreheads in affinity with his torment.' Gordon gave the sign of sympathy before continuing.

'Two of the Brethren went down into the grave, and one of them tried to lift our Master using the Entered Apprentice grip, but this would not hold. The other then tried the Fellowcraft grip, which also was insufficient. They having been unable to raise him, an enthusiastic and skilful Brother went down and took a firmer grip of the tendon of the arm and, with the help of the other two, lifted Master Hiram using the posture known as the Five Points of Companionship.'

Gordon was almost shouting now.

'The Brethren surrounding the grave cried out, "The architect is deceased; he is laid low".'

He paused and looked around before continuing in a normal speaking voice.

'When those craftsmen recounted their actions to King Solomon, he insisted that those cursory postures, grips, and phrases should identify all Master Masons throughout the cosmos, till time or fate should restore the true ones.'

Transferring his walking stick to his left hand, Gordon gave the signs in order, before transferring it back to his right hand.

'The Lodge which departed through the Gate of Wisdom,' he pointed with his stick towards the east of the temple, 'searched towards Joppa, and were meditating on whether to return to Jerusalem when, going by the entrance of a cave, they became aware of cries of intense mourning and grief. They decided to go into the cave to search for the source. They discovered the three missing overseers. The Lodge confronted them with the killing of Master Hiram, and, seeing there was no chance of escape, they made a complete confession of their misdeeds. They were trussed and restrained to be taken to Jerusalem, where King Solomon sentenced them to death in a manner which fitted the barbarity of their crime.'

Gordon pointed down to the Tracing-board, where it lay in the centre of the black —and white chequered floor of the Lodge.

'Master Hiram was reburied as close to the Holy of Holies as the Jewish law would allow. He was placed in a grave, from the centre three feet east, three feet west, three feet between north and south, and five feet or more perpendicular. He was not placed in the Holy of Holies, because nothing common or impure was allowed to be taken into there, not even the High Priest but once a year, and then not until after washing many times and carrying out many rituals of purification for the propitiation of sins, for the Jewish law said that the physical body was impure.'

Gordon indicated his white lambskin apron with his white-gloved hand.

'The fifteen trusty Fellows of the Craft who found Master Hiram attended his funeral clothed in white Aprons and Gloves, which they wore as symbols of their sinlessness.'

Gordon looked around the Lodge, before continuing.

'The decorations of a Master Mason's Lodge are the entrance, the vertical window, and the black and white flooring. The entrance was the porch which stood before the Holy of Holies; the vertical dormer window allowed the glimmer of light to enter the same; and the black —and white pavement was for the High Priest to walk on. The High Priest's duty was to burn incense to the honour and glory of the Most High and to pray fervently that the Most

High, with unbounded wisdom and goodness, would be pleased to bestow peace and tranquillity on the Jewish nation during the coming year.'

He pointed to the Tracing-board.

'The Tools with which our Master was slain were, as you have already been informed, the plumb rule, the level and the heavy setting maul. The coffin, skull and crossbones are emblems of mortality and allude to the untimely death of our Master, Hiram Abif, who was slain three thousand years after the creation of the world.'

He pointed towards the East, where the two lower Tracing-boards were displayed.

'The First-Degree Tracing-board dealt with the discipline of the body, and the Second with the culture of the mind.'

He pointed to the centre of the Lodge.

'But the Third-Degree Tracing-board deals with the awakening of the spirit. The simplicity of the Board masks its profundity, but it deals with matters deep within the centre of human concern. It has three main elements: the grave containing the mortal remains; the sprig of acacia which marks its head; and the tools scattered around the grave. The grave or tomb symbolises the body or human personality of the Candidate placed in it. Into that body has been infused a spirit, a psychic principle which elevates the animal nature into a rational being.'

Laboriously, with the aid of his walking stick, Gordon traced the steps from the west of the Lodge to the east, stepping over the Tracing-board as he went.

'In moving from west to east in this degree we are taught to step over the open grave of the Tracing-board symbolising that the Aspirant to be a Master Mason must learn to subdue his bodily urges, so making his ego his servant not his master.'

He turned and pointed to the flowering shrub at the head of the Tracing-board.

'The sprig of acacia, flowering at the head of the grave, represents the Centre, the ultimate core of our being beyond time and space. It springs into life, drawing sustenance from the corruption of the grave, showing how our spirit is not free to grow until the dominance of our physical principles has been allowed to die.'

He pointed first to the north and then to the south side of the Tracing-board.

'The tools scattered around the grave are of two types. Those in the dark north of the Board are the ambiguous implements of destruction and rebuilding. Ambiguous because the very tools which slew the master and brought about destruction and calamity also give you hope that we might reconstruct our personal temple. By our errors we learn wisdom and regrowth from the proper use of the tools which can bring us down. These spiritual tools symbolise the way in which we may hope to make contact with the light at our centre. The Plumb Rule tells us to apply uprightness to all parts of our being, our senses, our emotions and our mind. The Level shows us how these parts of ourselves are brought into balance. They are often unbalanced, and before our spirit can blossom we have to bring them into harmony and equilibrium. The heavy Maul symbolises the power of a strong and resolute will, which cannot be deflected from its objective.'

He pointed to the tools on the southern side of the Tracing-board.

'The tools, in the light of the southern side of the board, are tools which allow us to form the structure of our living temple. The Skerrit[*] allows us to locate and mark the area of the centre, the

---

[*] A device for drawing a circle about a centre point. It consists of a centre pin, a cord, and an attached scriber.

Scriber allows us to record our reflections and develop our meditations, whilst the Compasses allow us to measure our place within the great scheme of the cosmos.'

He turned to Paul, who reached behind his seat and clicked a switch. The five-pointed star about the Master's chair lit up. Gordon pointed to the eastern edge of the board.

'The mortal remains in the East are illuminated by the light of the bright Morning Star rising in the eastern sky. Few of us realise what disordered beings we are, and what labour is needed to bring our personality to awareness of the light at the centre. Either our sense-nature is uncontrolled or our emotions are ungoverned, or else our mind is undisciplined and incapable of concentration. These have to be squared, equalised and brought into harmonious function before our central spirit can blossom in the light of the centre.

'So, Brethren, the Tracing-board of the Third Degree sums up the meaning of the ceremony. The four points of the crossed bones meeting in the skull at the centre symbolise the Five Points of Fellowship which bring us to the centre. Yet this solemn symbol of mortality contains within it five points of hope, when illuminated by the light of the bright Morning Star rising in the east.

He looked directly at me as he spoke, pausing to emphasise each point. 'Practise those five points.

'Defend and maintain the five points of companionship.

'Let your grip given to a Brother Master be a certain assurance of companionship.

'Let your steps track through perils and risks, to join with his in forming a file of reciprocal protection.

'Meditate on the Sacred Law, but do not forget the deprivation and privations of your fellow humans and alleviate their needs and assuage their hardship, so far as may be done without damage to yourself or your family.

'Let your centre be a secure and mystical treasury to hold his genuine and legal secrets, when trusted to you.

'Lastly, do not denigrate a Master Mason's character behind his back, nor willingly allow others so to do. Stringently defend the virtue of those dear to him in the persons of his wife, his sister, or his child.'

He transferred his stick to his left hand before the final part of his memorised speech.

'To achieve Mastership, there must be a dying away of personal desire for worldly possessions and position, till every mundane allurement and ambition that would divert you from the goal ceases to attract. There must be a voluntary sacrifice and total obliteration of the personal ego, the sense of "myself" as something separate from other selves and having special rights of its own. There must be a purifying and a realigning of all the parts of one's bodily nature to the vital principle of the spiritual centre which hovers above the our lower personality like the sprig of acacia, but which is our true apex and root.

'The truths of this degree cut sharply across the world's wisdom and popular ideas, but denial and death of self is the inescapable law of our progress. Only personal labour can awaken these truths in you, and personal experience alone will verify them.'

He turned to Paul and gave a crisp Third-Degree salute.

'Brother Master, that concludes the description of the Third-Degree Tracing-board. But if any of the newly made brethren have questions, I will be happy to try and answer them.'

'Are there any questions?' Paul asked. I stuck my hand up and he nodded to me.

'Brother Gordon, I must admit my Raising was all a bit much to take in at the time, but this lecture has helped me understand some of the symbolism. But is there anything you would add to the formal lecture that you think might help me to become a better Mason?'

Gordon smiled at me.

'Well, Brother Robert, that moment when you are struck down and have to lie perfectly still while the Brethren process around your grave is a key to understanding how you need to develop. It tells you that the only end place for your ego is its death. The moment of Raising tells you to understand this and to make sure that you do not let your ego get in the way of developing your talents and skills within society; you must strive to create something which is greater than your ego. This is the purpose of building the living temple. It is to create an individual who can contribute to society and leave behind something more than they found – in other words, to leave the world a better place than it was when they entered it. That is the message of the Bright Morning Star. It is a message of hope for the future of mankind.'

I looked at the bright star blazing about the Master's chair, before nodding to him as he continued:

'The teaching about how to do this is contained in the working tools, the Tracing-board and the progression of offices which you will follow in due course. You must remember the key part of the Third-Degree ritual.'

He faced me and delivered that piece of ritual:

Let me now beg you to observe that the light of a Master Mason is darkness visible, serving only to express that gloom which rests on the prospect of futurity; it is that mysterious veil which the eye of human reason cannot penetrate unless assisted by that light which is from above. Yet even by this glimmering ray you may perceive that you stand on the brink of the grave into which you have just figuratively descended and which, when this transitory life has passed away, will again receive you into its cold bosom. Let the emblems of mortality which lie before you lead you to contemplate your inevitable destiny and guide your reflections to that most interesting of all human studies, the knowledge of yourself.

He smiled encouragingly.

'When you become a Master Mason, you must learn to let personal desire for worldly possession and position die away. You have to learn to control and suppress the wishes of your ego, so that you feel yourself a part of society, and indeed of creation as a whole. Only when you can stop fearing death do you realise that the work you do for others, such as teaching, research and charity, is more important than self-aggrandisement.'

I looked down at the new Master Mason's apron I was wearing. Gordon hadn't finished yet.

'A real Master Mason is one who has made the great act of self-denial, who has died the death of the ego and experienced the transformation it involves. It leaves you with no dread of death, for you have already been to your own funeral, and you know it is an inevitable complement to life. This freedom from fear of the future leaves you unfettered and able to make full use of your talents to build a structure, in your works, which will survive your physical death.'

He nodded to me, bowed slightly and then gave me a Third-Degree salute.

'So, Brother Robert, now you know the real secret of Freemasonry, and it is a secret which will free you from fear and help you achieve much. Use it well. Welcome to the study of the spiritual centre ... yourself.'

So now I had as much knowledge of the ritual as any newly made Master Mason could reasonably expect. But could I make sense of it?

For the next fifteen years I was to research the origins and contents of the ritual. On this long quest for understanding I met up with Chris Knight, and between us we wrote four books, all asking, Where did Freemasonry come from? I also wrote a book about the influence of seventeenth-century Freemasonry on the formation of the Royal Society. But in the course of all these researches I kept noticing there was an underlying spiritual dimension to the subject that it never seemed appropriate to discuss in books investigating Freemasonry's origins. For those books were asking where? not *how*? In this book I have finally returned to ask *how* Freemasonry affects an individual.

Over the years I have greatly enjoyed my Freemasonry. But often I have not been clear in my own mind why this was. The ritual seems to work a magic of its own, and working it makes me feel better about life in general. Over the last few years I have become fascinated by this spiritual aspect of the Craft and have tried to understand exactly how it functions. In the true tradition of the Second Degree this quest has led me into many surprising areas of modern scientific research.

At this stage of my quest I had completed the seven steps of Masonry:

1. The Question of Supreme Being – Am I interested in seeking purpose to life?

2. The First Degree – The study of my emotions.

3. The First Tracing-board – How the four quarters of personality work together.

4. The Second Degree – Developing my intellectual skills.

5. The Second Tracing-board – The Spiral path towards the hidden centre.

6. The Third Degree – Experiencing the death of my ego.

7. The Third Tracing-board – A way of integrating intellect, emotion and ego to free the spirit.

But I did not yet understand much of this teaching, and I went on to spend many years looking at the possible origins of this strange body of knowledge.

After all this study I have come to the opinion that Freemasonry is a remnant of an extremely ancient philosophical system that inspired monotheistic religion and many high-achieving individuals over the centuries – to name a few, Enoch the Jewish prophet; Hiram, the Phoenician King of Tyre; Jesus Christ, would-be messiah of the Jews and the inspiration of the Christian religion; and Earl William St Clair, the fifteenth-century founder of Freemasonry. But can it still work for anybody?

Where Next?

There are some 9,000 Masonic lodges in England and Wales and about another 1,900 in Scotland. If each lodge has at least thirty members, this means there are more than 300,000 Freemasons on the British mainland – and in that modest guess I have not included the large number of thriving women's lodges.

Masonic ideas have caught on widely and taken a firm grip upon the imaginations of so many people. Differences of race and language have not stopped its worldwide spread. Yet this success passes largely unremarked within the Craft.

Outside observers suggest that the diffusion of the Masonic system throughout the world must be because of some evil influence. But in my extensive studies of Freemasonry I have found no evidence to support this view.

So what *does* account for the wide appeal that Freemasonry has had during the last four centuries, and still has today?

Is it just a meeting place for social, fraternal and genial networking amongst folk who choose to split off into a distinctive fraternity with no deeper purpose than eating, drinking and chatting? Oh, and don't forget a few amateur theatricals thrown in ... before the Brethren get down to the serious business of eating their way through the rituals of the custard god.

This seems an incredible motive to support an organisation so firmly entrenched, so robust and so associated with movers and shakers over the years. Freemasonry has attracted kings (George V, George VI), archbishops (Dr Geoffrey Fisher), statesmen (Winston Churchill, George Washington, Benjamin Franklin), musicians (Haydn, Mozart, Liszt, Duke Ellington, Louis Armstrong), astronauts (John Glenn, Buzz Aldrin, Gus Grissom), writers (Arthur Conan Doyle, Walter Scott, Oscar Wilde, Anthony Trollope, Goethe, Pushkin), scientists (Alexander Fleming, Edward Appleton, Edward Jenner, Pierre Simon Laplace) and philosophers (Voltaire, Burke, Condorcet, Helvetius).

What is it that attracts such a wide range of people to Freemasonry? It has to be more than a charitable system promoting benevolence and philanthropy; that is not a good enough explanation for its long-term success. Masonry was not intended to be a high-grade Friendly Society, and its charitable efforts are a consequence of, not the reason for, its existence.

Is it a school of morality? Was it set up to promote peace and goodwill? This, too, fails to explain the facts. Why should you have to join a secret society, or enter into solemn obligations, to practise basic ethics?

Conspiracy theorists must be sadly disappointed that the Craft is not an engine for promoting the social and economic advancement of its members to the prejudice of non-members; a cover for political intrigue; or even a screen for propagating anti-religious ideas. But it isn't!

There remains one reason to explain the attraction of Freemasonry. That is the personal impact its ceremonial rites have on those who take part in them. Standing in open Lodge delivering ritual is highly satisfying. There is a veiled and deep 'something' in those rituals which speaks to latent needs in those who act them out. But what is it?

If I am ever to understand the spiritual appeal of Freemasonry, then I need to know more about how myth, ritual and symbolism work on the human mind. This is what I intend to investigate in the second part of this book.

In the tradition of the Second Degree, I will use the tools of science to help me understand what Freemasonry can offer if I am prepared to study it closely.

In name I am already an Initiate, but what does this mean? I want to understand Masonic Initiation on all its many levels. To do that, I must look more closely at how my mind works.

Part Two

The Hidden Mysteries of Ritual and Myth

The ritual I had been learning so carefully told me that Masonry is a high and serious subject. It committed me to solemn personal vows, which I wanted to take seriously. I wanted to feel the wonder of the centre once more, but I didn't know how to. What I really wanted to know was, how can I realise the truths outlined in the ritual and become *actually* – not just in name and form – an Initiate and a Master?

Chapter Eight

How does Ritual Work?

I am a Master Mason. So What?

Make no mistake about it, Freemasonry is very odd when you first encounter it, and as you progress it gets odder. If you are already a Mason, think back to how it first appeared to you. How did you become a Mason? Did you read about the Craft in anti-Masonic writing? Did a member of your family take you to a social event at the Lodge? Did you read a book exploring it? Try to view Masonry with the eyes of a child, not with the familiarity you have built up over many years. If you are not a Mason, then hopefully the previous chapters have showed you some of this inherent oddity.

How did I feel when I became a Master Mason? Strangely incomplete, yet in an inexplicable way fulfilled. At the outset, when I was interviewed by a panel of Past Masters, what I was joining had been virtually unknown to me. Now, after taking all the three degrees of Freemasonry, I was an initiate. But, although I took great pleasure in attending meetings, the Order remained largely unknown to me still.

I had learned how to memorise and recite large chunks of ritual. I had exposed various parts of my body to the curious gaze of assemblies of Brethren. At each stop on this journey I had been told, 'just do this next bit, and all will become clear to you'. But, until I decided to research it for myself, it never did.

I was now a Master Mason – I had a certificate from the United Grand Lodge of England to prove it. I had a pretty new blue-and-white pinny to wear, and was even allowed to keep my trousers on in Lodge. But I was not an expert in Freemasonry. Its ritual was spiritually stimulating but confusing, and I couldn't even say when the Order began, or why it was formed.

Then I began to study the origins of Freemasonry, and started to give lectures both in my own and in other lodges. In the course of this research I met Chris Knight and shared my bafflement and pooled my knowledge with him. At this time we wrote:

We shared the same frustrations concerning the vague conventional explanation of the origins of the Order. Our discussions became more frequent, and our interest grew as we sparked off each other, and it was not long before we decided to undertake a structured investigation with the joint objectives of identifying the character we knew as Hiram Abif and finding the lost secrets of Freemasonry. At that time neither of us believed that we had any chance of succeeding in this strange quest, but we knew that the journey would be interesting. We did not know it at the time, but we had just commenced one of the biggest detective investigations of all time, and our findings were going to be of major importance, not only to Freemasons, but to the world in general.[1]

The result of this co-operation was a series of international best≠selling books, *The Hiram Key*, *The Second Messiah*, *Uriel's Machine* and finally *The Book of Hiram*. These books were about where the Craft began, and what it was. The next thing I became interested in was how Freemasonry changed its members: how it made them better citizens, and how they in turn improved society. I went on to investigate that theme in *The Invisible College*, and *Freemasonry and the Birth of Modern Science*.

But there is yet another unanswered question that still bothers me. Why do I, and so many others, enjoy Freemasonry?

I had learned some truths from Masonry – and on the whole I am a better person for being part of it – but I had not become an initiate in any but the most formal sense. Most of my Brethren were in a similar plight, however eminent their titular Masonic rank; we were all as far from being Masters of the Mystic Science as any uninitiated person.

I needed to understand the psychological tools of Masonry. These are ritual, myth and symbolism. I decided to begin by looking at myth and its formal cousin ritual, two key aspects of the art of story-telling.

Story-telling Beings

Human beings like stories. When you offer to tell a young child a story she will clap her hands in anticipation of the joy it will bring her. She expects pleasure, she hopes for an experience to excite her imagination and transport her to emotional places she will enjoy visiting. And this love of a good story stays with us humans throughout our lives. In fact, if I were asked to say how humans differ from other primate species I might try suggesting we are the only species to tell each other stories.

The myths that groups of people create define their society's values and beliefs. And those myths can long outlast the people who first tell them. Charles Squire, an avid collector of ancient myths, explained the power of a good story and how it edified the people who preserved and retold it.

Of what profound interest and value to every nation are its earliest legendary and poetical records. The beautiful myths of Greece form a sufficing example. In threefold manner they have influenced the destiny of the people that created them, and of the country in which they were the imagined theatre. First, in the ages in which they were still fresh, belief and pride in them were powerful enough to bring scattered tribes into confederation. Secondly they gave the inspiration to sculptor and poet of an art and literature unsurpassed, if not unequalled, by any other age or race. Lastly, when 'the glory that was Greece' had faded, and her people had, by dint of successive invasions, perhaps even ceased to have any right to call themselves Hellenes, they have passed over in to the literatures of the modern world and so given to Greece herself a poetic interest that still makes a petty kingdom of greater account in the eyes of its compeers than many others far superior to it in extent and resources.[2]

The art of story-telling stretches back into the distant mists of time; I like to think it started at least in Neolithic times, perhaps even as far back as the Palaeolithic. It is an art which can change the way you think. We see just how powerful a working tool it is if we consider Scheherazade, legendary author of the *Tales of a Thousand and One Nights*, who avoided death by her story-telling skill. E.M. Forster – in his Clark Lectures at King's College, Cambridge, in 1927 – described skilful story-telling as 'the only literary tool that has any effect upon tyrants and savages'. Of Scheherazade he said:

Great novelist though she was – exquisite in her descriptions, tolerant in her judgments, ingenious in her incidents, advanced in her morality, vivid in her delineations of character, expert in her knowledge of three oriental capitals – it was yet on none of these gifts that she relied when trying to save her life from her intolerable husband. They were but incidental. She only survived because she managed to keep the king wondering what would happen next. Each time she saw the sun rising she stopped in the middle of a sentence, and left him gaping. 'At this moment Scheherazade saw the morning appearing and, discreet, was silent.' This uninteresting little phrase is the backbone of the One Thousand and One Nights, the tapeworm by which they are tied together and the life of a most accomplished princess was preserved. We are all like Scheherazade's husband, in that we want to know what happens next.[3]

Stories are a way we make sense of information. A list of facts is meaningless until it is arranged into a narrative we can relate to. And this is why much spiritual teaching is in the form of parables or myths. A parable is a short moral story, often told to convey a religious message, but a myth is perhaps the most basic form of story-telling we humans have ever developed, and it is certainly the oldest written form of story we have The first great myth is the Epic of Gilgamesh, the story of a king of Sumer, which dates from 3000 B.C.E. Its underlying theme is of a hero's quest to understand the purpose of life. This story was painstakingly inscribed in cuneiform on soft clay tablets and then baked in the sun, but this was done for a greater purpose than just fun or amusement: it was a way of conveying spiritual knowledge by telling a story.

The anthropologist Joseph Campbell studied myth and its place in the development of human society. He maintains that all myths are creative products of the human psyche, and story-tellers are a culture's myth-makers. He adds that mythologies are 'creative manifestations of humankind's universal need to explain psychological, social, cosmological, and spiritual realities'.[4]

A myth can show you what is important. In terms of an inner spiritual life – Campbell believed that all religions are founded on myths – they can make the most profoundly true statements about the human condition. This allows the underlying narrative of a myth to connect with the human spirit in ways that logic and reason cannot. It is certainly true that Freemasonry is based on a great sweeping myth.

If I wanted to understand Freemasonry, then, it seemed sensible to study myth and its relationship to ritual in greater detail. The first concept that Masonic ritual introduced me to was that of pilgrimage. I was blindfolded and then taken on a great trek round and round the lodge-room. Why?

Pilgrimage

Paul Devereux sees a pilgrimage as:

A pious, dutiful or petitionary journey to a holy place ... a spiritual quest or meditation packaged as a geographical journey; outer, physical travel with an inner destination. Pilgrimage is a deep human instinct.[5]

My Freemasonry had begun with a pilgrimage. The ritual called for me to travel, and in order to travel I had to be shown a path. The message of this was that, left in my ritually imposed darkness, I would not have been able to find my own way to the point where I could see the light. The pilgrimage was therefore a way of making real to me the difference between where I came from and where Freemasonry was planning to take me.

The dark journey of my Initiation took me out of normal routine, stripped me of all my normal tools and props of status. Anthropologist Victor Turner detects a key element in all pilgrimages, and one that fits in with what happens to a candidate entering the Masonic First Degree.

The pilgrim, like the initiate, is detached from the normal daily routine, and exists outside the security of the community, and while on the pilgrimage has not yet reached the secure context of the sacred destination. During this period the characteristics of the pilgrim are ambiguous. He passes through a cultural realm that has few or none of the attributes of the past or coming state. While on a pilgrimage the subject is literally neither here nor there. [6]

Devereux suggests that it is possible to make a mental pilgrimage by visualising the path you hope to follow, that this mental travel enables you to gain a deeper understanding of the levels of meaning which your pilgrimage impulse uncovers, and that this technique encourages mental and spiritual changes. [7] He seems to have detected a principle already known to Freemasonry. But where does the dark pilgrimage of Freemasonry take you? As I saw in my Third Degree, it leads to the greatest threat the human mind can conceive.

There is a price we pay for our human ability to think and plan: we become aware that one day we will die. When threatened, our brain causes a fear response that encourages us to either fight or flee the threat. With an increased ability to think in the abstract, we become able to imagine theoretical threats, such as our own future death; however, to protect ourselves from the petrifying effect of our fear, we develop myths and rituals to reduce the dread of our own demise.

The name given to this very human condition is 'existentialist angst'. Many mythical stories help us come to terms with this fear, and the Masonic pilgrimage forces those who follow it to confront the fact of death. This drive to understand the concept of personal death, and become comfortable with it, is part of the mystery of the Masonic centre.

Darryl Reanney, an Australian evolutionary biologist, studied the role that fear of death plays in human thought.

> *Death is unique. It is the one aspect of reality humans cannot look in the face. It is the ultimate paradox: it exposes a fundamental contradiction between the legacy of our genes and the legacy of our experience. ... The process of dying begins with conception; all that differs from person to person is their relative distance from the same finality ... towards which we, and all things mortal, inexorably progress.* [8]

The first written myth tells how a mortal king deals with this fear. When his friend Enkidu dies, Gilgamesh sets out on a great journey to seek a source of endless life.
Tablet X tells how he meets the bar-keeper Siduri and asks her for this great secret.

> *O, Siduri, you who are cupbearer to the gods, You who pour out for them the drink of immortality. You who provide life eternal. ... To you I make my plea. Behold, I am a stranger and I come to beseech your help.* [9]

Pascal Boyer, Henry Luce Professor of Individual and Collective Memory at Washington University in St Louis, looked at how story-telling creates social and religious systems.

Animals never move about for the sake of changing places. They are in search of food or safety or sex; their movements in those different situations are caused by different processes. The same goes for explanation ... minds consist of many different, specialised explanatory engines. Religious concepts are probably influenced by the way the brain's inference systems produce explanations without our being aware of it. ... The study of the social mind can show us why people have particular expectations about social life and morality and how this is connected to their supernatural concepts. [10]

Boyer is interested in how myths spread and persist, and he sees human belief systems as the result of a selection that is taking place all the time and everywhere. Anthropologists have now developed formal mathematical tools to describe culture transmission. The mechanism used to model this spread is called a meme, and he thinks it is memes which make us different from other species. [11]

So what are they?

Repetition and the Meme-ing of Life

The idea of a meme was first suggested by biologist Professor Richard Dawkins in 1976. This is how he unveiled the concept:

The laws of physics are supposed to be true all over the accessible universe. Are there any principles of biology that are likely to have similar universal validity? ... I would put my money on one fundamental principle. This is the law that all life evolves by the differential survival of replicating entities. ... I think that a new kind of replicator has recently emerged on this very planet. We need a name for the new replicator, a noun that conveys the idea of a unit of cultural transmission, or a unit of imitation. 'Mimeme' comes from a suitable Greek root, but I want a monosyllable that sounds a bit like 'gene'. 1 hope my classicist friends will forgive me if 1 abbreviate mimeme to meme.[12]

Dawkins's memes are tunes, ideas, catch-phrases, clothes fashions, ways of making pots or methods of building arches. He suggests that just as genes propagate themselves in the gene pool by leaping from body to body via sperm or eggs, so memes propagate themselves in the meme pool by leaping from brain to brain via the process of imitation. Writing in the introduction to a book by Susan Blackmore, he explains why he thinks the idea of the meme is important.

The word [meme] was introduced at the end of a book which otherwise must have seemed entirely devoted to extolling the selfish gene as the be-all and end-all of evolution. ... The real unit of natural selection was any kind of replicator. ... The genetic natural selection identified by neoDarwinism as the driving force of evolution on this planet was only a special case of a more general process that I came to dub 'Universal Darwinism'. ... But I was always open to the possibility that the meme might one day be developed into a proper hypothesis of the human mind.[13]

Dawkins spawned a whole new discipline. The philosopher Daniel Dennett, Professor of Arts and Sciences at Tufts University in Medford, Massachusetts, took up the idea and used it to develop a theory of human consciousness. He explains how he saw memes forming people's attitudes. I couldn't help noticing how this theory was expressing the same ideas as Charles Squire a century earlier, when he said that 'myths formed and defined societies', but Dennett takes the idea further and shows *why* this happened.

Once our brains had evolved entrance and exit pathways for the vehicles of language, they swiftly became parasitized by entities that have further evolved to thrive in just such a niche: memes. The outlines of the theory of evolution by natural selection are clear, evolution occurs whenever the following conditions exist:
1. Variation: a continuing abundance of different elements.
2. Heredity or replication: the elements have the capacity of creating copies or replicas of themselves.
3. Differential 'fitness': the number of copies of an element that are created in a given time varies, depending on the interaction between the features of that element (whatever it is that makes it different from other elements) and features of the environment in which it persists.[14]

Psychologist Dr Susan Blackmore extended Dennett's ideas and concluded that 'human brains and human minds are the combined product of genes and memes.'[15] She explains that the real function of memes is to provide a human brain with tools for thinking.

The ways we behave, the choices we make, and the things we say are all a result of ... a set of memeplexes [groups of co-operating memes] running on a biologically constructed system. The driving force behind everything that happens is replicator power. Genes fight it out to get into the next generation, and in the process biological design comes about. Memes fight it out to get passed on into another brain or book or object, and in the process cultural and mental design comes about.[16]

Moreover, Blackmore's research convinced her that 'the brain we have is a brain designed for spreading memes'.[17] How did this brain come about?

> *Memes could only come into existence when the genes had provided brains that were capable of imitation – and the nature of those brains must have influenced which memes took hold and which did not. However, once memes had come into existence they would be expected to take on a life of their own.[18]*

But is there a physical reality behind this idea that human brains evolved to act as hosts for memes? Or is it just a complicated way of saying that human beings like to listen to stories?

To answer this question I had to try to discover exactly where, and how, memes could be 'hosted'. I went back to see what Richard Dawkins had to say.

> *It [a meme] has a definite structure, realized in whatever physical medium the brain uses for storing information. If the brain stores information as a pattern of synaptic connections, a meme should in principle be visible under a microscope as a definite pattern of synaptic structure. If the brain stores information in 'distributed' form (Pribram 1974) [[19]], the meme would not be localizable on a microscope slide, but still 1 would want to regard it as physically residing in the brain.[20]*

So memes are formed as patterns of neuron connections inside our brains. But how are they formed? Had Dawkins considered this consequence of his theory? He had.

Plate 1
The First Degree Tracing Board (copyright www.tracingboards.com)

Plate 2
The Second Degree Tracing Board (copyright www.tracingboards.com)

Plate 3
The Third Degree Tracing Board (copyright www.tracingboards.com)

Plate 4
The Kirkwall Scroll
(copyright www.tracingboards.com)

Memes don't only leap from mind to mind by imitation, in culture. That is just the easily visible tip of the iceberg. They also thrive, multiply and compete within our minds. When we announce to the world a good idea, who knows what subconscious quasi-Darwinian selection has gone on behind the scenes inside our heads?[21]

Dawkins believes that memes are shaped within our minds by reflection and meditation, before being told as 'good' stories which then get passed on. They let us use raw data and turn it into usable information to direct our behaviour. This is a powerful idea, and it offers a simple explanation for why a human is different from, say, a pigeon – apart from the wings, of course.

Dennett explained that the crucial difference is the way we react to raw data and how we use it.

Meme vehicles [raw data] inhabit our world alongside all the fauna and flora, large and small. By and large they are 'visible' only to the human species, however. Consider the environment of the average New York City pigeon, whose eyes and ears are assaulted every day by approximately as many words, pictures, and other signs and symbols as assault each human New Yorker. These physical meme vehicles may impinge importantly on the pigeon's welfare, but not in virtue of the memes they carry – it is nothing to the pigeon that it is under a page of the National Enquirer, not the New York Times, that it finds a crumb.

To human beings, on the other hand, each meme vehicle is a potential friend or foe, bearing a gift that will enhance our powers or a gift horse that will distract us, burden our memories, derange our judgement.[22]

Freemasonry has developed powerful ways of telling stories and planting thoughts in the minds of its followers. But is it a 'gift that will enhance our powers' or a distraction to clutter up our memories with meaningless ritual? Instinctively, I felt it was a gift, but I was still a long way from understanding how it worked and what it might ultimately be capable of doing to me.

Reading more of Dennett's work confirmed this idea was worth pursuing. He believes that memes are a driving force behind the rise of human civilisation.

Significant memetic evolution is an extremely recent phenomenon, becoming a powerful force only in the last hundred thousand years, and exploding with the development of civilization less than ten thousand years ago. It is restricted to one species, Homo sapiens, and we might note that it has now brought us to the dawn of yet a fourth medium of potential R and D, thanks to the memes of science.[23]

The meme – Dawkins' evolutionary idea, which Daniel Dennett summed up as 'making our brain into a sort of dung heap in which the larvae of other people's ideas renew themselves, before sending out copies of themselves in an informational Diaspora'[24] – offers a possible theory to explain why Freemasonry has thrived and why it improves its members.

Ritual is a formal system of imitation. Could it be a deliberate structure for passing on memes? Is it a way of adapting a human's innate ability to imitate, to pass on useful life skills? Does Masonic ritual exploit something we are all born with?

Alison Gopnik, Andrew Meltzoff and Patricia Kuhl work on the psychological development of children. They found powerful evidence of the ability of very young children to imitate, and to learn by imitation.

One-month-old babies imitate facial expressions. ... It turned out there was a systematic relation between what the babies did, and what the babies saw. At first Andy did these experiments with three-week-olds. But to demonstrate that this ability was really innate, he had to show that newborn babies could imitate. ... He tested babies less than a day old; the youngest baby was only forty-two minutes old. The newborns imitated, too.

At first glance this ability to imitate might seem curious and cute but not deeply significant. But if you think about it a minute, it is actually amazing. There are no mirrors in the womb: newborns have never seen their own face ... [but] from the time we're born, we seem to link this deeply personal self to the bodily movements of other people, movements we can only see and not feel ... we know, quite directly, that we are like other people and they are like us.[25]

Harvard psychologist David McClelland, also noted that the ability to imitate and learn is closely linked to human achievement.

Mankind is engaged over space and time in a variety of social or cultural 'experiments' which involve different methods of economic, political, religious or social organization. Every so often a social 'mutation' occurs – a particularly fortunate combination of interests or leaders or methods of organizing different spheres of activity, a new development which leads either to growth in the economic or some other cultural sphere. ... The spread of such an obviously more successful way of dealing with the world occurs by 'diffusion'; that is, other people see the advantages of the new techniques and adopt them as soon as they learn about them.[26]

Is this the real secret of Freemasonry? When we put on our blue-and-white aprons are we learning how to cope with life? And does this mean it has spread by evolutionary pressure? Has Freemasonry latched on to a useful set of memes which promote achievement and help those they infect to become more comfortable in society?

Boyer thinks that while memes may be a good starting point for looking at how spiritual ritual works, there is more to this process than simple replication.[27] He talks about cultural epidemics.

Human minds are inhabited by a large population of mental representations. Most of them are found only in one individual, but some are present in roughly similar forms in various members of a group. ... The diffusion of particular representations in a group, as well as similarities across groups, can be predicted if we have a good description of which mental resources people bring to understanding what others offer as cultural material, in particular which inferential processes they apply to that material.[28]

Freemasons meet in groups, where the massed tutting of the older Brethen ensures that the newcomer conforms. Boyer lists the factors which make a spiritual system successful.

Some concepts happen to connect with inference systems in the brain in a way that makes recall and communication very easy. Some concepts happen to trigger our emotional programmes in particular ways. Some happen to connect to our social mind. Some of them are represented in such a way that they soon become plausible and direct behaviour. The ones that do all this are the religious ones we actually observe in human societies. They are most successful because they combine features relevant to a variety of mental systems. [29]

Certain principles and concepts are intuitive to human minds, and, when the right ones are brought together in a suitable framework, the resulting system works for its users. This means it survives and spreads. Particular types of cultural input are easy to acquire, because they match what we expect; such material needs little effort to assimilate it. But we have to remember Boyer's observation that 'we do not have the cultural concepts we have because they make sense or are useful, but because the way our brains are put together makes it very difficult not to believe in them'. [30] Freemasonry does not have to be sensible to succeed. It just has to appeal to our innate beliefs.

Examples of this are certain emotional rewards, often below the level of our conscious awareness, which trigger behaviour such as passing the salt before someone asks for it; these emotional effects are so small that we often do not realise what tipped our choice. Morality is another example. We get no clear reward when we behave morally, so why should it trigger positive emotions? Perhaps because behaving morally makes us feel comfortable with ourselves. Boyer points out that if a majority of individuals in a species feel this reward effect for moral behaviour, it gives that species an evolutionary advantage. But how do we rationalise our response to these subliminal rewards? Boyer says that human minds like to tell themselves stories that represent events as causally related. We want to put events in order, so that each one is the result of some other event and paves the way for what follows. [31] By identifying ourselves with moral heroes in exciting stories, we feel we are emulating them and sharing in their fame and glory. Then we have a reason for feeling good about moral behaviour.

Dr Andrew Newberg and Dr Eugen D'Aquili, brain scientists at the University of Pennsylvania, say the beginning of story-telling was an important step in the evolution of human minds.

Because of this knowledge of the potential threats all around them, early humans likely saw the world as a complex, endlessly dangerous place. ... Thankfully the big brain that generated these fears also provided a way to resolve them ... ideas to protect themselves – laws, cultures, religions and science, which enabled them to adapt to their world. All the lofty reaches to which human achievement has carried us ... can be traced to the mind's need to reduce the intolerable anxiety that is the brain's way of warning us that we are not safe. [32]

One of the ways we reduce anxiety is by making sense of the world. We see this in the theme of the Epic of Gilgamesh. By taking a series of separate events and turning them into a sensible and logical story, the story-teller gives an explanation for fate. When we realise we are going to die, this knowledge brings a whole range of related questions. Why are we born? Why do we die? What happens to us when we die? What is our place in the world? How can we live in this uncertain world and not be afraid?

If the story which is put forward to explain the events seems to be outlining a deep truth, then it can become a myth. So I needed to find out exactly how a good story turns into a myth.

The Making of Myth

A myth will always give information about a fear-generating fact.

Why is there evil in the world? The mythical answer is because Eve ate an apple, or Pandora opened a box she was not supposed to. Now we have someone to blame, and the problem is reduced to something understandable.

Joseph Campbell worked out that all myths can be reduced to a few common elements. First, they take a question of critical concern, such as where did mankind come from? Next, they pose the problem as a pair of apparently conflicting opposites. Finally, the myth reconciles the opposites by the action of spiritual powers in a way which stops humans needing to worry any further about the problem.

Here are some examples of a myth taken from Masonic ritual.

First, let's look at the creation of man. Masonic myth says that a supreme being, called by the metaphorical title of God, was sitting with his council of angels, and he had the idea of making man, so he asked them what they thought of this idea. Here's how the ritual tells the story:

When God in His eternal council conceived the thought of Man's creation, He called to Him the three ministers that continually waited upon the throne. And their names were – Justice, Truth, and Mercy. And He addressed them saying: 'Shall we make Man?' Justice answered: 'O God, make him not, he will trample on Thy laws;' and Truth also answered: 'O God, make him not, for he will pollute Thy sanctuaries.' But Mercy, dropping on her knees and looking up through her tears, exclaimed: 'O my God, make him, and I will watch over him with my care through the dark and dreary paths he will have to tread.'

And hearing Mercy's pleas God made man and called him Adam, and said to him: 'O Man, thou art the child of Mercy – go and deal with thy brother.'

According to this myth, which can be found in the 22nd Degree of the Ancient and Accepted Scottish Rite, God created man, despite the warnings that he would be untruthful and unjust, because of the intervention of the goddess of Mercy. So the story says that we may struggle to be truthful, we may not always deal fairly with our fellow men, but we can rely on Mercy, our spiritual mother, to speak up on our behalf and all will be well.

Another example is the question, what happens when we die? Again Freemasonic myth, to be found in the 28th Degree of the Ancient and Accepted Scottish Rite, has an answer.

There is no real death in nature; all is living. What we call death is change. The supreme reason, being unchangeable, is therefore imperishable. Thoughts, once uttered, are immortal. Is the source or spring from which they flow less immortal than they? How could the thoughts exist, if the soul from which they emanated were to cease to be? Could the universe, the uttered thoughts of God, continue still to exist if He no longer were?

In this myth, death is not an end, it is a change. It says that, just as we cannot see how a man's thoughts change, so we cannot see how death changes a spirit.

Newberg and D'Aquili think that our brains structure myths in this way because 'the mind makes sense of mythical problems using the same cognitive functions it relies on to make sense of the physical world'.[33] Myth-creation involves using the mind's causal or cognitive operator, which is the mind's ability to link abstract causes to real events. But this is only one of our mind's functions that create stories. The second is the binary operator: the mind's ability to reduce complex situations to simple opposites, such as up and down, or in and out. As Newberg and D'Aquili explain:

> When the cognitive imperative, driven by existential fear, directs the binary function to make sense of the metaphysical landscape, it obliges by interrupting that existential problem and rearranging it into the pairs of irreconcilable opposites that become the key elements of myth: heaven and earth, good and evil, celebration and tragedy, birth and death and rebirth; isolation and unity.[34]

Myths which satisfy our mind's structural needs sound good when we hear them; they resonate with us, reducing our dread of the unknown by telling an apparently sensible story about a nonsensical fear. If death is not an end but merely a change, then what is there to fear?

But telling a good story is only the beginning of understanding how ritual works. What happens when we act out the stories we invent?

Acting Out the Truth

When spring arrives in the Pennines, a strange ritual is carried out on the moors above my house. If I go for a walk in the early morning, when the dew is still on the grass, I am sometimes lucky enough to see mad March hares boxing in the mist. Two males will face each other, rear up on their hind legs and box with their front paws. They only carry out this strange ritual fighting dance in the spring, and it forms part of their mating behaviour.

For many years now, animal rituals have been a source of scientific study. Our television sets show us much more exotic examples than my local hares boxing. They bring into our living rooms images of bower birds building ornate decorated temples to procreation; the strutting of male peacocks, with their preposterous tails; the ritual mating flights of butterflies; or just the submission ritual of dogs seeking pack status. Ritual seems to have a biological basis in many animals, and this includes the human animal.

Much animal ritual is related to sex and mating. Pioneering evolutionary biologist Dr Michael Bastock first described the mating ritual of the silver-washed fritillary, a species of butterfly with brownish wings marked with black and silver. It is not noted for having a large brain or extensive memory skill, yet, for all its neurological limitations, this little creature carries out a complex courting ritual. When an amorous male spies a possible female consort he moves towards her in a purposeful manner. The coy female, if she is indeed another silver-washed fritillary, immediately takes to the air to move away from the male. The male then flies around her, performing a series of aerobatic looping circles to impress his intended lady love. He will fly so close that his wings almost brush her body. If she approves of the male she will continue in a steady, straight-line flight path while he displays his aerial skills around her. When she lands the two butterflies face each other in a rigid, unnatural posture before sniffing each other's scent glands; only then will this fussy female allow her suitor to couple with her. Bastock points out that before the male can mate he must carry out seven ritual acts, and the female must make the correct ritual response to each move for a successful courtship.[35]

A decade before he published his detailed study of animal courtship rituals Bastock had suggested that such complex behaviour in simple creatures might have a genetic cause.[36] And he has been proved right by recent evolutionary studies on the survival advantage of female coyness in mating rituals.[37] He spotted that the ritual worked for butterflies because it enabled two individuals, 'without any previous knowledge of each other, to identify a suitable mate by means of a neurological conversation'. He explained this as 'a biological resonance which was set up between the two insects caused by the repetitive rhythms causing their respective nervous systems to vibrate in harmony'.[38]

Do Masonic rituals work in a similar way? Are they just a sophisticated development of an insect mating ritual, modified for a species with a slightly larger brain? I needed to find out more about the neurobiology of ritual.

Ritual and the Brain

What do we experience when we take part in rituals? Newberg and D'Aquili say that, from a neurobiological perspective, 'human ritual has two major characteristics. First, it generates emotional discharges, in varying degrees of intensity, that represent subjective feelings of tranquillity, ecstasy, and awe; and, second, it results in mental states that are often explained as some degree of spiritual transcendence.'[39]

In 1992 a research group based at California State University carried out a review of the effects of taking part in various rituals, such as prayer, religious services, meditation and physical exertion.[40] They found that the benefits included lower blood pressure, decreased heart rate, lower rate of respiration, reduced levels of cortisol and positive boosts to the immune system. Newberg and D'Aquili point out that all these functions are regulated by the hypothalamus and the brain's autonomic nervous system, and they suggest that it is the rhythmic behaviours associated with many rituals that cause the change in mental states. Repetitive actions, such as dancing and singing, in ceremonies can have a significant effect upon the limbic and autonomous systems and produce what are described as 'intensely pleasurable feelings'.[41]

Combining repetitive actions with deliberately exaggerated gestures can induce electrical action within the amygdala region of the brain. This results in mild feelings of fear or awe.[42] Freemasonry has more than its fair share of extravagant gestures, and they are certainly used in a ritually repetitive way. When the Master raises his arms in the Grand and Royal Sign, all we assembled Freemasons feel the awe his action generates.

Furthermore, the cognitive setting in which ritual is carried out has a direct emotional impact on the participant's brain. This is where the story-telling sense of the myth combines with emotional arousal effects to produce a powerful means of imparting information. When you experience a sense of spiritual transcendence in a ritual setting, you often feel that you have had a close encounter with the source of order within the universe. If you are religious, you call this supreme being God. A scientist like me thinks it can take the form of a vision of the light and order at the centre.

Joseph Campbell saw a useful function of ritual as utilising mythology to reduce existential fear by helping us feel that there is some great creator who wants to be reunited with us and to whom we return when we die:

> *The one great story of myth; that in the beginning we were united with the source, but that we were separated from it and now we must find a way to return.*[43]

Newberg and D'Aquili say that 'the neurobiological effect of ritualized behaviours give ceremonial substance' to the myths which are acted out. By this they mean that, if powerful myths are acted out in a dramatic setting, we feel that we are a part of the truth the story seems to contain.

The most important function of ritual is to take a spiritual story and turn it into a spiritual experience. It takes something you believe in and turns it into something you can feel. Newberg and D'Aquili conclude that 'our growing understanding of neurological function leads us to believe that the ritual urge may be rooted in something deeper than the cultural needs of a given society. It suggests that humans are driven to act out their myths by the basic biological operations of the brain.'[44]

When we live out our myths they become real for us. This is something the system of Freemasonry exploits to the full.

But does it also have secrets about the effects of human posture?

Stand as I Do

As I related in the first part of this book, when I took my First Degree in Freemasonry I was told, 'You will therefore stand to me perfectly erect, with your feet in a form I will demonstrate to you.'

I then stood for quite some time in an awkward, off-balance and unnatural posture while the 'secrets' of the degree were revealed to me. My feet had been wedged together so I couldn't move them to get any relief and were braced in such a way that I couldn't make the slight movements which would normally keep me balanced. At the time, I felt this difficult posture was being used to create tension in my legs, and I suspected that this might be a ritual device to induce the release of stress hormones into my bloodstream and modulate my brain. This was something I would later find to be important.

Can gestures and postures enhance ritual responses? I decided to look more closely at the effects of posture on state of mind. I had heard mention of something called the Alexander Technique, which claimed to relieve a variety of mental, emotional and physical conditions by teaching people how to stand and sit correctly. Liz Hodgkinson, a well-known teacher of the method, says of it:

> *The Alexander Technique is basically a series of physical movements designed to correct bad posture and bring the body back into alignment, thus helping it to function efficiently, as nature intended. ... The idea is that, once you have learned to move your muscles and joints correctly, various ills of the body caused by wrong movement can then start to right themselves. The Technique is necessary because the vast majority of us move our bodies wrongly – often without realising that we are doing so, until health problems arise. ... Alexander himself believed that most of humanity's ills – mental, emotional and physical – are caused by the gradual and largely unconscious acquisition of bad habits.*[45]

This concept looked promising. The ritual of Freemasonry, strictly enforced by tutting ranks of wrinkly Brethren, insists that you can only learn things about yourself if you stand in a peculiar way. Could the work of Frederick Matthias Alexander tell me why?

Alexander was born in Wynyard, in north-west Tasmania, Australia, on 20 January 1869, the eldest of eight children. When he went to school he was a difficult pupil, because he consistently refused to take anything on trust; indeed he was such a pest that his father eventually had him taught at home by a private tutor. From early childhood he loved the theatre, and by the age of nineteen he was working as a professional actor in Melbourne. Then he found he had a serious problem for an actor: his voice kept failing during recitations. When this first happened he went to doctors for help, but medical treatment of the time could not cure it. The condition was getting so bad that Alexander often couldn't bring himself to accept many engagements, for he was uncertain of being able to get through a full evening's recitation. Then he lost his voice halfway through an important performance.

His doctor couldn't help. Alexander therefore began a careful observation of how he physically used his body when he was speaking in public. His student George Bernard Shaw later wrote, 'having the true scientific spirit and industry, he set himself to discover what it was that he was really doing to disable himself in this fashion by his efforts to produce the opposite result'.[46] In the end Alexander found out what was going wrong, and a great deal more as well. As Shaw went on to say, 'he established not only the beginnings of a far-reaching science of the apparently involuntary movements we call reflexes, but a technique of correction and self-control which forms a substantial addition to our very slender resources in personal education'.

Rheumatologist Dr Wilfred Barlow studied the Alexander Technique to try and help his patients. He found that Alexander's approach gave him a way of detecting their mental state; anxiety was always accompanied by acute muscle tension, and there was a close link between negative mental states and physical pain. 'In many ways,' Barlow said, 'it became clear that the mentally sick were physically tense. It is often impossible to separate the physical and the psychological aspects of a patients' condition.'[47]

By recording the electrical signals activating his patient's muscles, Dr Barlow found that all mental states, whether positive or negative, are accompanied by distinct physical movements. These may be slight, such as an increased rate of blinking, or very noticeable, as in the case of hyperactive children. Barlow concluded that states of muscular tension always occur when the patient is under emotional strain. But – more importantly for my study – he made the point that 'by learning the proper use of the muscles we can prevent negative feedback'.

My guess that the postures of Masonic ritual could be designed to create particular emotional states of mind was looking quite possible. Liz Hodgkinson confirms this, saying:

> Correct use of the muscles enables more positive feedback to be given to the mind, so that both mind and body can be freed from habitual tension. … The most valuable lesson that can be learned from an understanding of Alexander therapy is that the condition of our minds and bodies is very much in our control. To a very great extent, we can choose good posture, correct body use and positive thinking – or we can choose to be misshapen victims of ill-health and with a mind chock-full of negative, useless thoughts. [48]

A comment of Alexander's about his own technique echoes the experience of Masonic Initiation that I described earlier.

> We are confronted with the unquestionable fact that the subconscious can be 'educated' below the plane of reason. Acts very frequently performed become so mechanical that they can be repeated without any sense of conscious awareness by the operator. The pianist, after constant rehearsals, will perform the most intricate passage while his attention is engaged with an entirely unrelated subject, although it is particularly worthy of remark in this connection that when such an art as the performance of

music falls temporarily into such an automatic repetition, the connoisseur will instantly recognise the loss of some quality – generally spoken of as 'feeling' in the rendering. ...

The important point is the fact that the phase of being with which we are dealing becomes, as we progress through life, a composite of animal instincts and habits acquired below the plane of reason either by repetition or by suggestion. ... we share the qualities of the subconscious mind with the animal kingdom. For in the lower organisms no less than in that of humanity, this subconscious can be educated. The observations of naturalists now confirm the belief that the young of certain birds – the swallow has been particularly instanced – are taught to fly by the parent birds; whilst any one who has trained a dog will know how such a trick as 'begging' for food may become so habitual as to appear instinctive.[49]

I only found lodge meetings to be 'comfortable' after I had been taught how to stand and what to say. I did not feel at ease until the lessons had been repeated many times.

As Alexander points out, my subconscious mind was being educated by the repetition of the Masonic ritual.

Although I could now see what had happened, I still didn't know enough about the brain and nervous system to understand exactly how it worked.

Bringing Myth to Life

There are good and bad ways to get a story across. Freemasonry, though, is good at telling its stories. It knows that to be effective, a ritual must present the essential content of a mythical story in a behavioural context. This gives the myth neurological life within the participant's brain.

Pascal Boyer lists three important properties that successful rituals share:

1. A sense of specialness. Taking part in a ritual is not the same as acting in a play. What makes rituals special is that they create a sense that you have to perform it in the correct way, otherwise something terrible will happen – although there is often no explanation of how correct performance averts the danger. If you doubt the truth of this statement, just make a slip when delivering Masonic ritual in Lodge and see how much tutting you can provoke.

2. Consequences for social interaction. The First-Degree ceremony makes you a Mason. Before the ritual you were an ordinary human being; after it you have changed into a Brother.

3. A spiritual dimension. Many rituals are specifically religious and invoke God into the ceremony. Freemasonry invokes a belief that there is an ordering principle at the centre of the cosmos, and that its rituals help Freemasons approach, understand and relate to this centre.

Boyer points out that rituals that have all these properties are ones which are successfully transmitted. The folk who developed Masonic ritual seemed to know this instinctively.

But, before we Freemasons get too complacent, there is another aspect to consider. The endless repetition of three basic ceremonies can start to feel like a compulsive obsession. Is there is an element of Obsessive Compulsive Disorder (OCD) in the way rituals are carried out? Anthropologist Alan Fiske realised that OCD originates in areas of the brain that mediate the combining of our plans with our emotions.[51] He says that ritual can activate mental systems which make us feel comfortable. This was one of the first things I noticed about Masonic meetings: once I had gone through my three degrees, the later meetings became enjoyable. But does this mean I am simply a compulsive obsessive who has found a safe outlet for my odd behaviour?

Anthropologist Frederick Barth studied initiations into 'manhood' in New Guinea.

The secret knowledge [of initiation] is often vacuous or paradoxical. In many rites the candidates are taught that the secret of the rite is precisely that there is no secret, or that they will not be told until they reach a further stage of initiation. The rites promote a notion that knowledge is intrinsically dangerous and ambiguous.[52]

This sounds just like the lost secrets of the Master Mason. Having been given the 'secrets' the ritual said to me that they were not the 'real' secrets because those had been lost.

Rituals produce their effects in ways which are often not understood by the people who carry them out. Anthropologists describe rituals as having a transcendent flavour, meaning that, for the people who carry them out, the ritual seems to activate mysterious forces that can be sensed but not described. This was certainly something I could relate to; I was enjoying taking part in Masonic ritual; but I did not know why I found the meetings so uplifting. Boyer points out that 'you cannot perform rituals seriously without assuming that a prescribed series of actions will have a certain result and guessing at the same time that the series of actions as such cannot explain the result'.[53] He adds that 'the fact that people in a group perform important rituals together sharpens their perception that they are indeed a group with clearly marked boundaries'. The Tyler, standing at the door of the lodge with his sword in his hand, marks a clear boundary between Masons and non-Masons.

Boyer thinks that when our brains build religious concepts they use mental systems and capacities that are there anyway.[54] This implies that spiritual concepts are parasitic on other mental capacities that serve some evolutionary purpose and hence have become widespread in the gene pool. This is where the meme theory fits into his work. He points out that we can understand religion much better if we take into account that the processes underpinning 'belief' are the same in religion and in everyday matters.[55] Can these ideas help me understand Freemasonry?

He raises an interesting question about the conflict between religion and science. He talks of attempts by some scientists to create a purified religion, a metaphysical doctrine that retains some aspects of religious concepts. He identifies the key concept that there is a creative force, but it is difficult for us to know it, and it explains why the world is the way it is, etc. He asks if such a religion would be compatible with science and decides it would. But when he then asks if it is likely to become a successful religion, he decides not; he argues that it will not produce relevant insights into situations like death, birth or marriage. But what he has briefly described are the basic concepts of Freemasonry. He appears to be unaware that Freemasonry has been successful and uses exactly that concept. Freemasonry focuses only on death and birth, ignoring marriage as being outside its remit.

Masonry does not claim to be a religion, but despite Boyer's misgivings it is a successful spiritual system. Why is this? Boyer himself suggests an explanation and a way forward when he says:

Human minds did not become vulnerable to just any odd kind of supernatural beliefs. On the contrary, because they have many sophisticated inference systems, they became vulnerable to a very restricted set of supernatural concepts: the ones that can jointly activate inference systems for agency, predation, death, morality and social exchange.[56]

Its worldwide success shows Freemasonry fits this definition. So what are its real secrets? The ritual tells me these secrets are illuminated by symbols; therefore symbols are what I need to look at next.

[1] Lomas & Knight (1996), p. 17.
[2] Squire (1912), p. 1.
[3] Forster (1927), p. 41.
[4] Campbell (1988), p. 23.
[5] Devereux (2002), p. 51.
[6] Turner (1969), p. 46.
[7] Devereux (2002), p. 52.
[8] Reanney (1995), pp. 1–2.
[9] Temple (1991), p. 104.
[10] Boyer (2002), pp. 106–22.
[11] Boyer (2002), pp. 39–40.
[12] Dawkins (1976), p. 192.
[13] Blackmore (1999), p. xvi.
[14] Dennett (1990).
[15] Blackmore (1999), p. 11.
[16] Blackmore (1999), pp. 19–21.
[17] Blackmore (1999), p. 67.
[18] Blackmore (1999), p. 91.
[19] Pribram (1974).
[20] Dawkins (1999), p. 109.
[21] Dawkins (1999), p. 307.
[22] Dennett (1992), p. 204.
[23] Dennett (1992), p. 199.
[24] Dennett (1992), p. 207.
[25] Gopnik, Meltzoff & Kuhl (1999), pp. 29–31.
[26] McClelland (1961), p. 36.

[27] Boyer (2002), pp. 38–43.

[28] Boyer (2002), p. 43.

[29] Boyer (2002), p. 105.

[30] Boyer (2002), p. 154.

[31] Boyer (2002), p. 340.

[32] Newberg, D'Aquili & Rause (2002), p. 16.

[33] Newberg, D'Aquili & Rause (2002), p. 54.

[34] Newberg, D'Aquili & Rause (2002), p. 51.

[35] Bastock (1967), p. 68.

[36] Bastock.(1956).

[37] Wachtmeister & Enquist (1999).

[38] Bastock & Manning (1955).

[39] Newberg, D'Aquili & Rause (2002), pp. 88–90.

[40] Jerving, Wallace & Beidebach (1992).

[41] Gelihorn & Kiely (1972).

[42] D'Aquili & Newberg (1993).

[43] Campbell (1988), p. 58.

[44] Newberg, D'Aquili & Rause (2002), p. 86.

[45] Hodgkinson (1988), p. 1.

[46] Letter from Shaw quoted in Alexander (1969), p. xxix.

[47] Barlow (1991), p. 2.

[48] Hodgkinson (1988), pp. 34–35.

[49] Alexander (1969), pp. 51–60.

[50] Boyer (2002), p. 169.

[51] Fiske & Haslam (1997).

[52] Barth (1975), p. 23.

[53] Boyer (2002), p. 268.

[54] Boyer (2002), p. 146.

[55] Boyer (2002), p. 57.

[56] Boyer (2002), p. 154.

Chapter Nine

How Does Symbolism Work?

Worth a Thousand Words

Q: What is Freemasonry?
A: A peculiar system of morality, veiled in allegory, and illustrated by symbols.

As an Apprentice Freemason I worked hard to burn this question, and its answer, deep into my mind. But how *can* symbols explain a peculiar system of morality? I now had some idea of how myths can be allegories of innate truths. I'd looked at story-telling and learned a little about how myths could be brought alive by ritual. So much for allegory, now I had to find out about symbolism. But where to start?

The most common form of symbolism, and one which we all know, is language. Words are verbal or written symbols. How a word sounds, or what shape it takes when written down, doesn't really matter. It is the ideas, images and emotions that it carries to the mind of the person who hears it which count. This form of symbolism carries ideas directly from brain to brain.

Steven Pinker is Professor of Psychology at the Massachusetts Institute of Technology. He sees the symbolism of language as a unique skill of humankind.

You and I belong to a species with a remarkable ability: we can shape events in each other's brains with exquisite precision. I am not referring to telepathy or mind control or the other obsessions of fringe science; even in the depictions of believers these are blunt instruments compared to an ability that is uncontroversially present in every one of us. That ability is language. Simply by making noises with our mouths, we can reliably cause precise new combinations of ideas to arise in each other's minds. The ability comes so naturally that we are apt to forget what a miracle it is.[1]

This awesome gift, our ability to blend new ideas into our minds, lies at the heart of our Masonic ritual. When we listen to a Brother, standing in the centre of the lodge, telling us the traditional history, that story lives afresh in our minds. But how do symbols help this process? Often during the ceremonies you are asked to consider landmarks, suggesting that these symbols will help you grasp a subtle idea. This was the view of Joseph Fort Newton, a Masonic sage who died in 1950, who said of Masonry's use of symbols:

The old time Masons did not need to go to hidden teachers to learn mysticism. They lived and worked in the light of it. It shone in their symbols. It is the soul of symbolism that every emblem expresses a reality too great for words. Masonry is mystical, as music is mystical, like poetry, and love, and faith, and prayer, and all else that makes it worth our time to live; but its mysticism is sweet, sane, and natural, far from fantastic, and in no wise eerie, unreal or unbalanced. Of course, these words fail to describe, as all words must, and it is therefore why Masonry uses symbols.[2]

This is poetic, but not very helpful when trying to understand how symbols might convey something that words cannot. But, as I thought about this, I realised there is a system of symbols which does exactly this. We have a specialised system of symbols for mapping the hidden mysteries of nature and science: it is called mathematics. Maths is a discipline which uses clearly defined tokens. Its symbols have agreed relationships which accord to sensory data. And they can explain things which do not translate into words.

A good example of this type of system is the geometry of Euclid. Geometry defines a small number of basic symbols, such as the point, the line and the plane; it then uses rules to fix the ways these primary concepts work together. These few symbols and the ways they act on one another are the basis for all other statements and concepts. The geometric image of Pythagoras's theorem which hangs from the collar of a Past Master of the Craft is a symbolic assurance about the nature of the sides of a right-angled triangle.

Einstein said about the language of maths:

The super-national nature of scientific concepts and scientific language is due to the fact that they have been set up by the best brains of all countries and all times. In solitude, and yet in cooperative effort as regards the final effect, they created the spiritual tools for the technical revolutions which have transformed the life of mankind in the last centuries. Their system of concepts has served as a guide in the bewildering chaos of perceptions so that we learned to grasp general truths from particular observations.[3]

In words that are almost Masonic, Einstein describes maths as a 'spiritual tool to transform mankind'; math symbols enable an adept to understand and share deep truths which often cannot be put clearly into words.

By claiming it is 'illuminated by symbols' Freemasonry says its system can harness the power of a symbolic idiom. But can geometric shapes really offer new modes of thought? Can the symbolism of Freemasonry be used to decode its 'secrets'?

Geometry begins with a series of general postulates: for example, 'a straight line is the shortest distance between two points'. From these principles conclusions can be deduced. So the method falls into two steps. First, discover the basic principles – those from which no simpler principles can be deduced – and then draw the conclusions which follow from them.

Setting up principles to serve as a starting point for later deductions is the most difficult step. There is no general way to work out what is important and what is not. Early geometricians had to wrestle the general principles out of nature. They looked at groups of empirical facts to see if there were any general features that would allow them to set up rules or theorems. Once the rules were worked out, deduction followed on deduction. This process leads to new facts, extending far beyond the reality that gave rise to the symbols: you may only be told the length of one side of a triangle and its angles, and the principles of geometry will then let you deduce everything it is possible to know about that particular triangle. But, without basic principles, there is no foundation to build deductions upon. Single isolated theorems will not help understanding, unless they can be related to an overall theoretical framework.

You have to learn how to manipulate all the symbols, and how they work together, before you can use them to solve problems. Many Freemasons never gain this critical mass of understanding. They grasp only sections of the ritual and meaning, but in general their impression of the whole symbolic system remains disjointed.

Until you learn the spiritual principles underlying the Order, your understanding is limited. You remain stuck at the stage of science before the work of Newton. Before calculus there was no way to work out the orbits of the planets around the sun. Once Newton had formulated the key role of gravity, pulling towards the centre of the solar system, everything about the motion of the planets became clear. It was now possible to use maths to predict when the Bright Morning Star would appear on the horizon.

I was beginning to suspect that Freemasonry might be drawing on a set of extremely ancient symbols to provide a language to discuss deep spiritual matters that are difficult to put into words. The Craft defines the meaning of its symbols by analogy. This means that people of different backgrounds can use them to share ideas. They don't have to adopt any specific religious dogma. The scientist can talk to the Christian, the Moslem to the Jew, and all can use a common language of spiritual symbolism. At best it is a calculus of the spirit. The symbols are abstract and geometric but carry deep meaning. The lozenge, the triangle, the line of the pillar and the circle all seem simple, almost crude, symbols. But I was soon to find that they are a key part of the symbolic heritage of the human race.

The Oldest Symbols

The most ancient symbols drawn by human hand that have yet been discovered are 70,000 years old and were found in South Africa. Here is how *The Times* reported the find:

> *A pair of decorated ornaments unearthed in a South African cave have been dated at more than 70,000 years old, proving that human beings could think abstractly and appreciate beauty much earlier than is generally accepted. The engraved pieces of ochre, a type of iron ore, are by far the oldest examples of symbolic art. ... The earliest similar objects from Europe were made less than 35,000 years ago...*
>
> *The find at Blombos Cave, 180 miles from Cape Town in the Western Cape, ... indicates that not only did the first human beings evolve in Africa and spread throughout the world, but that they became mentally sophisticated by the time they did so. ...*
>
> *The pieces of ochre, one 2 in. long and another 3 in. long have no practical function and were clearly intended for decorative or ritual use. This proves that the people who made them must have been capable of subtle thought, and probably indicates that they spoke a language of syntax and tenses, Professor Henshilwood said.[4]*

And what did these long-dead *Homo sapiens* choose to carve on their pieces of ochre 70,000 years ago? The symbol is identical to the one carved into the Junior Warden's pedestal in my present Lodge; it is the shape outlined by the square and compass when conjoined: a diamond shape (archaeologists call it a lozenge). The humans living around Blombos Cave, users of the earliest symbols yet discovered, used a symbol which Freemasonry still uses today.

The late Marija Gimbutas was Professor of European Archaeology at the University of California. She studied the evolution of human symbols and found that they had real meaning for the people who drew them. She also held out a hope that we might rediscover their message.

Symbols are seldom abstract in any genuine sense; their ties with nature persist, to be discovered through the study of context and association. In this way we can hope to decipher the mythical thought which is the raison d'être of this art and basis of its form. … My primary presupposition is that they can be understood on their own planes of reference, grouped according to their inner coherence. They constitute a complex system in which every unit is interlocked with every other in what appears to be specific categories. No symbol can be treated in isolation; understanding the parts leads to understanding the whole. I do not believe that we shall never know the meaning of prehistoric art and religion. Yes, the scarcity of sources makes reconstruction difficult in most instances, but the religion of the early agricultural period of Europe and Anatolia is very richly documented. Tombs, temples, frescoes, reliefs, sculptures, figurines, pictorial paintings, and other sources need to be analysed.[5]

In *Uriel's Machine* I put forward the suggestion that the meaning of the lozenge was to record the angle between the shadows cast by the winter and summer solstice sunrises, a subject I will discuss more fully later. I decided to check if this applied to these very first lozenges, and found that at the latitude where they were found this angle was 57°. Having drawn this angle out as an apex on a sheet of tracing paper, I then displayed a photograph of the Blombos lozenges on my computer screen. I overlaid my calculated angle on to the 70,000-year-old drawing, carefully moving the paper image over the computer image – and my lines and the lines of the ancient artist were a perfect fit. Marija Gimbutas is right. These symbols are not abstract. They show the range of movement of the sun on the horizon over the seasons of the year.

Gimbutas links the lozenge with Goddess worship. My work has linked much of the Masonic ritual of Solomon's Temple with the Venus goddess of the Phoenicians, Baalat-Gerbal,[6] and the Egyptian Goddess Ma'at.[7] Baalat-Gerbal was symbolised by a headdress of two curved horns, similar to those of a cow or a stag, and she has close parallels with the Norse Goddess Freyja. The founder of Freemasonry William St Clair had Norse ancestors who built a temple dedicated to Freyja near Trondheim, a matter I will return to later in this book. This temple incorporated Masonic-type pillars at its eastern entrance.[8]

Gimbutas looked at the use of Goddess symbols over thousands of years.

What is striking is not the metamorphosis of the symbols but rather the continuity from Palaeolithic times on. The major aspects of the Goddess of the Neolithic – the birth giver, ... the fertility- and life-giver, ... and the death-wielder – can all be traced back to the period when the first sculptures of bone, ivory or stone appeared, around 25000 B.C.E., and their symbols – vulvas, triangles, breasts, chevrons, zig-zags, meanders, cup-marks – to an even earlier time. The main theme of Goddess symbolism is the mystery of birth and death and the renewal of life, not only human life but all life on Earth and indeed the whole cosmos. ... This symbolic system uses cyclical not linear time.[9]

The most important symbol of Freemasonry, the square and compasses, is made up of two overlaid chevrons. This fact is concealed when the Lodge is closed. The square and compasses are only opened and overlaid to form two chevrons when the immediate Past Master places them on the volume of the sacred law, as the Lodge is opened. But can symbols implant new combinations of ideas into a receptive mind as simply as words can? It soon became clear that they can.

Can You Read Symbols?

Professor Gimbutas says that a simple way to draw a woman's pubic area is to outline a V. This graphic shorthand is used everywhere, from the sketches of Leonardo to the graffiti on the walls of male toilets. She lists vast numbers of female figures with chevrons symbolising genitals. As an example, she quotes a table of forty-seven variations on the female chevron symbol taken from the Neolithic Vinca culture that flourished in the Balkans around 5000 B.C.E.[10]

Her description even made its way into popular thrillers. Dan Brown's fictional hero, Harvard symbologist Dr Robert Langdon, is told by Marie Saunière, the equally imaginary curator of Rosslyn Chapel Trust, that the downward pointing triangle 'is the chalice which represents the feminine'.[11] I wonder where that idea came from?

After 5000 B.C.E. a new version of this female symbol appears – again one that is still used in the modern Craft. It is the net, and its formal cousin the chequerboard. This symbol was widespread through central Europe from 5000 B.C.E. onwards. Gimbutas reports over 2,000 caves with chequerboard patterns carved into them, from the Paris basin of France down to Sardinia, with the earliest dating from the Neolithic. I was reminded of the chequerboard floor and the net covering of the pillars in the Second–Degree Tracing-board when I read her comments on the significance of this symbol.

> *In the Early Neolithic, the net motif and pottery painting emerge at the same time. The net's symbolic importance is indicated by the thick borders that frame it from the beginning — bands, lozenges, triangles, squares and circles. … The intimacy of the net with the pubic triangle, uterus, and egg suggests it symbolises an embryonic substance capable of giving life … emphasizing the life-giving power of the Goddess.* [12]

Her description of the triangle and lozenge borders brought to mind both the pavement of the lodge and the border of the First-Degree tracing. But she was talking about symbols that dated back over 7,000 years, and, in the case of the lozenge, ten times longer. Whatever else you might think about the symbols of Freemasonry they must have an emotional appeal if people have drawn and redrawn them so many times over the millennia.

The lozenge shape also has a practical use: it can be used, almost like a postcode, to indicate latitude. [13] This has an important symbolic purpose in connection with farming. If we think of the ritual planting of seed as part of a religious motivation for farming, then the shape of the Goddess symbol, when drawn by the seasonal movement of the sun's rising point on the horizon, can tell you if your seed will grow at that latitude. When the first cultivated grains were exported westward from the plains of Anatolia, around 9000 B.C.E., the ability to measure latitude would have been an important piece of sacred knowledge. [14]

And how easy the problem of measuring latitude becomes once you know how to project a lozenge from the movements of the sun. I first realised this whilst building a primitive orbit gauge, called a horizon declinometer, as part of the research for the book, *Uriel's Machine*. I noticed that the pattern of the shadows cast by the markers of the winter and summer solstice sunrises and sunsets forms the shape of a St Andrew's cross. The exact angle of the X, which varies according to the latitude at which it is measured, is formed by the shadows creating two apex-facing triangles (see *Uriel's Machine* for a detailed discussion of this process).[15] Gimbutas says that twin triangles have been used to represent the Goddess since 5000 B.C.E.[16] Is it just chance that this link with the seasonal movements of the sun is preserved in Masonic ritual?

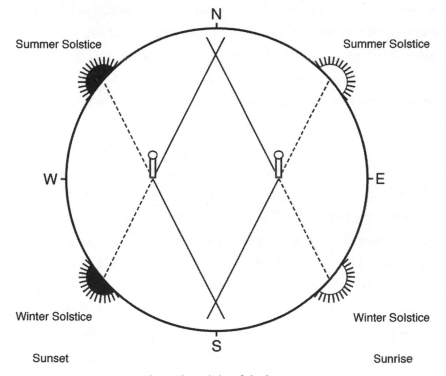

Fig 1: The origin of the lozenge
At the rising and setting of the sun at the two solstices cast by the two posts, aligned east-west, form a lozenge which is distinctive for each latitue. The circle represents the visible horizon.

At any latitude a distinctive St Andrew's cross is produced; its angles may differ, but the basic pattern is always the same. This symbol is a shorthand way of representing the movement of the sun over a full year and in the past could well have been used to represent this concept. At the latitude where William St Clair built the Temple of Roslin the solstice angles produce a perfect square, and that is where modern Freemasonry began.

The lozenge is a common motif in the famous passage-grave at Newgrange in Ireland, as it is at many other Neolithic sites. If the lozenge angles are derived from the geometry of the sun's rays, a potential solution to its symbolic meaning is clear. The diagonal cross of the year has four legs which represent the direction of solstice sunrises or sunsets, but the shadows created by the solstice marker poles can also be drawn out as a diamond-shaped lozenge, that will vary in its angles according to latitude.

So each latitude has a distinct lozenge. In the north the lozenge is tall and thin, while as you go nearer the equator it gets shorter and fatter. At 55° North the shadows cast by the rising sun form a regular square with four right angles. Places south of this latitude produce increasingly wider diamonds, and as one moves further north the diamonds become taller. This unique shape is why a lozenge can be used to identify a location in the way that a post code or a zip code does today. This process is fully described in *Uriel's Machine*.[17]

In 1999 treasure-hunters digging near the central German town of Nebra uncovered a cache of bronze weapons and a small bronze disc. Laminated on to the disc are gold images of the sun, the moon and a sky map of 32 stars. On opposite edges of the disc there are two golden arcs, which coincide exactly with the angles between the summer and winter solstice sunrises and sunsets.[18] This find, dated to

1600 BCE, confirms the idea, first published in *Uriel's Machine*, that the movement of the sun on the horizon was observed and recorded in Europe in the late Neolithic and early Bronze Age. Looking at the Nebra disc, I was reminded of the First-Degree Tracing-board – which also encodes the positioning of the candidate on the summer and winter solstice sunrise lines of the lodge – and I couldn't suppress the romantic thought that it might have served the same purpose.

Archaeoastronomer Dr John North came to a similar conclusion about the origin of the lozenge symbol.

> *Suppose, for example, that a religious architect were to have marked out two parallel lines towards the rising midwinter sun and then to draw across the two parallel lines [two more parallel lines] (with the same spacing) towards the setting midwinter Sun. A lozenge-shape would result, its angles depending on geographical latitude and local horizon. ... The fact remains that like the cross of Christianity or the crescent of Islam, the lozenge and chevron could easily have been taken over from an older symbolism and given a precise meaning, before being eventually repeated again and again without much thought of it.[19]*

But what is this older symbolism that North is assuming? Marija Gimbutas has shown that the lozenge is a key symbol of Goddess worship. She explains its survival simply.

> *The old European sacred images and symbols were never totally uprooted; these most persistent features in human history were too deeply implanted in the psyche to be uprooted. ... The Goddess's religion went underground. Some of the old traditions, particularly those connected with*

birth, death and earth fertility rituals, have continued to this day without
much change in some regions; in others they were assimilated into Indo-
European ideology.[20]

My experience of the Craft says that these symbols have a deep
emotional appeal, and the more I sit in Lodge and gaze at them, the
more attractive they become. In the light of Professor Gimbutas's
comments I wondered to what extent evolution had hard-wired an
instinctive attraction for these symbols in my brain. There is no doubt,
from her work, that these symbols have been continually redrawn for
thousands of years. Then I found a piece of work which explains what
it is about the human brain that causes this symbol to be attractive.

The Instinctive Appeal of Art

Betty Edwards is Professor of Art at California State University. She
is also a well-respected working artist. Her long-term passion is
teaching her students how to draw. However, whilst studying methods
of teaching, she applied the work of Jerome Bruner and Roger
Sperry, neurobiologists who discovered the different skills of right
and left hemispheres of the brain. Their ideas led her to develop new
ways of teaching drawing which helped her students to make better
use of the right side of the brain.[21]

Her results were astounding, even with her most unpromising
students. She became famous for her ability to teach the technique of
drawing. But she also noticed that, as she encouraged her students to
actively draw from the right hemisphere of their brain, they tapped
new veins of creativity.

Edwards made a breakthrough in understanding how symbols work. She spotted that creative thought requires a unique blend of the verbal, analytical mode from the left side of the brain with the visual, perceptual mode of the right side. Learning to read, write and recite ritual trains only the verbal mode. She suggested that learning to see and draw was a good way to train the visual side of the brain. When both modes are able to work as equal partners, one mode enhances the other, and together they release human creativity. Her idea of training the mind to use verbal memory and develop the visual appreciation of symbols seems to resonate with the way Freemasonry stimulates its followers. But Edwards came up with confirmation of Gimbutas's idea that some symbols are embedded deep in the human psyche.

Edwards found that her students could see meaning in drawings. This is how she explains the process.

Working with drawing students, I often recall that experience when they suddenly see that drawings (and other works of art) have meaning. I am not, of course, referring only to drawings of things – portraits, landscapes, still-life subjects. That kind of meaning – what a drawing is – can be summed up in a few words. But meaning is also expressed in the parallel visual language of a drawing, whether it represents recognizable objects or is completely non-objective. This different kind of meaning requires a different kind of comprehension. A drawing, to be comprehended for meaning, must be read by means of the language used by the artist, and that meaning, once comprehended, may be beyond the power of words to express. Yet in its parts and as a whole, it can be read. [22]

She is talking about the meaning a symbol can convey, which may be something that is difficult to put into words. This is exactly what Freemasonry claims when it says it is 'illustrated by symbols'.

Edwards believes that 'drawings' – that is, marks on paper with or without a recognisable image – can be read like a language. She thinks that abstract symbols can reveal to the person making the marks – as well as to the viewer – what's going on in the mind of the mark-maker.[23] She began to test with her students the idea that drawings can represent pure expression even if devoid of realistic images. She found marks on paper can reveal thoughts of which even the thinker may be unaware.

In 1940 George Orwell wrote an essay called 'New Words'.[24] He put forward the idea that it would be a useful exercise to make 'thought visible', speculating that words limit our ability to describe what happens in our minds: 'Everyone who thinks at all has noticed that our language is practically useless for describing anything that goes on inside the brain.' Orwell suggested that a way forward was to invent new words, an idea he refined in the 1949 novel *Nineteen Eighty-Four* and turned into the concept of Newspeak. But he realised that chaos would result if everybody constantly invented their own new words to describe similar mental events. Then he decided that what was needed was to make thought visible.

In effect, it must come down to giving words a physical (probably visible) existence. Merely talking about definitions is futile; one can see this whenever it is attempted to define one of the words used by literary critics (e.g. `sentimental', 'vulgar', 'morbid', etc.). All meaningless – or rather, having a different meaning for everyone who uses them. What is needed is to show a meaning in some unmistakable form, and then, when various *people have identified it in their own minds and recognized it as worth naming, to give it a name. The question is simply of finding a way in which one can give thought an objective existence.*[25]

He wondered if film might be the way to communicate mental processes. He pictured himself sitting in a private cinema watching his thoughts unfold on a flickering screen.

If one thinks of it, there is very little in the mind that could not somehow be represented by the strange powers of the film. A millionaire with a private cinematograph, all the necessary props and a troupe of intelligent actors could, if he wished, make practically all of his inner life known. He could explain the real reasons of his actions instead of telling rationalised lies, point out the things that seemed to him beautiful, pathetic, funny, etc. – things that an ordinary man has to keep locked up because there are no words to express them. In general, he could make other people understand him ... though putting thoughts into visible shape would not always be easy.[26]

But the Craft, with its technique of illuminating with symbols, may have been ahead of him in the game. Its symbols are always placed on show during its ceremonies.

Now let us return to the work of Betty Edwards. She is convinced that drawing allows people to express ideas or feelings that are too complicated or imprecise to fit into the straitjacket of words. She says 'drawings can show relationships that are grasped immediately as a single image, where words are necessarily locked into a sequential order'.[27] Words have to be processed in single file, while the ideas in symbols can march into your mind in line abreast.

She makes the point that words, and the sequential thinking that goes with them, have dominated human life since our species invented writing. So now it is difficult for us to imagine that there might once have been a *visual* language for translating experience, one which did not use words. And yet this language of symbols is open to everybody. Mathematics and science require at least minimal levels of training; even nature, if her secrets are to be penetrated, demands the use of advanced techniques of science, meditation, or philosophy – but symbols can speak directly to our emotions.

Betty Edwards set out to train her students to use this innate visual, perceptual language. She showed them how to apply it in parallel with verbal, analytical thought processes. In this way she rediscovered an older tradition of insight.

Sir Francis Galton, a cousin of Charles Darwin, was interested in the principles of heredity. In the nineteenth century he wrote a study of human genius, in the course of which he noted the way his own mental process worked.

It is a serious drawback to me in writing, and still more in explaining to myself, that I do not so easily think in words as otherwise. It often happens that having been hard at work, and having arrived at results that are perfectly clear and satisfactory to myself, when I try to express them in language I feel that I must begin by putting myself upon quite another intellectual plane. I have to translate my thoughts into a language that does not run very evenly with them. I therefore waste a vast amount of time in seeking for appropriate words and phrases, and am conscious, when required to speak on a sudden, of being often very obscure through mere verbal maladroitness, and not through want of clearness of perception.[28]

Betty Edwards found a way round this problem using an approach she called analog drawing. She told her students to draw images which portrayed human qualities or emotions, such as anger, joy, tranquillity, etc., and to draw them without making use of any words or well-known symbols, such as hearts and flowers for love. This is her explanation of how the exercise was to be done, using the example of anger:

Think back to the last time you were really angry. Without using words at all, even to label the event or the reason for your anger, feel within yourself what the anger was like. Imagine you are feeling the emotion again, that it flows from deep inside you, then down into you arm, down into your hand, and into the pencil, where it emerges from the point of the pencil to record itself in marks that are equivalent to the feeling – marks that look like the felt emotion.[29]

She carried out this exercise with a large number of students and reproduces many of their images in her book.

One of her results stands out: the images of femininity. Many of the analog drawings on the quality of being female surprised her. They were what she described as 'an odd structure of crossed forms, a structure that was totally unexpected'.[30] Betty Edwards may not have expected the result, but Marija Gimbutas would have known the images well. The drawings showed nets, chequerboards, chevrons and lozenges; symbols that Gimbutas says are 'associated with the primary aspect of the Goddess, that of life-giving moisture of the Goddess's body – her breasts, eyes, mouth and vulva'.[31]

Betty Edwards' pupils were not archaeologists nor were they trained in the history of art. She says this about how her students were able to call forth such basic icons of femininity:

The really surprising thing is that students unacquainted with art were able to generate intuitively such a subtle and expressive visual analog.[32]

Is there something deeper in the human brain which has evolved to react to certain visual shapes in an emotional way? Perhaps there is. Whilst reading the work of brain scientist V.S. Ramachandran I found a clue which set me off on a whole new train of research as to how Freemasonry might work.

Keyed Responses

You have little control over what makes you sweat. Many strong emotions cause you to sweat, which makes it possible for scientists to monitor what is happening in parts of your brain that you are not aware of. This unconscious urge to sweat is called Galvanic Skin Response (GSR). When you feel strong emotions your brain makes you sweat, and – since sweat is a good conductor of electricity – the more you sweat, the easier it becomes to pass an electric or galvanic current across the surface of your skin. You don't even have to be consciously aware that this subliminal sweating is happening for it to be measured.

Scientists have known about GSR for many years – it is one of the key elements of polygraph or lie detector testing – but it was only recently that scientists at London University's Wellcome Department of Cognitive Neurology used functional magnetic resonance to scan brains to see exactly which parts caused the sweating. The areas involved are the left medial prefrontal cortex, the bilateral extrastriate visual cortices, and the cerebellum – in other words, the parts of the brain which make us sweat are the parts which create our emotions.

GSR happens when our attention activates these emotional parts of our brain, which are in the limbic system, an area that reacts below our normal level of consciousness. It is an evolutionary response which attracts our attention to events outside our bodies and then makes us feel an emotional response to the stimuli.[33] A formal definition of GSR is:

The change in the electrical resistance of the skin following stimulation, an easily measured variable widely used in experimental studies. A change in electric conductivity of the skin caused by an increase in activity of sweat glands when the sympathetic nervous system is active, in particular when the organism is anxious.

This is a very useful response if you want to study how people respond to symbols, or to emotionally charged ideas – and that is exactly what V.S. Ramachandran, Professor of Neuroscience at the University of California, used it for. He described the GSR machine as measuring 'gut reaction, or the subconscious visceral self'.[34]

The GSR meter passes a small electrical current across the surface of the test subject's skin. To use it, you place one contact on the thumb and the other on the forefinger, then connect both to the machine, which then displays skin resistance on a meter. When the subject experiences an emotion their skin resistance changes, because their involuntary release of sweat allows more current to pass. The degree of change can be read from the meter or plotted in a time sequence. It is not the absolute level of skin resistance which matters, but how it changes, and this tells an observer that the subject is experiencing emotion, or arousal.

According to Professor Ramachandran,

The limbic system gets its input from all the sensory systems — vision, touch, hearing, taste and smell. The latter sense is in fact wired directly to the limbic system, going straight to the amygdala. This is hardly surprising given that, in the lower mammals, smell is intimately linked with emotion, territorial behaviour and sexuality. The limbic system's output is geared mainly towards the experience and expression of emotions.[35]

Having studied epilepsy-sufferers, he is aware that there are two types of seizure. The most common occurs in the motor cortex of the brain and results in the massive, muscle-twitching type of fit that most people associate with this illness. But some of his patients experienced less obvious fits in their limbic systems. He described this limbic epilepsy:

The most striking symptoms are emotional. Patients say that their 'feelings are on fire', ranging from intense ecstasy to profound despair, a sense of impending doom or even fits of extreme rage and terror. Women sometimes experience orgasms during seizures, although for some obscure reason men never do. But most remarkable of all are those patients who have deeply moving spiritual experiences, including a feeling of a divine presence and the sense they are in direct communication with God. Everything around them is imbued with cosmic significance. ... I find it ironic that this sense of enlightenment, this absolute conviction that Truth is revealed at last, should derive from the limbic structures concerned with emotions rather than from the thinking, rational parts of the brain that take so much pride in their ability to discern truth and falsehood.[36]

Epilepsy is defined as a chaotic electrical state of the brain. Brains are made of a large mass of specialised cells, our neurons, which transmit electrical signals. To understand epilepsy you need to know that a neuron is:

a specialised cell that acts upon another cell by transmitting an electrical pulse called an action potential, by which it releases a specialised chemical called a neurotransmitter.[37]

The problem with epilepsy is knowing the difference between what a single neuron does and how it acts when it gets caught up in a crowd. The brain has two systems of keeping all its neurons in touch with each other. One is chemical, the other electrical. (I would eventually discover that both systems have an important role to play in the way Freemasonry works its creative magic, but more of that later.) The first neurological system to attract my interest was the electrical one.

Electrical activity within the brain can be recorded by wires placed on the outside of the skull. At one time composite 'brainwaves' were plotted on a chart. Now new ways of brain scanning make it possible to churn out computer plots showing which groups of neurons are active as their owner is thinking.

A device called an electroencephalogram (EEG) measures the voltages created by the triggering of groups of neurons, plotting them on a chart recorder, and the printout shows what are commonly called brainwaves, the electrical outputs of a brain. The trace has a height (which is the amplitude of the voltage pulses), a frequency (how often the pattern repeats itself in a fixed period of time) and a form (the shape it makes as it repeats). These patterns were first examined in

1929 by a German psychiatrist, Hans Berger. The type and pattern of electrical waves that spill out of your mind vary according to how excited your are: if you are awake and alert you generate low-amplitude waves with a fast frequency, but if you relax you generate long, slow waves of greater amplitude, called alpha rhythms. When you are asleep you generate delta waves, which have a higher amplitude with a repetition frequency of between 1 and 2 cycles/sec. Brainwave patterns start early in life; they have been recorded in foetuses from the age of about three months, using electrodes placed on the mother's abdomen. Other slow rhythms, called theta rhythms (in the range 4 to 7 cycles/sec) and delta rhythms appear in younger children who are awake, but after you reach the age of about ten these slow rhythms only appear when you are sleeping.[38]

Let's go back and think about the chaotic interior of a brain during an epileptic attack. What is happening electrically inside a brain when the subject's eyes glaze over, he rolls on the floor and foams at the mouth as his body thrashes about? It's as if an electrical storm is taking place in the brain. Brainwaves having a period of 3 cycles/sec, with a distinctive 'spike-and-wave' shape, show on the EEG charts of people undergoing an attack. A number of studies show there are parts of the brain which act as centres of attraction for the 3-cycles/sec epileptic waves and multiply them throughout the brain. The epileptic waves start in some groups of neurons which are easily excited in the brains of sufferers.[39]

The external symptoms this causes are described in a standard textbook as:

lip-smacking, chewing, gagging, retching, or swallowing. Some patients may perform a variety of complicated acts that seem to blend with normal behaviour. Usually the behaviour is inappropriate. A few patients may assume bizarre positions. Some patients have fugue states. Fortunately, outbursts of aggressive behaviour are extremely rare, but these outbursts can occur. Often the patient is not responsible for his actions.[40]

The brain has to form a critical number of neuron links before the epilepsy can appear – if your brain is too simple you can't suffer from it. But, as Professor Ramachandran points out, some forms of epilepsy only affect your emotions. What interested him was this: does this special form of epilepsy change the way a person thinks?

One of the theories he looked at is that epileptic fits in the limbic system form new spiritually aware pathways in the subjects' brains, which change their personality. He tested this out by looking at patient's galvanic skin response as they looked at images and words. He showed them random series of images and symbols of several types. They consisted of words for ordinary objects (vase, table, shoe, etc.) and familiar faces of members of their close family mixed in with unfamiliar faces. He also showed them sexually arousing words and pictures, and violent and horrible images. Amidst these images, designed to arouse, repel or be neutral, he added a number of religious words and symbols. The results were surprising: there had been a selective amplification of the GSR to religious words and symbols, and also a reduction in response to other categories, such as the sexually loaded ones.

The one clear conclusion that emerges from all this is that there are circuits in the human brain that are involved in religious experience, and these become hyperactive in some epileptics. We don't know whether these circuits evolved specifically for religion or whether they generate other emotions that are merely conducive to such beliefs.[41]

When I read this I wondered if a similar type of effect could be measured with the symbols Gimbutas had found to have been appealing over the millennia. I decided to test a range of symbols with my students, to see if any of them caused a GSR response. Some did – and they were the Neolithic ones taken from Gimbutas's work.

I took a set of twelve shapes – six drawn from modern contemporary jewellery, and six symbols used in Neolithic jewellery from Gimbutas's illustrations – and reproduced them on cards. I set up a GSR meter between the thumb and forefinger of the right hand of each member of a group of twenty students. Once their baseline reading stabilised, I showed each subject a card and allowed them to look at the image for at least a minute, until their GSR settled again. Then I noted the reading, before showing them another image. When I analysed the results I found that the ancient goddess symbols showed a consistent change in galvanic skin response. The implication of this test was that the goddess symbols did cause a subconscious emotional response in my test subjects. But what I couldn't tell from this data was if that response was positive or negative. Did they like these goddess symbols, or did they find them upsetting? The response was subconscious, so there was little point in asking the subjects; the only sure way to find out was to conduct a larger survey and ask different questions.

I then took a sample group of about 250 students from all over the world and asked them to rank the same set of images in terms of attractiveness. I drew the sample set from a wide range of cultures and writing systems. They consisted of three equally sized groups of subjects from British, Asian and Chinese cultures, and of people first taught to read in three different writing systems, using three different methods of recording words. These were Graeco-Roman alphabets,

Chinese pictograms and Asian/Arabic scripts. I also tested equal numbers of females and males in each culture/alphabet group.

For each test subject I first collected the demographic data – this consisted of their culture, writing system and sex. Next I placed the same twelve images that I had used for the GSR test, printed on to cards, on a table in front of each subject in turn and asked them to examine them. They were told to look at each image individually and tell me when they were satisfied they had sufficient time to have seen them all in as much detail as they wanted. Then I asked them to give me the one they found most attractive. I recorded the number and placed the card out of sight. I then asked them to pick the most attractive of the remaining images. This process continued until there was only one image left. In this way I created a ranking system, with each image having a possible rank value from twelve down to one. When I had completed the full sample I calculated an average attractiveness score for each image.

If all the images had appealed equally, all the scores should have tended towards an average of 6.5, but they didn't. I expected to find a certain amount of random variation in the values, so I used a chi-square test to see if any values showed a statistically significant level of attractiveness. Over every group of sex, culture and first alphabet, three images showed a statistically significant level of attractiveness: and each used different combinations of the lozenge and spiral.[42]

Marija Gimbutas observed:

Old European culture flourished in an enviably peaceful and creative civilisation until 1500 B.C., a thousand to 1500 years after central Europe had been thoroughly transformed. Nevertheless, the Goddess religion and its symbols survived as an undercurrent in many areas.

Actually many of these symbols are still present as images in our art and literature, powerful motifs in our myths and archetypes in our dreams.[43]

These findings suggested a new question. Did these symbols survive because they were instinctively appealing? Or were they shapes which some evolutionary force had shaped our brains to like? And if human brains are hard-wired to like particular symbols, what is the evolutionary pay-off for this? Could this explain the peculiar appeal of Masonic symbolism? The square and compasses form a lozenge shape, and that, I had found, both evokes a galvanic skin response and is attractive and pleasurable. But what of the other symbol which figures so highly in attractiveness across all the cultures and writing systems I investigated?

The spiral is the hidden symbol of the Second Degree. Where does this fit into Gimbutas's chronology of symbolism? She says that the spiral appears as a design on pottery in south-east Europe around 6300 B.C.E. and then spreads westwards. By 3500 B.C.E. the symbol was widespread throughout Europe and had become associated with the life force of the Goddess.

The spiral often appears in the centre of a dish or bowl, and around it are circles in panels or bands; these usually number twelve or thirteen, perhaps symbolising the year cycle with its twelve or thirteen lunar months.[44]

My investigation of ritual showed that symbols enter our visual system via the optic nerve and, when processed directly by the limbic system of the brain, can have a subconscious emotional impact. The clues I found in the published research on how our brains use symbolism and symbolic reasoning show that this hidden process can be more flexible than concrete concepts.

Freemasonry has developed a language of myth to veil its secrets, and a language of symbols to illustrate its truths. But what are these truths? They are secrets of the spirit, and as a scientist I believe that your spirit exists only within the environment of your brain. One way and another, my quest to understand Freemasonry was far from over; I seemed only to have generated more questions, rather than answers. So, if I wanted to understand how the human spirit responds to Freemasonry, I now needed to know more about the human brain that houses it.

[1] Pinker (1994), p. 15.
[2] Fort Newton (1921), p. 50.
[3] Einstein ([1941] 1982), p. 270.
[4] Henderson (2002).
[5] Gimbutas (2001), p. xix.
[6] Lomas & Knight (2004), pp. 93–185.
[7] Lomas & Knight (1996), p. 143.
[8] Liden (1969).
[9] Gimbutas (2001), p. 3.
[10] Gimbutas (2001), p. 6.
[11] Brown, D (2003).
[12] Gimbutas (2001), p. 81.
[13] Lomas & Knight (2000), p. 236.
[14] Diamond (1997), p. 104.
[15] Lomas & Knight (2000), pp. 173, 236–61.
[16] Gimbutas (2001), p. 265.
[17] Lomas & Knight (2000), pp. 173, 236–61.
[18] http://www.archlsa.de/sterne (accessed August 2004).
[19] North (1996), p. 503.
[20] Gimbutas (2001), p. 318.
[21] Edwards (1979), p. 26.
[22] Edwards (1987), p. 38.
[23] Edwards (1987), p. 56.
[24] Orwell (1968), p. 87.

[25] Orwell (1968), p. 87.

[26] Orwell (1968), p. 87.

[27] Edwards (1987), p. 66.

[28] Galton (1869), p. 78.

[29] Edwards (1987), p. 67.

[30] Edwards (1987), p. 92.

[31] Gimbutas (2001), p. 99.

[32] Edwards (1987), p. 92.

[33] Critchley, Elliott, Mathias & Dolan (2000).

[34] Ramachandran & Blakeslee (1999), p. 248.

[35] Ramachandran & Blakeslee (1999), p. 177.

[36] Ramachandran & Blakeslee (1999), p. 179.

[37] Freeman (1999), p. 33.

[38] Van de Castle (1994), p. 232.

[39] Pincus & Tucker (1978), p. 13.

[40] Pincus & Tucker (1978), p. 9.

[41] Ramachandran & Blakeslee (1999), p. 188.

[42] This experimental work was reported in a paper given at the 2004 Orkney Science Festival.

[43] Gimbutas (2001), p. 318.

[44] Gimbutas (2001), p. 279.

Chapter Ten

Our Ritual Brain

The God Experience

Is there a science of transcendental consciousness hidden in the rituals and symbols of Freemasonry? Well-known Masonic writer Walter Wilmshurst thought so:

> *Both Freemasonry and religion deal with the same subject and lead to the same goal, but in the approach to it there is a marked difference. If we translate now our philosophical reasoning into familiar religious terms we recognise that a transcendental condition of consciousness, is that which is within you. The Mason learns this as a science, and so has an exact scientific understanding of truths about which the non-initiate has but shadowy notions; he knows what others must only conjecture.*[1]
>
> *But can Freemasonry really be a science of the spirit? A science as I understand the term?*

There is a common thread which runs through all religions. It suggests that humans have an inbuilt longing to connect with something larger than themselves. Albert Einstein wrote about it in a 1930 article.

> *Common to [all religions] ... is the anthropomorphic character of their conception of God. In general, only individuals of exceptional*

endowments, and exceptionally high-minded communities, rise to any considerable extent above this level. But there is a third stage of religious experience which belongs to all of them, even though it is rarely found in a pure form: I shall call it cosmic religious feeling. It is very difficult to elucidate this feeling to anyone who is entirely without it, especially as there is no anthropomorphic conception of God corresponding to it.

The individual feels the futility of human desire and aims and the sublimity and marvelous order which reveal themselves both in nature and the world of thought. Individual existence impresses him as a sort of prison, and he wants to experience the universe as a single significant whole.[2]

He went on to pose a challenge:

How can cosmic religious feeling be communicated from one person to another, if it can give rise to no definite notion of a God and no theology? In my view, it is the most important function of art and science to awaken this feeling and keep it alive in those who are receptive to it. ... In this materialistic age of ours, the serious scientific workers are the only profoundly religious people.

Has Freemasonry developed a way of conveying this deep spiritual insight – the insight that Einstein calls 'the third stage of religious experience', which has 'no definite notion of a God and no theology'? This would be possible if the human brain has evolved modes of transcendental thought that can be accessed using myth, ritual and symbolism. Freemasonry certainly has this effect on me. I find it gives me a chance to discuss and enjoy spiritual experiences without having to compromise my scientific views. To understand how Freemasonry works I will have to look at the infant science of neurotheology, the science of how and why the brain might evolve a concept of god.

Einstein called this awareness of transcendence a 'cosmic religious feeling' and said that even scientists feel it. The new scientific discipline of neurotheology says that for a belief in God to be so widespread there must be an objective explanation.

A human being's grasp of the world enters the mind as trains of electrical pulses carried by nerves from the body's extremities to the brain. Once in the brain these pulses create a model of reality that evolved to help us survive and compete in a hostile world. All DNA-based animal life, from the simplest flatworm wriggling in the sand to Albert Einstein thinking great thoughts, uses the same type of electrically powered cell to relate to the world.[3] There are certain basic features of neurologically-controlled behaviour that the ancestors of any animal alive today got right. They must have learned how to navigate their world safely, avoiding becoming trapped or being eaten, have found and mated with members of their own species, and have found things to eat (any creatures that failed in these key tasks did not survive to pass on their DNA). And once blind old Mother Nature chanced to develop a specialised cell that could perform these tasks, she used it over and over in many creatures. The evolutionary step forward was the nerve cell called a neuron.

All animal brains are made up of tangles of neurons. The difference between the simple brain of a flatworm and the startlingly creative brain of Einstein is a matter not of principle but of complexity. As animal brains become more capable, so their internal connections become more complex. And it is the complex interconnection of the human brain that allows it to conceive the idea of a god.

The first scientist to publish a detailed analysis of how the structure of the human brain can create a belief in a god or gods was Dr Michael Persinger, a psychologist and head of the Neuroscience Research Group at the Laurentian University in Sudbury, Ontario. In the introduction to his 1987 book *Neuropsychological Bases of God Beliefs* he wrote:

> *An objective understanding of the God Experience is more than just another philosophical pursuit. Reports of meaningful and profound relationships with gods, such as Allah, Jehovah, Yahweh, or even the Great Cosmic Whole, are extraordinarily frequent behaviours. One brief episode of the God Experience can change the life of an individual. When embedded within the rules of human culture, a collection of these experiences can form the dynamic core of a religious movement.*[4]

This 'God experience' is a form of the 'cosmic religious feeling' that Einstein described. During a God experience the subject feels his self unite with all space-time (which may be called Allah, God, Cosmic Consciousness, or given some other idiosyncratic label, depending on the beliefs of the subject – Persinger reports it called 'a mathematical balance', 'consciousness of time' or 'extraterrestrial intrusions'). The people who have these incidents describe them as either 'spiritually mystical states' or 'peak experiences'.

Persinger's starting point is that the human brain differs in structure from those of all other species. He saw that the emergence of human society only became possible after the evolution of large frontal lobes in the brain, which enabled humans to inhibit impulsive actions and to anticipate the future. This ability was a key factor in making it possible to live together in co-operative groups, without which we would not be able to sustain complex societies, for it helps us to think in a focused logical manner. As he says, 'People who cannot inhibit irrelevant responses do not talk or think in clear and crisp patterns. These people free associate, talk nonsense and confuse words and phrases.'

Our brain's frontal lobes allow us to create the idea of time. Being able to predict and anticipate helps us survive, and groups who develop these skills evolve successfully. But Persinger also spotted a downside to this rosy picture. Along with the ability to look forward to the future came the faculty to anticipate our own death, and this could incapacitate us, causing feelings of doom about our personal demise. But we would not have become a successful species without some means of thwarting this mental paralysis. Unless we had come up with ideas to balance the terror of personal extinction, the continued existence of the human mental phenomenon known as the self could not have been maintained; this mental construct 'would have been fragmented by the persistent, gnawing realization that death could come at any time'.

Persinger says that one of the secrets of our success as a species lies in our capacity to have 'God experiences'. He tested people with various degrees of damage to their temporal lobes and found a range of different responses. But even in the most damaged patients he noticed that these God experiences do not occur all the time: they come in short bursts during periods of personal crisis, or after ingesting chemicals or following repetitive rituals. When troubles bore down too heavily on his patients, and their life appeared worthless and futile, they could suddenly experience a sense of understanding and purpose. And this change in attitude was always sudden and total.

He found that the mental flips happened when the patients' brains suffered something called a temporal lobe transient.[5] (This is a form of epileptic fit occurring in the emotional regions of the brain, which has none of the normal physical side effects but has profound effects on the feelings of the patient.) He predicted that these emotional fits should occur with a wide distribution in both frequency and intensity even in healthy individuals. Most people would experience mild forms, perhaps every year or so, but a small percentage would have intense and extreme bouts. He found evidence in the literature for such variation,[6] and pointed out that, if stripped of their poetic language, then the writings and teachings of many religious leaders of ancient times show clear evidence of temporal lobe transient effects, putting them at the extreme end of this range.[7]

Persinger lists the key factors that increase the chances of having a God experience:

Low levels of blood sugar;
Fatigue;
Lack of oxygen;
Anxiety;
Temporal lobe instability caused by epilepsy.

Persinger went on to study people who considered themselves religious and compared them with people who had God experiences.[8] He found they split into four main groups.

GROUP 1 people never had any significant God experience and did not attend church or any other type of ritual meeting regularly. Members of this group tended to be young; as people got older they became more likely to drift into one of the other three groups.

GROUP 2 people reported religious or mystical experiences they believed to be real but did not attend a church until after their experience. They tended to repeat whatever stimulus prompted the first occurrence of a God experience. Typical triggers were things such as introspection, meditation, occult practices, or psychedelic pursuits. This was the most eccentric group. Its members showed signs of neuroses and an overriding belief that 'there is an eternal and infinite force'. Persinger found they tended to be attracted to radical religious factions who would cultivate repeat God experiences and demand high emotional loyalty. He also found this group was highly egocentric.

GROUP 3 members attended church regularly but never had mystical experiences. For them religious belief was a buffer against life anxiety, and they found the religious rituals calming and reassuring. They were the most conformist group.

GROUP 4 people were regular churchgoers at the time they had a mystical event. They tended to suffer from clinical personality disorders, and Persinger found they lacked self-discipline and had no self-direction outside their religion.

Persinger suggests:

The God Experience has had survival value. It has allowed the human species to live through famine, pestilence and untold horrors. When temporal lobe transients occurred, men and women who might have sunk into schizophrenic stupor continued to build, hope and plan. ... [it] has allowed people to feel righteous as they bashed the skulls of others who dressed a little differently or described God in a foreign accent. When temporal lobe transients occurred each soldier felt that somehow he would survive the battle.[9]

He also points out that there is a threat in the God experience. This is the assumption of total righteousness adopted by religious extremists.

Unfortunately there are several negative features of the God Experiences. They nurture a resistant strain of egoism. Although masked by a pleasant smile, religions encourage the conclusion that the believer is somehow special and unique. ... Each believer feels that his or her experience is more true and more real than those of others. Friendly lip service is given to liberal understanding. Sometimes maverick peacemakers attempt to show that all religions are different experiences of the same thing, but deep down the feelings of uniqueness remain.[10]

On the plus side, he points out, this brain utility can reduce existential anxiety. It can 'change human beings from trembling, incapacitated primates into confident, creative individuals'.

Recent studies have shown that practising some form of religious or spiritual belief improves mental and emotional health. It can reduce rates of drug abuse, alcoholism, divorce and suicide. Spiritual practices such as meditation, prayer and taking part in ritual services reduces feelings of anxiety and depression, boosts self-esteem, improves the quality of interpersonal relationships. This often results in a more positive approach to life.[11]

Other research has found that ritual practice plays a part in good health, by affecting the body's nervous responses.

A quiet prayer, a stately hymn, or an hour spent in meditation, can activate the body's immune system, lower heart rates and blood pressure, restrict the release of harmful stress hormones into the blood and generate feelings of calmness and well-being.[12]

It would seem that the human brain has evolved structures that make it easy to believe 'there is an eternal and infinite force'. Is this feature of human neurology a factor in the spiritual impact of Freemasonry? Persinger had looked at the negative effects of the God experience on members of religious groups, but he did not study Freemasonry, which teaches through its ritual:

No man truly obeys the Masonic law who merely tolerates those whose religious opinions are opposed to his own. Every man's opinions are his own private property, and the rights of all men to maintain each his own are perfectly equal. Merely to tolerate, to bear with an opposing opinion, is to assume it to be heretical, and assert the right to persecute, if we would, and claim our toleration as a merit.

Persinger's pioneering work inspired others. Andrew Newberg and Eugene D'Aquili of the University of Pennsylvania, carried out brain scans of people having a religious experience. Buddhists meditating and nuns praying were subjected to brain scans to see just what was happening at moments of religious ecstasy. The scientists' most startling result occurred when they carried out a scan of the brain of the Buddhist meditator just as he achieved the state of samhadi: the state that Persinger calls the 'God experience'.

Newberg and D'Aquili set out to study the altered states of mind in which mystics experience the absorption of their self into something larger. To do this, they developed a way of taking freeze-frame snapshots of brain activity.

There are three main ways to scan brain activity. These are Positron Emission Tomography (PET), Functional Magnetic Resonance Imaging (fMRI) and Single Photon Emission Computed Tomography (SPECT). The first two give a real-time scan of brain activity as it is happening. This can be a useful diagnostic tool for medics, but for an investigator of spiritual experience those techniques have severe limitations. The most important is that, in order to scan the brain of a person having a God experience, the subject must have the experience whilst lying in the scanner. However, it is not in the nature of such experiences to be producible on demand, so another way of taking a snapshot at a key moment in time had to be devised.

The solution found by Newberg and D'Aquili was to inject a radioactive tracer into the bloodstream of the subject at the moment of maximum intensity. This harmless tracer was absorbed into the brain tissue at the points of key activity, and remained there for a number of hours afterwards. In this way it gave a freeze frame of the brain activity at the time it was injected. The SPECT scanner could subsequently produce scans of the density of the tracer within the subject's brain.

With this technique it was possible to wait for the test subject to achieve their meditative target and then inject the tracer. Then the researchers had a couple of hours to take a scan of the subject's brain.

The Buddhist monk, who was highly experienced in the art of meditation, was allowed to deliberate in peace but was to indicate to the researchers in an adjacent room as he experienced his peak. At that moment they injected radioactive tracer into his bloodstream, freezing the state of his mental electrical activity for later SPECT scanning.

What they found was a mechanism to explain the mental 'God experience' that Persinger had discovered.

Two Pillars of Our Brains

Some three-and-a-half million years ago a naked ape by the name of Lucy was walking upright around the side of a lake in Africa's Great Rift Valley when she had the misfortune to fall into a bog. Luckily for us her bones were preserved, and so we know about one of our species' earliest ancestors. This upright walking ape, with a brain about the size of a modern chimpanzee's, is the ancestral mother of us all. But, although Lucy walked tall, she didn't have a cerebral cortex, that swelling of our modern heads which makes us mentally human.[13]

Some 3,300,000 years later one of her daughters, Mitochondrial Eve, was still living in Africa and had grown a much larger brain, but was always in two minds about everything.[14] Eve's brain had expanded to three times the size of Lucy's, had evolved a cerebral cortex and split into two hemispheres. Each hemisphere had a fully functioning mind, and her two minds 'talked' to each other via a bundle of nerves called the corpus callosum. The right hemisphere controlled the left side of her body and the left hemisphere the right side. Her right brain was good at seeing shapes and patterns, while her left brain was better at gossiping. But the inherent duplication and redundancy of this set-up gave her species a considerable survival advantage. We see this even today: when a part of a stroke victim's brain has been destroyed, they can learn to use another part to carry out the lost function.

This complex brain configuration has not changed in the subsequent 200,000 years, and we are wired up the same way Mitochondrial Eve was. Our left hemisphere looks after verbal language, analysis and maths. The right hemisphere thinks in a more abstract way, uses non-verbal or symbolic reasoning as well as carrying out visual-spatial perception, and is where we feel emotion.[15]

The two hemispheres work together in a normal healthy brain, because they are connected by the nerve fibres of the corpus callosum. But the two sides of your brain do not share all their information. The link via the corpus callosum has not yet evolved far enough to enable our hemispheres to share complex thought patterns: they can only exchange nuances.[16] Newberg and D'Aquili say about this binary nature of the brain:

The generation of human conscious awareness, in all its multilayered fullness, depends on the harmonious integration of both sides of the brain.[17]

There are four main functions which allow our mind to understand the world, and these are shared between the two hemispheres.[18] Each of our senses – sight, sound, smell, touch and taste – has a primary reception area in the brain. And each hemisphere handles the raw data received from its opposite side of the body. These specialised areas combine the sense inputs of our brains to create our impression of the outside world.

THE VISUAL ASSOCIATION AREA

We are not consciously aware of the rough visual patterns, the single points of light similar to the individual pixels in a computer screen, that are registered by the primary visual area. This level of detail is organised by secondary visual areas which match the jumble of lines, shapes and colours into an image our mind has learned to recognise. Say, for example, I am looking at a woman. The primary image, compiled from the triggering of thousands of separate rods and cones in the retina, will have features like length and colour of hair, characteristic body shape, fashion of clothing, etc., all mixed up together. The stage of recognition will use memories stored in other parts of my brain, drawing information from both hemispheres, to place this image in the context of my past experience. When it does I can recognise my wife.

If the visual association area of my brain were damaged, then I would lose the ability to recognise people or objects I know. Newberg and D'Aquili believe that this area also plays a major part in spiritual experiences. These often involve visual images, suggesting that the type of impulsive vision that occurs during meditation or prayer comes from this part of the brain. But not all images in the mind originate from the input of the senses, and visions or realistic memories can be reproduced by electrical stimulation of these areas of the brain during surgery.[19]

THE ORIENTATION ASSOCIATION AREA

There are two orientation areas: one in my right hemisphere gives me a sense of where I am in space, while a similar area in my left hemisphere controls my knowledge of where my body ends and otherness begins. When they work together, these areas combine to give me a sense of what makes up my self and where the rest of the world that is not part of me begins.

Again, Newberg and D'Aquili maintain that when an individual loses control of their sense of self, the orientation area can develop a sense of mystical and religious experience – meaning a state of mind like Persinger's God experience.

THE ATTENTION ASSOCIATION AREA

This part of the prefrontal cortex is the region of the brain that runs our decision-making processes. Its main function is to enable us to focus our attention, and some researchers have gone so far as to describe this area as the seat of the will.[20] This is where we form our intentions and decide how we will act. If this area of the brain is damaged we become unable to maintain our will long enough even to complete sentences. We also become incapable of experiencing emotion, and indifferent to what is happening around us. In this state we can become dangerously disconnected from society.[21] This is thought to be because of the high level of interaction between the prefrontal cortex and the limbic system, which is the key area of the brain that controls emotional responses throughout the body.[22]

THE VERBAL/CONCEPTUAL ASSOCIATION AREA

Here we generate abstract thoughts and then turn these thoughts into words with which to share concepts with other people.[23]

Newberg and D'Aquili say of this area:

This area houses other important brain functions, such as causal thinking, that are associated with how we create myth and ultimately how myth is expressed in ritual.[24]

It is the integrated perceptions of these four areas of the brain, distributed and often duplicated in the two hemispheres, that enable us to be aware of the reality of the world. We depend on the overall accuracy of this interpretation for our success as a species. But the downside of building good mental models of reality is that we get to perceive our own existence, and then to extrapolate from this to our personal death. At that point all our emotions, sensations and thoughts convince us that we are more than the gooey mess inside our skull that we call our brain. Our power to visualise the world is so potent that we become convinced that we cannot just cease to be when our brain ceases to function and we die.

Yet our brain evolved our mind. Only when the heat of our African homeland forced the evolutionary jump to Mitochondrial Eve's greater brain complexity did its neural networks become complex enough to support the consciousness we call mind.[25] We are born without self-awareness, and it is only the somatic evolution of viable neuronal pathways during early childhood which creates our mind and our consciousness.[26] But, at the other end of life, diseases such as Alzheimer's can destroy our minds whilst leaving our grey, gooey mess alive. So how does our mind link to our body?

Four States of Mind

Our large brains cause problems. They utilise much of the energy we consume when our body is resting – within two minutes of being starved of oxygen the brain starts to die. To maintain a working brain involves a high cost in terms of the need to search out food. And the size of our brain causes tremendous difficulties for the females of our species, who have to pass large-headed babies through their birth canals; having large-brained children increases their risk of death in childbirth.

But as a species we obviously think size matters. Not content with having a brain that can only just pass through a woman's birth canal, within our first two years we grow it into a much larger one. Again it costs our species dear, in terms of the high dependency of young children who cannot fend for themselves. To pay such a high price in terms of energy overhead, reproductive risk and dependency of offspring must have an evolutionary advantage, or we would have died out long ago. So what is the advantage of being big-headed?

The answer? We are remarkably versatile in how we adapt and exploit our environment. Our twin brains sustain a highly efficient twofold bodily control system that speeds us up when it matters and slows us when it is safe to do so. We have both an arousal and a quiescent system. Both are part of the same autonomic nervous system, but they produce very different effects.

Let's look at how this works in terms of the four key actions any creature must carry out for its species to survive – what biologists often call the four 'F's . When stimulated by any event there are four possible ways to respond: fight it, feed on it, flee from it, or have sexual fun and reproduce with it. As far as survival is concerned, when not enjoying one of the four f's we can just sit around resting.

Most of the time our autonomic nervous system looks after the housekeeping that keeps our body alive. You don't have to consciously will your heart to beat, your lungs to pump, or your stomach to digest. This is probably just as well: if you had to think about doing these things, you wouldn't have any spare time to concentrate on not being eaten by a predator or run down by a bus. However, when you are threatened, are attracted to a potential sexual partner or need to climb a tree to pick an apple to eat, then your body adjusts its functioning – and your autonomic arousal system takes care of this. Your respiration will increase, your blood pressure rise, and your muscle tone prepare you for action: in other words, your body will be set up to act. This is the flight or fight response that readies your body to preserve your life from threats. It is what makes your heart race when you hear an unexplained bump in the night, or makes you move to protect yourself when you think somebody is about to lash out at you.

If your body stayed at this high level of alertness and preparation for action, it would quickly wear you out. This is why you have the autonomic relaxation system. Your quiescent system conserves energy, regulates your sleep patterns, induces relaxation, controls the digestion of your food and grows new cells to repair your body.

Most of the time your two control systems work together. An increase in alertness turns off the relaxation system, and vice versa.[27] But there are occasions when they can both be active at the same time. One such occasion, which most adults will have marvelled at, is the state of sexual climax. When our arousal system reaches a condition of saturation, the neural activity spills over into the quiescent system, causing an ecstatic rush of energy. The state of hyper-arousal combined with intense relaxation has a deep emotional effect on you. It is a sexual reward system that evolved a long time ago to encourage you to share your DNA.

Elaine Morgan studied the ancient genesis of orgasm.

The [evolutionary] problem was a fairly simple one: how to induce animal A and animal B to get together for purposes of procreation. The answer would seem to be simple, too: Let them enjoy getting together.

What conceivable evolutionary purpose would be served by going only halfway to this solution, by making animal A desirous and pleasure-seeking and rewarded by pleasurable sensations, and animal B merely meek and submissive and programmed to put up with it? Every piece of circumstantial evidence we possess concerning animal behaviour points to the conclusion that the sexual drive is a mutual affair – that both sexes feel a need, both are impelled to satisfy it, and both experience copulation as a consummatory act.[28]

This neural reward mechanism, which triggers both our arousal and quiescent autonomic nervous systems at the same time, has been giving out emotional incentives for procreation since before Lucy walked the African veldt. And the part of our brain that creates emotional response is the limbic system. Persinger[29] and Ramachandran[30] agree with Newberg and D'Aquili that the limbic system is closely involved in mystical and spiritual experiences. Was this where I might find clues to help me understand how Freemasonry works?

Many animals have brains with a limbic system, and its evolutionary advantage is not in question. It provides aggressiveness to find food, supplies fear to avoid predators and gives the emotional attraction to drive its owner to mate and care for its young. But the limbic system not only drives our emotions, it also drives most of our involuntary control functions. It is not under our conscious control, so whatever effect it has on us, we experience it as something external to our mind, even though biologically it is part of our brain.

Newberg and D'Aquili found four extreme autonomic states that our brains can move between.[31]

Hyper-Quiescence: a state of relaxation normally only experienced during the deepest sleep. But Newberg and D'Aquili point out that it can also be induced by the use of slow and deliberate rituals, such as chanting or group prayer. The state is one of 'oceanic tranquility and bliss in which no thoughts, feelings or bodily sensations intrude upon consciousness'.

Hyper-arousal: the opposite of hyper-quiescence, this occurs when we feel excitement combined with alertness and deep concentration. It is the state of mind entered by marathon runners, motor racing drivers and fighter pilots in combat. Newberg and D'Aquili describe it as happening when we need to take instantaneous decisions based on processing vast amounts of sensory input where conscious thoughts could be a dangerous distraction. People who experience it say it is like effortlessly channelling vast quantities of energy through their consciousness, resulting in a quintessential flow experience.

Hyper-Quiescence with rousal breakthrough: When the arousal system achieves high levels of activity, Newberg and D'Aquili say, there are certain mental conditions in which the normal balanced reaction between the arousal and quiescent systems is over-whelmed, resulting in intensely altered states of consciousness. In meditation and contemplative prayer, powerful quiescent activity can result in sensations of great bliss, but when quiescent levels reach maximum, the arousal system can simultaneously erupt, causing an exhilarating rush of energy. Someone who experiences this state while concentrating upon some object may feel as if he were being absorbed into that object.

Hyper-arousal with quiescence breakthrough: This is a trance-like state that occurs for brief moments during sexual orgasm. Newberg and D'Aquili say that there are non-sexual means of achieving this state of mind; the examples they cite are intense and prolonged contemplation, rapid ritualistic dancing or stimulating repetitive ritual.

As I mentioned, Newberg and D'Aquili carried out a electrical scan of a Buddhist monk's brain at the moment he achieved the state of samhadi. Their result showed how the two autonomic limbic systems combine to produce a spiritual high.

They took a base line scan of their subject's brain activity when he was resting. They injected the tracer when the subject indicated he was achieving meditative bliss. Now they had a picture of his brain activity at this key moment, which the subject, Robert, also described:

First, he says, his conscious mind quiets, allowing a deeper, simpler part of himself to emerge. Robert believes that this inner self is the truest part of who he is, the part that never changes. For Robert, this inner self is not a metaphor or an attitude; it is literal, constant and real. It is what remains when worries, fears, desires and other preoccupations of the conscious mind are stripped away. He considers this inner self the very essence of his being.[32]

When they studied the SPECT image the researchers found that the Orientation Association Area (OAA) in his brain was overloaded, which meant it was 'temporarily blinded and deprived of the information it needed to do its job'. They concluded that this would mean that the OAA would not be able to find any borders between Robert's self and the rest of the world. The implication of this is that 'the brain would have no choice but to perceive that the self is endless and intimately interwoven with everybody and everything the mind senses. And this perception would feel utterly and unquestionably real.' Newberg and D'Aquili call this process 'deafferentation'.

The OAA needs a constant stream of sensory information to do its job well. When that stream of data locating us in the physical world is interrupted, the OAA has to work with whatever information is available, resulting in less precise definitions of the boundary of the self. A sensory overload interrupts this awareness of the physical world and results in a God experience.

They repeated the experiment with a group of Franciscan nuns at prayer and found similar effects.

Persinger's God experiences, the sense of the self being absorbed in something much larger, are not the result of emotional mistakes or simple wishful thinking; they are observable neurological events, which are well inside the range of normal brain function. And this research shows that spiritual experiences do not have to be symptoms of mental illness. Everybody has the mental mechanism to experience these things, although few achieve the mental heights or meditative depth of the more extreme practitioners of spiritual contemplation.

Newberg and D'Aquili showed that there is a range of mental states which are associated with a whole range of transcendental experiences. They range from 'a mild sense of spiritual communality felt by members of a congregation, to the deeper states of unity triggered by more intense and prolonged religious rites'.

But, then to add to this innate source of fun, Persinger replicated part of this range of electrically powered mystical experiences using a helmet that creates pulsing electromagnetic fields. He showed that an externally generated pattern of electrical pulses forced on to the brain can also reproduce this natural subjective effect. On his university website he says:

After writing the Neuropsychological Bases of God Beliefs (1987), I began the systematic application of complex electromagnetic fields to discern the patterns that will induce experiences (sensed presence) that are attributed to the myriad of ego-alien intrusions which range from gods to aliens. The research is not to demean anyone's religious/mystical experience but instead to determine which portions of the brain or its electromagnetic patterns generate the experience.[33]

It seems there are different ways to create 'real' spiritual experiences within the human brain. One is electrical, as I already knew from my experience with thunderbolts. This natural electrical state can be induced by stress, ritual, or meditation. But there is another independent communication system operating within our brains, that also can create ecstatic experiences. Now I needed to consider how this might impact on spiritual events.

Our Chemical Brain

In the autumn of 1970 a young graduate chemist from Bryn Mawr College began work on a PhD at John Hopkins University. She would soon discover a whole new system of communication between brain and body, based on a group of molecules, now known as peptides. But she was unusual for a research scientist of that period, in that she was interested in the sort of things that often make scientists uncomfortable. Let her speak for herself.

Measurement! It is the very foundation of the modern scientific method, the means by which the material world is admitted into existence. Unless we can measure something, science won't concede it exists, which is why science refuses to deal with such 'nonthings' as the emotions, the mind, the soul, or the spirit.[34]

Dr Candace Pert's work provided another key piece in the jigsaw of scientific findings that I was putting together to help me understand how Freemasonry works and why I enjoy it so much. I had been assuming that the key to understanding the effect of ritual and myth on the brain lay in studying the electrical effects within the neurons. I suppose there are two main reasons for this.

1. I first encountered the state of consciousness that lies at the spiritual centre of Freemasonry when an intense electrical field zapped me during a thunderstorm.

2. All my early reading in neurology focused on the electrical properties of the brain and looked at ways of using electrical analogues to model intelligence. So perhaps it is not surprising that I thought of the human brain as simply a more complex version of the neural nets I model on my computer.

I came to the problem with a mindset that assumed all inner brain workings, even for complicated levels of mental activity and behaviour, could be determined by studying the synaptic connections between neurons. As an electrical engineer I felt comfortable with the ideas of Prof Walter Freeman of the University of California. He says that synapses, the points where neurons join together, form the networks and define the neural circuits whose electrical pulses control every aspect of perception, integration, and performance in a human mind.[35]

But Candace Pert added a new dimension to this idea. She says:

Enter a new theory of information exchange outside the bounds of the hardwired nervous system, focused on a purely chemical, nonsynaptic communication between cells. ... Studying the ton of new data on numerous neuropeptides and their receptors ... Something was wrong. If peptides and their receptors were communicating across the synapse from each other, they should be only minuscule distances apart, but their location was not conforming to this expectation. Many of the receptors were located in far-flung areas, inches away from the neuropeptides. So we had to wonder how they were communicating, if not across the synaptic gap. ... the way in which peptides circulate through the body, finding their target receptors in regions far more distant than had ever previously been thought possible, made the brain communication system resemble the endocrine system, whose hormones can travel the length and breadth of our bodies. The brain is like a bag of hormones! Our view of the brain, and the metaphors we used to describe it, were permanently altered.[36]

This was a revelatory idea for me. Everything I had read about 'cosmic consciousness' and 'the God experience' had made me think of it as an electrical phenomenon, but here was another dimension that could perhaps explain the powerful and positive emotional content of Masonic teaching. I wanted to know more.

She was making the point that the ways of linking the brain and body were far more complex and far-reaching than a simple electrical network allowed for. She was talking of a mechanical communication system. Her system used molecules as dispatch riders to carry messages about the body, each message-passing molecule being made up of a string of amino acids, the building blocks of life. They carry the ionic charge of electricity across the open gap from axon to dendrite at every synapse. But if the charged molecules given off by a 'firing' axon cannot bind on to the surface of the receiving dendrite, then no electrical signal is transferred. You can't use just any molecule; it's got to be one that fits.

Dr Pert found that a typical neuron could have millions of receptors on its surface, and each one is a keyhole in which only a single key shape fits. She views the receptors that cluster on the synapses of neurons as 'sensing molecular scanners', explaining that, just as our eyes, ears, nose, tongue, fingers and skin act as sense organs, so do neuron receptors, except they work at the microscopic level of single molecules. She puts it more poetically:

> [I] like to describe these receptors as 'keyholes,' although that is not an altogether precise term for something that is constantly moving, dancing in a rhythmic, vibratory way. All receptors are proteins. And they cluster in the cellular membrane waiting for the right chemical keys to swim up to them through the extracellular fluid and to mount them by fitting into their keyholes – a process known as binding.
>
> Binding? It's sex on a molecular level![37]

One example stood out clearly: she had looked at the role of sex hormones in the brain. She pointed out that soon after the existence of neural receptors had been proved, the keyholes for sex hormones were 'unexpectedly identified in the brain and then ignored' by the research establishment. Yet the effect of testosterone or oestrogen on the developing brain of a foetus was already known to affect a child's sexual identity.[38]

The way these complex chemical chains, known as peptides, affect such a basic personality variable as sexual orientation should have suggested that perhaps the electrical network system was not telling the complete story. But everybody knew that the electrically pulsating neurons were the key to how human minds worked – so the chemical brain was ignored. Perhaps at this point it is just worth reminding ourselves what neurons are and how they work.

A neuron looks like a very tiny daffodil plant, with a stem, a bulb and lots of little roots, called dendrites. That bulb is the cell body, the long stem is called the axon, whilst the flower that forms the terminal ending is called the synapse. Neurons receive signals from other neurons via their dendrites. When enough dendrites are excited, the electrical potential within the cell body rises to a level called the trigger potential, and the neuron 'fires'. As it does so it sends a pulse of electrical power along the axon towards the synapse area, where the pulse is passed on to the dendrites of other neurons. Simple isn't it? Tickle enough of the neuron's roots and it sends a compulsive sneeze or a giggle up its stem, so its flower tickles the roots of the next neuron in line. Who said thinking can't be fun?

All right, I admit that there is perhaps a little more to the theory than that. But, looking at the brain through this electrical model, my point is that neurons are digital in operation: they either work or they do nothing. There are no half-measures in neuron triggering. They either reach a threshold voltage (between 50 and 70 mV) and trigger, or they just sit there quietly. Neurons that trigger cause thoughts, and without triggering neurons you don't have memories, reflexes or consciousness. You need memory and reflex and conscious thought before you can have a personality.

But Candace Pert had brought a new complication to this idea. The synapse is where the axon of one neuron connects to the dendrite of the next, but there is a physical gap. The electrical charge is carried across the gap by ionically charged molecules. What Dr Pert brought to the party was news that some charged molecules would be received by the dendrite whilst others would not. The neurotransmitters had a chemical code of their own which could modulate the operation of the electrical system.

She had brought into this model of the nervous system a second nervous system that took longer to operate but had the capability to communicate throughout the body. But it was not just the fact there was a second nervous system that caused ripples, it was that it was older, in evolutionary terms, than the electrical system. She pointed out that peptides were being made inside cells long before neurons had developed; in fact peptides were passing messages between cells before brains evolved.

Before the scientists discovered the function of peptides (the key) and receptors (the keyhole each peptide fits into), neurotransmitters had been thought of as just a means of transporting the electric signal across the synaptic cleft. They were thought to work like a switch, either on or off. But Dr Pert and her colleagues found these coded molecules could cause complex and fundamental changes when their keys fitted into keyholes within the brain and other organs of the body.

These receptors have come to be seen as 'information molecules' – the basic units of a language used by cells throughout the organism to communicate across systems such as the endocrine, neurological, gastrointestinal, and even the immune system. Overall, the musical hum of the receptors as they bind to their many ligands, often in the far-flung parts of the organism, creates an integration of structure and function that allows the organism to run smoothly and intelligently.[39]

Pert knew that 'mind'-altering drugs such as heroin, marijuana, Librium, and PCP ('angel dust') could only work if there were receptors for them inside the brain. All these drugs were extracted from plants, but the ligands (key-type molecules) changed the state of consciousness of the brain they entered. The implication of this was that everybody's brain must be full of keyholes waiting for a consciousness-changing drug to turn them on. As she said, it doesn't matter if you are a lab rat, a First Lady, or a dope addict, everyone has the same mechanism in their brain to create bliss and expanded consciousness.

We knew that the brain receptor didn't exist to serve as a binding mechanism for external plant extracts, such as morphine and opium. No, the only reason that made any sense for an opiate receptor to be in the brain in the first place was if the body itself produced some kind of substance, an organic chemical that fitted the tiny keyhole itself – a natural opiate.[40]

As a species we had to have evolved this range of special keyholes to match peptides that our own body systems manufacture and use. But for what purpose? Amorous hamsters provided the answer.

Dr Pert had realised that for a heroin addict the effect of the drug was similar to that of a sexual orgasm. She suspected that the blissful pleasure experienced during orgasm was a result of the body manufacturing its own mind-changing substances, called endorphins.

The endorphin molecules were the natural body chemicals that the opiate receptors in the brain had evolved to receive.

Morphine, which is widely used by the medical profession as a painkiller, as well as nullifying pain also causes a pleasure 'high'. A few years ago I broke my elbow in a horse-riding accident and had to have a number of extremely painful operations on it. In the immediate aftermath of an operation I was given intravenous morphine and lay for a timeless period in a state of untrammelled bliss. It was like the immediate afterglow of good sexual experience without any of the accompanying muscular contractions or consequent messiness. Then, as the trauma of the operation receded, I was weaned off the morphine and back to reality. At which point I suddenly noticed that my arm hurt like hell. Yet during the period of most severe pain I had been on cloud nine and hadn't even noticed the hurt.

It has been known for some time that orgasms can cure headaches. Dr Catherine Blackledge explains:

> *Orgasm is a potent analgesic. That is, female orgasm increases a woman's threshold to pain (the point at which an externally applied increasing pressure becomes painful); in other words, orgasm has a pain-suppressing effect. Critically though, female orgasm does this without affecting a woman's response to tactile or pressure stimulation (it is not an anaesthetic and does not dull sensations). Startlingly, studies show that woman's pain thresholds increase by over 100 percent as a result of orgasmic vaginal and cervical stimulation.*[41]

This finding was confirmed by an extensive survey carried out by Drs Komisaruk and Whipple.[42]

The golden hamsters Dr Pert and colleague Dr Nancy Ostrowski used in measuring the change in endorphin levels in the brain during the sex act were no doubt happy in their final moments. As she explains:

We used hamsters ... because of their predictable cycle of sexual behavior – two minutes of licking this or that, three minutes of humping, etc., and the act was complete. The males are extremely prolific, ejaculating about twenty-three times per cycle. ... Nancy would inject the animals with a radioactive opiate before copulation, and then, at various points in the cycle, decapitate them and remove the brains. Using autoradiographic visualization of the animals' brains, the two of us were able to see where endorphins were released during orgasm, and in what quantity. We found that blood endorphin levels increased by about 200 percent from the beginning to the end of the sex act.[4]

Dr Pert went on to study 'jogger's high' and provided a physiological validation of the phenomenon. The exercise increases the level of endorphins in the blood, and these affect the endorphin receptors in the brain and induce pleasure. Next she went on to study the role of natural opiates in the experience of ecstasy during human orgasm. Reluctant to chop off the heads of her test subjects as they were humping away, she had to develop a less dramatic means to collect her data.

All her pairs of volunteers agreed to chew parafilm (which generates saliva) at various moments during sexual intercourse and then to spit into test tubes. From analysis of endorphin levels in the saliva, Dr Pert concluded that human orgasm is accompanied by the release of our own pleasure chemicals into our brains and bloodstreams.

Dr Pert had noticed that Dr Donald Overton of Temple University drugged some rats with an artificial peptide that locks into receptors in their brains and bodies and then taught them to run a maze. Whilst drugged the rats would remember that learning, but would forget it when not drugged. This led her to suggest that peptides not only affect our emotions but also have an effect on what we remember.

Just as a drug facilitates recall of an earlier learning experience under the influence of that same drug for the rat, so the emotion-carrying peptide ligand facilitates memory in human beings. The emotion is the equivalent of the drug, both being ligands that bind to receptors in the body. What this translates into in everyday experience is that positive emotional experiences are much more likely to be recalled when we're in an upbeat mood, while negative emotional experiences are recalled more easily when we're already in a bad mood.[44]

This finding has an important evolutionary implication. It helped the ancestral apes who mothered our species decide what to remember and what to forget. The female primate who fell in love and remembered how to find her way back to the gentle male who gave her food is far more likely to be one of our maternal great-grandmothers than the flibbertigibbet who got lost and was eaten by bears.

Elaine Morgan made the point that

Love as a concomitant of sexual relations is not a recent romantic invention. Right from the start, when the hominid put his arms around his female and kissed her, it was not only to make her shut that row. As when a mother hugs and kisses a howling baby, it was done out fondness too. He didn't like to see her frightened, and the demonstrations of goodwill and affection ... would tend to arouse in him the same warm feelings that they aroused in her. While primate sex is a fleeting and comparatively impersonal business, the other primate bonds whose elements were now being incorporated into it were more personal and long-lasting.[45]

Candace Pert could explain why this was. She realised that the emotional high of love, or the opposite emotion of fear, would help fix our great-great-grandmother's memories. As she explained:

Just as drugs can affect what we remember, neuropeptides can act as internal ligands to shape our memories as we are forming them, and put us back in the same frame of mind when we need to retrieve them. This is learning. Emotional states or moods are produced by the various neuropeptide ligands, and what we experience as an emotion or a feeling is also a mechanism for activating a particular neuronal circuit simultaneously throughout the brain and body – which generates a behavior involving the whole creature, with all the necessary physiological changes that behavior would require.[46]

These ideas also raise the question, is there a special kind of peptide for each emotion we feel? Dr Pert suggests this might be so, but a specific answer requires more research. However, there is one last piece of evidence that peptides play a much larger role in the pleasure of orgasm than most of us realise. A study by Komisaruk, Gerdes and Whipple found that women who had suffered severe spinal injuries, leaving them entirely without feeling in the lower half of their body, could still experience orgasm brought on by genital stimulation even though they could not feel the touch. They showed all the usual orgasmic pleasure responses including the changes in heart rate and blood pressure.[47] It would seem that Dr Pert's peptides can affect the pleasure centres in the brain without need of electrical connection via the nervous system.

But I am interested in how all this helps me understand Freemasonry. The Craft deliberately makes its candidates uncomfortable, and sometimes even afraid. It then rewards them and makes them feel good. I began to wonder if the purpose of the emotionally powerful enactments of myth and ritual was to cause interaction between chemical peptides and electrical brainwaves. Armed with this knowledge of the electrical and chemical nervous systems I was now ready to revisit the teachings of Freemasonry. My next task was to use my newly acquired understanding of the brain to look more closely at the spiritual implications of Masonic ritual.

[1] Wilmshurst, unpublished journal notes.
[2] Einstein ([1930] 1982).
[3] Colbert (1980), p. 80.
[4] Persinger (1987), p. ix.
[5] Persinger (1983).
[6] Bear & Fedio (1977).
[7] Dewhurst & Beard (1970).
[8] Persinger (1984).
[9] Persinger (1987), p. 138.
[10] Persinger (1987), p. 4.
[11] Worthington, Kurusu, McCullough & Sandage (1996).
[12] Jevning, Wallace & Beideback (1992).
[13] Johanson & Edey (1981), p. 46.
[14] Brown, W.M. (1980).
[15] Joseph (1996), p. 23.
[16] Marzi (1986).
[17] Newberg, D'Aquili & Rause (2002), p. 21.
[18] Joseph (1988).

[19] Penfield & Perot (1963).

[20] Libet, Freeman & Sutherland (1999), p. 46.

[21] Raine, Buchsbaum, & Stanley (1994).

[22] Pert (1998), pp. 73–93.

[23] Kandel, Schwartz & Jessell (2000), p. 84.

[24] Newberg, D'Aquili & Rause (2002), p. 31.

[25] Ornstein (1991), pp. 55–66.

[26] Edelman & Tononi (2000), pp. 82–92.

[27] Kandel, Schwartz & Jessell (2000), p. 138.

[28] Morgan (1972), p. 97.

[29] Persinger (1993).

[30] Ramachandran, Hirstein, et al. (1997).

[31] Newberg, D'Aquili & Rause (2002), pp. 40–42.

[32] Newberg, D'Aquili & Rause (2002), p. 2.

[33] http://laurentian.ca/neurosci/_people/ Persinger.htm (accessed August 2004).

[34] Pert (1998), p. 21.

[35] Freeman (1999) p. 21.

[36] Pert (1998), p. 139.

[37] Pert (1998), p. 23.

[38] Moir & Jessel (1989), pp. 38–52.

[39] Pert (1998), p. 27.

[40] Pert (1998), p. 64.

[41] Blackledge (2003), p. 295.

[42] Komisaruk & Whipple (2000).

[43] Pert (1998), p. 103.

[44] Pert (1998), p. 144.

[45] Morgan (1972), p. 129.

[46] Pert (1998), pp. 144–5.

[47] Komisaruk, Gerdes & Whipple (1997).

Part Three

Uncovering Antient Treasures

So far in this book I have looked at scientific studies of myth, symbolism and the effect of ritual and posture on the brain and the state of its mind. Now I need to go back to the seven steps of Masonry that I described in Chapter Seven and what they might be trying to teach me. And so it is time to return to the work of a Masonic teacher who might help me understand.

Walter Leslie Wilmshurst takes a startlingly different view of the Craft to most workaday Masons. He links the strange state of mind I went through in the midst of thunderstorm, to the secret knowledge at the centre of Freemasonry.

Chapter Eleven

The Meaning of Masonry

The Mystical Mason

Fifteen years after his death, Walter Leslie Wilmshurst was honoured by the Lodge he founded. It published a book entitled The *Life and Work of W.L. Wilmshurst.* As I write, a copy sits on my desk; a translucent paper jacket protects its dark blue board cover, but under the flimsy tissue it shows the ravages of damp. I open it, pleased to find the inner pages survive untainted. The subtitle expresses how his Lodge felt about WLW, as they came to call him: 'One of the World's greatest Masons – deepest Mystics – and most perfect of English gentlemen.'

The flyleaf shows a photograph of a short, rather tubby, bald man in a wing collar, plain white shirt and black bow tie. Over the shirt he wears a black dinner jacket with broad satin lapels. His dark eyes are averted to his left, as though he is not happy to face the camera. The edges of his mouth turn down in an expression of sombre composure he must have used regularly as a solicitor. His right hand almost disappears behind his back but the splayed fingers of his left hand are thrust to the front of the picture; they rest on a dark, shrouded table. The awkwardness of his stance suggests he wants to draw attention to the ancient ring he wears on his fourth finger. Following a tradition started by WLW, the current Master of the Lodge of Living Stones, the Lodge he founded, still wears that second-century Gnostic Christian ring to Lodge meetings.

Wilmshurst was fifteen when he came to Huddersfield in 1893. Having just left public school in Surrey, he was articled to a reputable firm of solicitors, Moseley and Co., whose senior partner was a friend of his Uncle Ben. Six years later Walter qualified as a solicitor; on Saturday 22 June 1888 he finished work at lunchtime and went out with his friends from the Huddersfield Choral Society to celebrate his coming of age. Within a few weeks he rented an office in Kirkgate and set up his own practice – which he ran until his death on 19 July 1939.

As a young, ambitious solicitor Walter wanted to set himself up in the social hierarchy of the thriving woollen town, so, on the advice of Mr Moseley, he applied to join his local lodge of Freemasons. And thus, at six o'clock on the chilly winter evening of 11 December 1889, young Walter was stripped of his worldly goods. He was dressed in a crude white linen suit which was adjusted to display various parts of his body. Then, in a state of hoodwinked darkness, he was taken into Huddersfield Lodge No. 290. The second Wednesday of the next month he was passed to the Second Degree and, without any pause for reflection, was raised to a full knowledge of the 'secrets' of a Master Mason in February 1890.

He said of this experience:

Often the three Degrees are taken rapidly, sometimes in three successive months. It is unlikely that in so brief a time you will grasp their implications in full. You have been furnished with a system of instruction in spiritual advancement too rapidly to grasp fully. You are expected to focus your future life on it. But it may take you years of thought and effort to work out how to do so.

Our rituals may not open your mind at the moment they are given. You may not see immediately the light and deeper perception of Truth which Initiation offers. Often you will have to carry out further spiritual work to attain the higher order of consciousness. But sudden awakening can happen if you come properly prepared in heart and intention. Some derive a truly magical stimulus, a permanent quickening of their spirit's dormant or repressed faculties during the rite. But this desirable result could occur more often if everyone involved in the ritual grasped just what he or she was doing and worked together more closely to bring it about.

Usually the quickening of consciousness reveals itself slowly and gradually. It comes as the result of reflection upon the Craft's doctrine and symbolism, and from attempts to follow the path of life and mapping out its teaching.

I did not find this statement until I put together a complete view of Wilmshurst's thoughts on Masonic Initiation. I began with his book *The Meaning of Masonry*, and a paper he gave to the Masonic Study Society in London in 1925 entitled 'The Fundamental Philosophic Secrets of Masonry'. In it he said:

There are philosophic secrets concealed within the Masonic system. They are to be distinguished from the merely formal secrets imparted ceremonially.

By these secrets is not meant information that can be imparted or withheld at will, but truths inherent in the system itself; truths needing to be extracted from it, like poetry or music from the printed page, by personal effort, and [which] can be recognised as truths only by the responsiveness of the soul after deeply meditating and assimilating them.

Hence we are taught them by means of signs, tokens and perfect points of entrance, meaning appropriate faculties of perception and understanding. Inward truths and mysteries are inevitably secret from those who lack the faculty to perceive them.

Secret orders always exist for initiation into these secrets and mysteries, and in these days when we see our own Order so little concerning itself with such things but preferring to direct its energies rather to social and secular purposes, it is useful to reflect that the sole justification for a secret Order is that it is intended to provide specialised instruction and combined fraternal effort for those desirous to draw apart from these activities of the outer world and enter a quiet sanctuary where they may contemplate and attain personal realisation of things which must always be outside the consciousness of the uninitiated.

This was my first clue that WLW thought that Freemasonry is a science of self-awareness. It seemed to hint at the state of expanded consciousness I had known in the middle of that intense electric lightning field.

I have spent years looking for the origins of Freemasonry, and written a number of books about it. But I keep returning to the fact that Freemasonry contains secret knowledge. It helps individuals to grow spiritually and to become more comfortable with themselves and their place in society. But how does it do this? Does Wilmshurst have the answer?

His book *The Meaning of Masonry* is strange. He seems to know more than he is prepared to write about. He admits this in the introduction, when he says:

In giving these pages to publication care has been taken to observe due reticence in respect of essential matters. An elementary and formal secrecy is requisite as a practical precaution against the intrusion of improper persons and for preventing profanation.[1]

This abstruse book was written 33 years after Wilmshurst joined Masonry. So it took him some time to arrive at the rather guarded views he expresses in it. The main clue to his real meaning shows when he says:

Our present Masonic system was compiled and projected as an expression of the ancient doctrine by a group of minds which were far more deeply instructed in the old tradition and secret science than are those who avail themselves of their work today.[2]

Wilmshurst read widely. He was as at ease with the writings of the Greek philosopher Plotinus as he was with the mystical Christian prose of Meister Eckhart, St John of the Cross, and St Teresa. He knew the works of the Indian mystic Ramakrishna, the Christian gnostic Georgi Gurdjieff and his pupil, philosopher Peter Ouspensky, as well as that investigator of enhanced states of mind R.M. Bucke. He also owned a well-thumbed illustrated copy of Budge's translation of the Egyptian Book of the Dead. Wilmshurst's library, his private papers and his working notes have been preserved, and whilst researching this book I have made full use of them. All the otherwise unattributed quotations from Wilmshurst in this book are taken from his notebooks and annotations, as preserved in this library.

Towards the end of *The Meaning of Masonry* he talks about the intent of this 'ancient doctrine" saying:

The system of Speculative Masonry is an experiment upon the mind ... promoting the science of human regeneration ... but understanding depends upon the gift of the supernal light, which in turn depends on our desire for it. If wisdom is widowed, all Masons are the widow's sons. We seek her out and labour for her as for hidden treasure.[3]

Was he talking about the great flame-coloured cloud that I saw with my electrically overloaded neurons when the thunder god hitched a ride in the back of my Jeep?

In his private notes he went much further, seeing the spiritual purpose of Freemasonry as:

To pass from mere manhood and carnal understanding to conscious Godhood whilst we are still in the flesh. It is the realisation of our fundamental unity and identity with the ultimate of ultimates.[4]

He goes on:

If this, then, be the purpose and goal of Initiation, the fundamental hypothesis and philosophic secret of Masonry is the solemn fact that God and the human soul are in essence a unity, not a duality, and the sole intention of our Initiatory system is, by instruction and discipline, to bring about in each of us the conscious realisation of that unity.[5]

He has put into words how I felt just before the ionisation resistance of the atmosphere above Queensbury broke down in a shaft of lightning.

But WLW is talking about a state of consciousness that he got to by precise discipline of his mind, not about some hysterical act of faith, or even a physical effect on the neurons of his brain. This is Persinger's 'God experience'. Wilmshurst makes this clear later in the same paper.

Masonry is not non-religious, but super-sectarian, and is directed to secrets and mysteries of being with which popular religion does not deal. It is ontological and philosophic, but not theological.[6]

In a paper published in the Occult Review in March 1924 he described this state of mind more fully and called it 'cosmic consciousness'. He defines it as:

An inner vision which transcends sight as far as sight transcends touch, and a consciousness in which the contrast between the ego and the external world and the distinction between subject and object fall away.[7]

Walter Wilmshurst, the mystical Mason, knows all about the state of mind that Newberg, D'Aquili, Persinger and Ramachandran measure and describe. He has experienced his mind expanding to fill the cosmos. And he didn't need a thunderstorm to trigger it. What's more, he is claiming that the function of Masonic ritual is to teach its followers to reach this state. Having enjoyed my first taste of it, I was interested to learn how I might visit that mystical realm again.

The Mystical Path to the Centre

After fifty years of studying the problem Wilmshurst decided that Freemasonry teaches that a human is made up of four segments, each forming a fourth part of a circle. The circle represents the totality of being which a Master of the Craft will try to balance in all its parts. When this is achieved the spirit becomes a complete and rounded whole with its focus on the centre, and only when this balance is achieved can the light at the centre be seen. This is the moment of expanded consciousness, or Persinger's 'God experience'.

Wilmshurst says 'each daily step in Masonic knowledge should help us develop our Masonic skill, so that we grow in our ability to perceive this great light and harmony which lies at the centre of our being'. Only when we learn to perceive 'the light unquenchable' within our own mind, do we become a Master Mason. Then we know what he calls 'cosmic consciousness': the state of mind I first met as an involuntary reaction to a lightning bolt.

He created a diagram to show the spiral path which he followed as he learned how to discipline himself to be able to achieve the state of mind to see the light at the centre. To reach a state of 'cosmic consciousness', he claimed that, as his spirit circled around this knowledge of himself, he moved through four parts of a circle. This diagram shows the sequence of symbols he contemplated as he moved towards the centre.

The first quarter represents his physical body, and this deals with controlling the irrational urges of the flesh.

The second quarter is his rational mind, which can control and counterpoise the irrational body.

The third quarter is his emotional mind, which can be swayed by both rational and physical elements, and is influenced by whichever is allowed to dominate.

The fourth quarter is his spirit. He calls this a supra-rational principle, which can know the transcendental nature that unifies the universe.

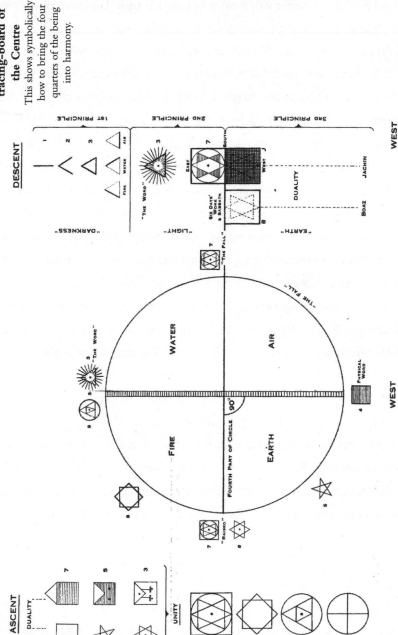

Fig 2: Wilmshurst's tracing-board of the Centre

This shows symbolically how to bring the four quarters of the being into harmony.

Only when the first three quarters are brought together in harmony can they support the spirit's search for the great light, which Wilmshurst says he found at the centre (the point which, he reminded us, is 'that from which no Mason can err').

He goes on to explain how each of the Degrees contributes to our spiritual journey.

The First Degree helps us develop a rational mind. It teaches us how to bring our intellect into balance with the irrational urges of our flesh. This degree offers us postures, a Lodge structure to focus our thinking, and a set of symbols and spiritual tools. Only when we balance our rational mind against our bodily urges, and learn how to use posture, symbolism and the spiritual tools are we ready to move on the Second Degree.

The Second Degree helps us to balance our intellect and our emotions. We learn how to discriminate between the irrational urges of the flesh and the truth of the spirit. We are given more postures, tools and symbols to strengthen our rational mind. We learn to handle our emotions, so that we are ready for the revelation of a blazing star of truth that is as yet only visible as darkness at the centre. In this Degree we meet the spiral symbol which teaches that practice makes perfect, and we must continue round the spiral path as each circuit brings us closer to the centre. The postures affect our body and feed hormonal responses into our rational minds to help us learn to subdue emotion.

But before we can proceed to the Third Degree we must be prepared to let go of our ego and self-regard.

In the prime of your physical and mental powers this sublime degree will call upon you to undergo a crucial trial. It does not involve the physical

end of your bodily life, but it does involve the permanent death of your
ego. This experience will endow you with the knowledge, powers and
qualities of a Master.

In the Third Degree we allow our ego and rational mind to die. Only then 'our spirit may be reborn as the keystone of our being and be supported in its quest to attain the vision of light which emanates from the centre'. This ritual of death and rebirth stills the urges of our body, our intellect and our emotions and brings forth our suppressed spirit. Few Master Masons realise this state during the ceremony. It is only prolonged meditation on the meaning and symbols of the degree that achieves the expansion of consciousness.

Wilmshurst says that in the Third Degree the circle of our being is rendered complete. It is made perfect once we have mastery over its four component parts. When you can do this you are a Master of the Craft and you will have been through a radical transformation of your mind and a regeneration of your entire nature. Now you will be ready to allow the light of the centre to flow through fresh channels in your brain and to internalise the true secret of the Craft. This awakening enables you to know the transcendental state of mind that Wilmshurst says is seeing the 'light unquenchable'.

Wilmshurst has his own answer to the question 'What is Freemasonry?' He says the Craft is a discipline of practical spiritual learning that leads to the transcendental centre of our mind. Once there, for brief moments of ecstasy, we experience what it is to become a part of everyone and everything in existence.

At each stage of spiritual progress we improve ourselves. We gain skills in concentration, memory, empathy, charity and goodwill.

He says Freemasonry is based on three grand principles: Brotherly

Love, Relief and Truth. In our social meetings we practise brotherly love; through our charitable giving we practise relief; but we often neglect the inquiring and intellectual Masonic quest for truth. This, he says, should be the driving force behind our urge to make visible the light of the centre.

He tells us that the path to the centre is threefold. First, we need to perfect our work in the Lodge, by understanding ritual and its use. Second, we need to expand our understanding by free and open discussion of the meaning and purpose of the spiritual journey that is Freemasonry. And, finally, by daily use of the postures, symbols and spiritual tools of the Craft we must develop the power of our spirit. If we internalise this teaching, he promises that we will achieve the transcendental state of mind that is our 'unprovable proof' that we have understood the inner mystery of the Craft.

Wilmshurst says Freemasonry is 'a spiritual system of self-improvement which helps individuals achieve their full personal potential, and also encourages them to take a full and active part in improving the lot of society in general'. But it is not a religion, although it uses some components of the religious beliefs of its followers. It is a way to understand and develop your spirit.

A Science of Mysticism

That lightning strike in Queensbury changed my attitude towards mysticism. I kept finding statements, in Wilmshurst's work and in the writings of the mystic thinkers, saying that initiation is an experimental science, not something that can be learned from a book. An initiate can communicate the system and rituals to follow but not the result of travelling the spiritual path.

To understand initiation you cannot just think it, you must do it. That was the great secret of the thunderbolt. I lived the ecstasy of awareness of the centre. I knew what it felt like and I wanted to learn how to do it again. But to a scientist this knowledge poses an interesting dilemma. How can electrical interference with my sensory input data, or dedicated Masonic meditation, cause such a magical experience as awareness of the centre?

My conscious self is on the end of a telegraph wire. The wire is the axon of a neuron which connects my brain to my senses. Everything I know of the outside world arrives via that axon as a series of Morse-code-like dots and dashes of voltage pulses.

All nerves work in the same way, so if the nerves from my eyes were connected to the auditory areas of my brain, then I would hear light. I know this to be true because it is exactly what happened when I heard the 'zizz' of the electric field of the lightning strike. The sphere of my intellectual knowledge is limited by my personality, and the external termini of my sensory nerves limit the range of my understanding. Imagine what would happen if somehow all my senses got cross-wired. I might taste the redness of a sports car, touch the scent of new-mown hay, hear the tang of a lemon, see the pure tones of a flute, and smell the softness of a baby's skin. How could I describe the world I was experiencing to someone whose senses were not scrambled? I couldn't.

The intense electric field of the lightning storm that I described in the Prologue kicked my brain into a different state of perception. When that happened I could understand why Wilmshurst wrote in his notebook:

Ours is an experimental science. We can but communicate our system, never its result. We come to you not as thinkers but doers. Leave your deep and absurd trust in the senses, with their language of dot and dash, which may possibly report fact but can never communicate personality. If philosophy has taught you anything, she has surely taught you the length of her tether, and the impossibility of attaining to the doubtless admirable grazing land which lies beyond it. One after another, idealists have arisen who, straining frantically at the rope, have announced to the world their approaching liberty; only to be flung back at last into the little circle of sensation. But here we are – a small family it is true, yet one that refuses to die out – assuring you that we have slipped the knot and are free of those grazing grounds. This is evidence which you are bound to bring into account before you can add up the sum total of possible knowledge; for you will find it impossible to prove that the world as seen by the initiate, unimaginable, formless, dark with excess of bright, is less real than that which is expounded by the youngest and most promising demonstrator of a physico-chemical universe.

But is it possible to learn how to achieve this state of cosmic consciousness at will? As I was thinking about this matter, I happened to be reading the manuscript of an autobiography by a more experienced writer, who has been a good friend to me. And he had thought a great deal about this problem; in fact his first successful book, The Outsider, was about this subject.

The Outsider's Mind

At the age of sixteen Colin Wilson decided to kill himself. In his autobiography he tells how he stood with an open bottle of hydrocyanic acid in his hand, about to drink from this vessel of death.

Then an odd thing happened. I became two people. I was suddenly conscious of this teenage idiot called Colin Wilson, with his misery and frustration, and he seemed such a limited fool that I could not have cared less whether he killed himself or not. But if he killed himself, he would kill me too. For a moment I felt I was standing beside him, and telling him that if he didn't get rid of this habit of self-pity he would never amount to anything.

It was also as if this 'real' me had said to the teenager: 'Listen, you idiot, think how much you'd be losing,' and in that moment I glimpsed the marvellous, immense richness of reality, extending to distant horizons.[8]

At a moment of great stress Colin felt a form of the cosmic consciousness which Wilmshurst says is the centre of Freemasonry. They seem to agree that this state of mind is closely linked to death. Colin thinks that many people who achieve something original in literature or philosophy have been tempted by the idea of suicide. He explains this is on the grounds that anyone who looks into this abyss achieves a separation of their real self from their inessential self, a process which is like being reborn. These ideas are like those of Wilmshurst:

The methods of the initiating officers and the nature of the experience itself must be lived to understand its effect. No one ever understands without experiencing them. It is an experience in which your consciousness is withdrawn and rendered dead to all earthly concerns. It is introverted and directed backwards through psychic darkness towards the centre. This is the source and root of its own being, and there it passes into union with the light of the cosmic centre which is the source and inspiration of our personal spirit. It is an experience of which it has been said it either finds you in a state of sanctity or leaves you so.

The sublime event forces you to conscious awareness of your mortality. It establishes a union between your human spirit and the cosmic ego. By reknitting your lower, carnal personality with your centre (your higher self, or spiritual principle), you become perfected. After this experience you will be an initiate master.[9]

Colin explains how he had been worrying about his girlfriend being pregnant. Then he found she was not. The relief of the discovery tipped him into an enhanced state of mind.

What struck me so clearly was that what I was seeing – this immense depth of mystery, beauty, magic that seemed to be exhaled from the sea and Exmouth peninsula beyond it – was quite objective. It was really there, all the time. The mechanism of tension and relief had merely pulled aside the veil as the curtains of a theatre open to reveal the opening scene. But if that was so, then man should be able to induce mystical ecstasy by simply learning to see things as they are. How? Obviously, by somehow learning to reproduce the mental process that had just been revealed to me.

My basic insight here was not a new one: it is Blake's recognition that things would be seen as 'infinite' if the doors of perception were cleansed. But at this point, my scientific training took over. What precisely was the nature of the mental act that would clear the doors of perception?

Human beings possess certain curious powers that distinguish them from animals; not only their ability to be raised into a trancelike state of delight by poetry or music, but to induce sexual excitement – and even an orgasm – without the actual presence of the sexual object. No animal can masturbate without the presence of some stimulus; only man has this power to build up a complex set of responses in the mind by imagination alone.

In the same way, there is no reason why man should not learn to brush aside these veils of indifference and habit that separate him from reality. It is simply a question of reproducing the mental act. [10]

But how is it to be done? What are the disciplined steps needed to return to the ecstasy of the centre? This is Wilmshurst's view:

The popular appeal of Masonry and the tendency of its members to be content with its surface attraction have resulted in the original idea of a lodge becoming neglected. It was conceived as a small community devoting itself in privacy to corporate work of a philosophical nature. This was for the intellectual development and spiritual perfecting of its members. Social amenities should be secondary incidents. It is desirable to revive these ideas if you want to revive the spiritual dimension of the Craft.

The strength and worth of a lodge does not depend upon numbers and popular attractions. It rests on the quality of the corporate life of its members. It depends on their united and consistent co-operation towards a common ideal. Its success relies on their ability to form a group consciousness.

He went further, adding:

The Craft is not a monastic community, it is a discipline of the secret that is adapted to people who live in the real world, and who discharge domestic and secular duties. It does not call upon you to follow any uniform rule of life such as is followed in an enclosed order. It leaves you to live your life in your own way but helps you acquire your own way to harmonize your outward and inward lives.

It does, however, make definite provision in three respects. These guidelines constitute a rule of life.

1. It emphasizes continual obedience to Moral Law.

2. It calls for 'daily progress in Masonic Science' by practising some form of helpful study, reflection or meditative practice, suitable for your taste and temperament.

3. It provides the symbolism of the working tools and the Tracing-boards for daily contemplation and reflection.

It is advised that you should pay attention to these points. This especially applies to the personal use of the symbolic working tools and Tracing-boards, which cannot be too closely or too often pondered upon and applied.

If you fail to practise the simpler and elementary enjoinders of the Craft, how can you hope to perceive its more advanced and concealed teachings?

Wilmshurst's idea is to follow a path of focused meditation. He suggests using the spiritual and mental tools of the Craft to bring about the desired mental state.

But, as Colin Wilson noticed, there is a common feeling which is similar to the bliss of cosmic consciousness. It is sexual orgasm.

Newberg and D'Aquili describe a state of mind they call hyper-arousal with quiescent breakthrough. This trance-like state occurs for brief moments during sexual orgasm, though there are also non-sexual means of reaching it: they give examples such as intense and prolonged contemplation, rapid ritualistic dancing, or stimulating repetitive ritual – and they might have included almost getting struck by lightning. It seems that the state of bliss that occurs when an initiate becomes aware of the centre is a brain state that the blind watchmaker of evolution latched on to, to encourage humans to share their genes.

The main thrust of Wilmshurst's Masonic study claims that Freemasonry is a highly evolved system of spiritual arousal. If he's right how does it work?

The Evolution of Cosmic Consciousness

Jane Austen didn't quite say, 'It is a fact universally acknowledged that men and women have orgasms as a result of brain arousal during sex,' but biologist Dr Catherine Blackledge did. She thinks that the spiritual bliss of one of Wilmshurst's mystical heroines, St Teresa, is like sexual orgasm.

> *Pleasure or pain? Ecstasy or agony? ... St Teresa swoons backwards, lost in the moment, surrendering to her sacred vision. She moans, her lips parted, her face suffused with sensation, her eyes closed. The folds of her clothing stream and flow from her body, fluid as water, caressing her contours, as above golden rays of light surge down from heaven, and the angel of her lord prepares to pierce his flame-tipped spear through her heart, again and again.* The Ecstasy of St Teresa, *[Gianlorenzo] Bernini's sculpture of the Spanish saint of Avila in intimate communion with her god, is both glorious and disturbing, supremely capable of inducing shudders in unsuspecting onlookers.*[11]

Dr Blackledge observes that to some people Bernini's seventeenth-century image of religious ecstasy verges on the blasphemous. They 'see in it an emblem of eternal orgasm'. But, once you realise that the state of mind of a spiritually initiated saint is also the natural state of the sexually aroused brains of normal humans, then you understand. St Teresa's brain is freeloading on the behavioural reward that evolution came up with to encourage us to bear children. Putting it simply, orgasm is a reward mechanism that encourages primates to share their DNA. But the way it works offers a clue to cosmic consciousness.

Wilmshurst said about St Teresa's visions:

St Teresa's mystical experiences were legion. They included the stigmata, i.e., the imprint of the five wounds of the Crucifixion, levitation, clairvoyance, clairaudience, etc. She, too, had an experience, which she terms the 'orison of union,' which corresponds closely by its description to cosmic consciousness.

In this orison of union [says St Teresa], the soul is fully awake as regards God, but wholly asleep as regards things of this world, and in respect of herself. During the short time the union lasts she is, as it were, deprived of every feeling, and, even if she would, she could not think of any single thing. Thus she needs to employ no artifice in order to assist the use of her understanding. In short, she is utterly dead to the things of the world, and lives solely in God. ...Thus does God when He raises the soul to union with Himself suspend the natural action of all faculties. But this time is always short, and it seems even shorter than it is. God establishes Himself in the interior of this soul in such a way that, when she returns to herself, it is wholly impossible for her to doubt that she has been in God and God in her. This truth remains so strongly impressed on her that, even though many years should pass without the condition returning, she can neither forget the favour she received nor doubt of its reality. If you ask how it is possible that the soul can see and understand that she has been in God, since during the union she has neither sight nor understanding, I reply that she does not see it then, but that she sees it clearly later, after she has returned to herself, not by any vision but by a certitude which abides with her and which God alone can give her.

She did not perceive them in their proper form, and nevertheless the view she had of them was of a sovereign clearness and remained vividly impressed upon her soul. This view was so subtle and delicate that the understanding cannot grasp it.[12]

Wilmshurst quotes St Teresa's account of intense passion as evidence for a mystical state of mind in an initiate. Dr Blackledge also quotes from St Teresa, from the manuscript Life, written in 1565:

The pain was so great that I screamed aloud; but simultaneously I felt such infinite sweetness that I wished it to last eternally. It was not bodily but psychic pain, although it affected to a certain extent also the body. It was the sweetest caressing of the soul by God.

Perhaps we should not be surprised that St Teresa struggles to describe her intense sensations. As Dr Blackledge points out:

Descriptions of orgasm often defy exactitude. What, after all, is one expressing? Is it a pinnacle of pleasure and passion, or simply seconds of sweet, streaming, exquisite suffering? Is it a blissful evanescent and ecstatic moment when a person can stand outside one's conscious life and self, or just deliciously pleasant muscular contractions centred on and around a person's genitalia? Orgasm, it seems, is paradoxical.[13]

Oxford-educated anthropologist Elaine Morgan is quite clear why we have orgasms. As I have previously mentioned she says:

Every piece of circumstantial evidence we possess concerning animal behaviour points to the conclusion that the sexual drive is a mutual affair, that both sexes feel a need, both are impelled to satisfy it, and both experience copulation as a consummatory act.[14]

I have already mentioned recent research by Dr Blackledge, which showed that the ecstatic state of mind we feel during orgasm does not dull the senses.[15] Instead it heightens the state of consciousness by suppressing distracting pain from other parts of the body. And Blackledge agrees with Elaine Morgan that orgasm evolved in mammals as a means of enhancing sexual selection. She says:

While it is certainly true that today human female orgasm is not essential for conception to occur, I believe that the influence orgasm continues to have on egg extrusion and movement (ovulation and whether implantation occurs), as well as sperm transport and sperm transfer, points to the origin of this pleasurable muscle and nerve phe¬nomenon. [The] orgasm – the rhythmic, forceful, rippling contractions and relaxations of genital muscles – evolved from the female's need to control and co-ordinate the transport of both ova and sperm within her reproductive anatomy. With its accompanying symphony of hormones, the (orgasmic) muscular contractions of female genitalia do indeed manage to orchestrate egg and sperm movement, often with an exquisite amount of precision. Reproductively speaking, it is to every female's advantage to be able to achieve this manipulation of egg and sperm movement inside herself. The result, if a female is allowed free choice of mates and free movement of her genitalia, is conception with the most genetically compatible partner, and hence optimally successful sexual reproduction.[16]

The state of bliss we call orgasm has proved itself a useful tool for evolution. All humans descend from a long line of successful sexual reproducers, so we have all inherited the ability to enjoy orgasms for sexual purposes. But is it possible that the bliss of cosmic consciousness is a spiritual spin-off that our brains evolved when becoming orgasmic? There is nothing sexual about Masonic ritual, but could it be using this brain state in some other way?

Colin Wilson looked at this idea of non-sexual peak experience. He says:

> *What happens at these moments of intensity suddenly brings our happiness into focus, as a slight twist on the adjustment wheel of a pair of binoculars can make a scene stand out sharp and clear. ... This leads to the interesting recognition that most of our values – the things we love – are hidden most of the time, as if in a mist. We all have at least several hundreds of reasons for happiness, beginning with being alive. We value our homes, our security, our families, our possessions; yet except in rare moments of sudden delight – what Maslowe called peak experiences – these values remain below the threshold of consciousness.* [17]

He is talking about an idea that figured in Wilmshurst's analysis of the intent of Masonic ritual. WLW said that control of the emotions and the intellect leads to the restraint of a distracting ego and allows the spirit to shine through. Colin looked at this from a different perspective. He recognised that a lot of human actions take place below the level of conscious awareness, and he describes the actions of the autonomic neural systems, that handle most of our bodily responses, as our 'robot'.

The central problem of human consciousness is connected with the 'robot', the mechanical part of us. As highly complex beings we need to be able to do a great many things mechanically, from breathing to driving the car and talking foreign languages. In fact, our 'robot' does most difficult things far better than we can do them deliberately. ... This 'robot' can be extremely dangerous sometimes. ... When I do something with interest or pleasure, it has the effect of charging my vital batteries, just as a car's batteries are charged when you drive it. When I do things 'automatically', there is little or no charge or 'feedback'. If I get overworked, or into a state of depression, the 'robot' takes over, and I may live for weeks or months, or even years, in a devitalised, mechanical state, never putting enough energy into anything to realize that this state is abnormal.[18]

But is it possible to encourage the occurrence of these positive peak experiences? Colin thinks so.

Once we recognise that the intensity with which we 'see' the world depends completely on the amount of 'interest' we put into the perceptive system, we begin to gain a kind of precarious control over our own moods and peak experiences. I say precarious because self-consciousness is a fairly new stage in human evolution, and to begin with, we are likely to find this kind of control as awkward as walking a tightrope.

Peak experience, cosmic consciousness and the 'God experience' are different views of a state of mind that is central to Masonic ritual. But cosmic consciousness is different from orgasm; it lacks the muscular contractions and the emission of fluids. However, it does lead to the experience of bliss and satisfaction. Could this be the elusive reason why Freemasons so enjoy carrying out their rituals?

Could this be why I enjoy Freemasonry?

The degree to which most Masons experience this intense state seems to vary. But one feature of all the descriptions I read, which are confirmed by my own experience of an intense electric field, tell me that these states of consciousness are not continuous; they are discrete and separate. The change from one state to another is instantaneous. When I was almost struck by lightning I moved from a sense of foreboding to cosmic bliss in an instant, without any perception of how the change occurred. It was a sudden transition from one stable state to another, quite different one. The brain is made up of linear, saturating subsystems, and this gave me a clue about where to look during my quest to understand how Masonic ritual works. The only systems I know which show a characteristic flip from despair to bliss, from darkness to light, from high to low, are chaotic ones. So it is the mathematics of chaos I need to think about next.

The Chaos of Orgasmic Response

René Thom (1923–2002), Professor of Mathematics at the Institut des Hautes Etudes Scientifiques at Bures-sur-Yvette near Paris, created a new branch of maths called catastrophe theory. It describes how slowly changing linear forces acting on a system cause abrupt changes in its overall state. These ideas have wide application to physics, biology and the social sciences, and Thom explains them in a book called *Structural Stability and Morphogenesis*.[20]

He was interested how a gradually changing force will not seem to have any effect at first, but, if it continues, then some types of system can become unstable. They will jump rapidly from one stable state into another. He developed a graphical method of showing this effect by projecting the movements of a point on a plane on to a folded surface. Two interacting parameters, such as the arousal and quiescent systems of the brain, can be shown by a plane, and the states of consciousness by a surface, on which there can be both fold curves and cusp points where two fold curves meet. Small changes in the parameters can cause dramatic jumps in states of consciousness. Thom called these jumps 'elementary catastrophes' and classified the types of surfaces that cause them. (N.B. Thom uses 'catastrophe' in a technical sense, to describe a sudden change from one stable state to another; that does not imply that the change is undesirable. I will continue to use the word in this emotionally neutral, jargon sense throughout this chapter.)

His obituary, in *The Times* observed that one of his inspirations was Christopher Zeeman's use of dynamic systems to model the brain. The inspiration was mutual, as the piece goes on to add:

Many mathematicians and scientists were inspired by Thom's genius, including Zeeman, who brought catastrophe theory to Britain and to the attention of the international mathematical community, and who developed many applications in the biological and behavioural sciences. One of the limitations of catastrophe theory, however, is that it is qualitative rather than quantitative (that is, invariant under smooth rather than just linear changes of co-ordinates), making it difficult sometimes, but not always, to test models numerically: indeed, there have been several notable successes ...

The main contribution of chaos theory so far has been to give a better understanding of unpredictability, of how small perturbations in the initial conditions of a deterministic system can give rise to large variations in the ensuing motion.[21]

The type of chaotic system I am interested in has two control inputs: the brain's arousal and quiescent systems. Thom called this a 'cusp'-type catastrophe. By modelling the various states of awareness, ranging over 'flow consciousness', orgasm, meditation, sleep and cosmic consciousness, with this method you can see how the mind can flip rapidly from one state to another.

Newberg and D'Aquili say that orgasm happens when an electrical overload trips in the neurons which normally cause the restful quiescent effect. Recent research by Dr Jozsef Jansky of the National Institute of Psychiatry and Neurology in Budapest lends weight to this idea.

He reports the case of a 31-year-old Hungarian woman with epilepsy. She told him that she had orgasm-like feelings just before she had a seizure. Checking further, he found that 22 cases of a so-called 'orgasmic aura' just before epileptic seizure had been noted since 1945.[22] Some of these reports had good enough brain-activity records for him to zero in on the part of the brain that caused their orgasms: the right-brain region of the amygdala. This is the part of the brain that creates emotional response, where Newberg and D'Aquili found the centre of transcendental bliss. Jansky suggested this orgasmic aura might be caused by an electrically stimulated release of hormones.

This is a clue as to why cosmic consciousness is sometimes easy to reach and at other times almost impossible. For an electrical spill-over to occur, the brain has to be supplied with enough of the right types of neuropeptides. Candace Pert's work suggests the most likely hormones are oxytocin and vasopressin. These two hormones are known to be important in producing high-quality REM sleep, and Pert showed that they contribute to the post-orgasmic feeling of well-being. Oxytocin is made by the hypothalamus, then stored in the posterior pituitary gland, and at certain stages of arousal is suddenly released into the bloodstream. When this happens it turns on the both the quiescent and arousal systems at the same time.

Dr Mary Carmichael of Stanford University in California studied oxytocin levels among women and men during masturbation and orgasm. The blood concentrations of the hormones were measured continuously using venous catheters. The observed levels during self-stimulation before orgasm were higher amongst women than men, but both sexes showed increased levels. During orgasm women generated higher levels of oxytocin than men; multi-orgasmic women reached a higher peak of oxytocin concentration during their second orgasm. Carmichael noted that during male orgasm the release of oxytocin helps to induce contractions of the prostate and seminal vesicle. [23]

She also found that hormones of the adrenalin family inhibit the release of oxytocin. These are the hormones our bodies release when we are frightened or cold. They are emergency arousal hormones to give us energy to protect ourselves by fighting or running away, and they turn off the quiescent system. This suggests that to reach cosmic consciousness, without external electric stimulation, you need to be aroused but not alarmed. You need your body to release oxytocin, but without activating adrenalin to cancel out the oxytocin's effects on the quiescent system.

Excitatory neurotransmitters make actions happen, whilst inhibitory neurotransmitters reduce activities. Oxytocin, which excites the neurons of the quiescent system and calms you down, is released in large quantities from the posterior pituitary gland under certain conditions of arousal, particularly skin pressure, touching and nipple stimulation. When I read this I couldn't help remembering the prick of the dagger against my naked breast during my Initiation. The release of this hormone is why a hug or a cuddle can make you relax and give you a sense of well-being. But what of the arousal system? This is turned on by adrenalin, which is both a hormone and a neurotransmitter.

Because adrenalin drives our fight-or-flight response, it has to be activated and inactivated quickly. It is made in a part of the brain called the adrenal medulla and stored in the chromaffin granula. Just like oxytocin, it is released into the bloodstream in large quantities when your body is exposed to an appropriate form of arousal.

A release of adrenalin affects your sympathetic nervous system (heart, lungs, blood vessels, bladder, gut and genitalia). It will be triggered in response to physical or mental stress and binds to a special group of transmembrane proteins: the adrenergic receptors. Then it increases the heart's rate and intensity of beating; it dilates bronchi and pupils; and causes vasoconstriction, sweating and reduced clotting time of the blood. Blood gets shunted from your skin and viscera to your skeletal muscles, coronary arteries, liver and brain.

It seems that the balance between stress and arousal affects your state of consciousness. Applying this knowledge to René Thom's model of cusp catastrophe I could now draw a diagram of the possible states of consciousness that happen.

The cusp surface moves according to the degree of adrenalin (tense) or oxytocin (relaxed) that is released into your bloodstream. Too much adrenalin blocks access to cosmic consciousness (spiritual arousal), while too much oxytocin puts you into REM sleep.

I suppose it's not really surprising that the path to sexual orgasm always remains open, except under conditions of extreme stress. This brain function evolved in the earliest primates as a reward for DNA-sharing during procreation, and it does its job very well. We seem to be the only primate species to have adapted its features to allow us to gain all the extra survival benefits of spiritual experience. But the mechanism still has rough edges – in particular, unless we balance our mind/body system between relaxation and arousal, we cannot reach this elusive state. All the mystical writings confirm that this can take years of practice. I was fortunate to experience the intense electric field of an impending lightning strike, which imposed an electrical balance on my arousal and quiescent systems despite the state of my hormonal balance.

A single-cusp catastrophe model shows what happens. Let's start by looking at the reliable mechanism of sexual arousal. This is shown below.

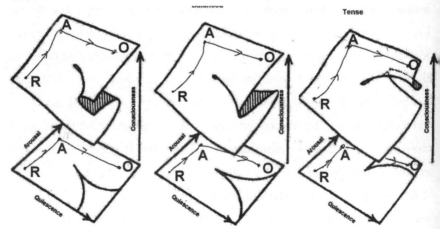

Fig 3: The sexual route to orgasm

The lower plane shows possible combinations of Arousal and Quiescence and the states of consciousness this can cause with different degrees of relaxation. Point O. represents the transient state of sexual orgasm. The route to orgasm is caused by increasing arousal.

The lower graph shows all possible levels of arousal and quiescence. The path to orgasm starts at **R**, when both autonomous systems are at a normal state of excitation. As sexual activity increases, the arousal system increases in activity, but it also stimulates the production of oxytocin. At point **A** your mind is at a state of flow consciousness, what Newberg and D'Aquili call hyper-arousal. If the stimulation continues, the build up of oxytocin triggers quiescent breakthrough, and you become fully aroused and fully quiescent at the same time. This is point **O**, where you experience the bliss of orgasm. You just tasted Mother Nature's reward for procreating.

The level of consciousness is shown on the upper graph. It follows a folded surface whose shape changes with the balance between tension and relaxation. This tried and tested system of sexual arousal and reward has served all primates well for millions of years; we are all descended from a long line of ancestors who were motivated to procreate by it. But the mechanism has other possibilities, and humans have exploited one. Michael Persinger pointed out our brain's ability to have 'God experiences' has powerful survival value: it makes our species resilient, and enabled our ancestors to keep up their hopes and keep trying through famine, pestilence and untold horrors. Anything that gives survival advantage, and can be passed on via DNA, offers the chance of selective development. According to the science of neo-Darwinism this is the main engine which drives evolutionary change.[24]

Evolution cannot plan ahead; it has to use what is there. The awareness of self that the two-lobed brains our species evolved offered a route to increase forward planning. But it also offered the possibility of despair when we realise that we must die. Persinger said that this ability to experience what we think is god can change human beings from 'trembling, incapacitated primates into confident, creative individuals'. So how did Mother Nature manage this neat trick? Thom's catastrophe theory shows a way.

As in the previous diagram, the lower plane shows the possible states of the quiescent and arousal systems. As before, the path to bliss starts at point **R**, where both systems are in a normal unaroused state, but it follows a different route. The subject does not seek physical stimulation but meditates, trying to calm and still the mind and body, so increasing the ability of the quiescent system to move to point **M**. Should you become too relaxed, then you drift off into a dreamlike state of near sleep and stay on the lower level of consciousness, as the slight spill-over into arousal can only move you to point **B**. Although this is very relaxing, it does not lead to the more intense state of cosmic consciousness which Wilmshurst describes. You

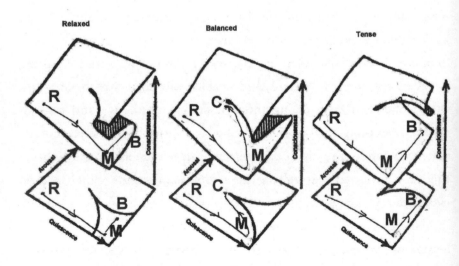

Fig 4: The spiritual route to orgasm
The lower plane shows possible combinations of arousal and quiescence and the states of conciousness this can cause with different degrees of relaxation. Point **O** represents the transient state of spiritual orgasm. This route is caused by increasing quiescence.

become blocked by the blind alley of the cusp and fail to reach a more intense state. This is shown in the left-hand element of the diagram. The right-hand element shows what happens if you are too tense. With considerable effort to suppress intrusive thoughts you may struggle to point **M**; if you hold that state long enough an arousal spill-over can occur, but it only moves you to point **B**, the same dreamlike state of relaxed arousal. The step up in consciousness and the overwhelming of your sense of self just does not happen.

The middle diagram shows what happens if your tension and relaxation are in perfect balance. You move from **R** to **M** and then, as your arousal system is tripped in, you move up the smooth edge of the cusp to point **C**: the state of mind about which Wilmshurst says:

When you thus cease to be finite, you become one with the infinite. This sublime condition is not of permanent duration and only now and then can it be enjoyed.

Small wonder this state of mind can only 'now and then be enjoyed'. The conscious mind is trying to use an autonomous subconscious reward mechanism to reach a state of mind that is not only extremely enjoyable but extremely elusive. It involves bringing two mental systems, one chemical and one electrical, into perfect balance and then holding that state. It is like balancing a marble on the tip of a ballpoint pen. It's possible, but hard to keep up and takes lots of practice.

But are Wilmshurst's teachings about the mystical state of oneness with creation at the centre of Masonry, really ancient? Did he perhaps simply invent the idea and then notice similarities with Masonic ritual? To check that out I will need to consider the oldest Masonic document still in existence. Does that contain anything to support Wilmshurst's thoughts?

Also, Wilmshurst says that the purpose of Freemasonry is to map out a spiritual path to inner knowledge. But how can I be sure that this was Masonry's original purpose? Is it really a continuation of an ancient spiritual tradition? And, if it is, how did it evolve into such a successful system of spiritual arousal? A fortuitous meeting with a leading brain scientist, in a hotel overlooking Kirkwall Harbour in Orkney, was to provide more clues.

[1] Wilmshurst (1922), pp. 8–9.
[2] Wilmshurst (1922), p. 88.
[3] Wilmshurst (1922), p. 170.
[4] Wilmshurst (1925).
[5] Wilmshurst (1925).
[6] Wilmshurst (1925).
[7] Wilmshurst (1924).
[8] Wilson (2004), pp. 3–4.
[9] Wilmshurst (ed. Lomas) (in press).
[10] Wilson (2004), pp. 3–4.
[11] Blackledge (2003), p. 251.
[12] Wilmshurst (1924).
[13] Blackledge (2003), p. 251.
[14] Morgan (1972), pp. 97–8.
[15] Blackledge (2003), p. 295.
[16] Blackledge (2003), p. 292.
[17] Wilson (1990), p. 223.
[18] Wilson (1990), p. 224.
[19] Wilson (1990), p. 225.
[20] Thom (1975).
[21] Times (2002).
[22] Jansky, et al (2002), pp. 302–4.
[23] Carmichael, Humber, et al. (1987), p. 27.
[24] Dawkins (1988), pp. 1–23.

Chapter Twelve

The Puzzle of the Kirkwall Scroll

To Begin at the Beginning

In September 1999 I was invited to lecture at the Orkney Science Festival on the same day as Karl Pribram. Pribram, a sprightly man in his early eighties, is Emeritus Professor of Stanford University and the Director of the Center for Brain Research and Informational Sciences at Radford University. His energy and enthusiasm would not be out of place in a man a third of his age.

He was at the Festival with his wife, the writer Katherine Neville, who also was speaking. After the day's lectures I joined them both, and the Slovenian physicist Dr Andrej Detela of the Jozef Stefan Institute in Ljubljana, for dinner at the Kirkwall Hotel. It was a fascinating evening. Karl has spent most of his life exploring the properties of the brain and its structure, and the after-dinner talk ranged widely over quantum physics and brain science, with Karl telling us about his work for NASA. He also outlined his ideas on the nature of consciousness. As he was talking about the transition from sleeping to waking, I took the chance to ask him about something that has puzzled me for years.

Sometimes when I am awakened by early morning sunlight I can be aware of my body, but not of who or where I am. I'd noticed that over a brief space of time – objectively, it could be no more than a few seconds – I would find myself becoming aware of who I was and then remembering my history. I asked Karl if it was possible that, as I awoke, I could be living through a stage of consciousness in which I existed without any concept of self. This state seemed to share some characteristics with the state of religious bliss that Newberg and D'Aquili found in their brain-scan studies.

Karl launched into an impromptu lecture on the nature of self-awareness, during which he spoke of the difference between 'primary' and 'higher-level' consciousness. He explained that, before I could have any sense of self, I had to have primary consciousness.

'It is an ability to generate a mental scene in which you can integrate a large amount of diverse data to relate your immediate behaviour to the demands of your environment,' he said, his eyes twinkling as brightly as the Kirkwall harbour lights through the window behind him.

He went on to say that this level of consciousness is similar to the sort that a dog experiences, or that a young baby may have before it learns to talk. Awareness of self is built on the inputs provided by the senses, and is only possible once your brain develops an ability to construct and connect past and future scenes. So you have no sense of self until you can remember your past and extrapolate your future. This wisdom seems to have been absorbed into the teaching methods of Freemasonry.

'This acquired memory,' Karl went on to explain, 'is a physical property of the brain.'

When I awoke without a concept of who I was, I was experiencing the state of primary consciousness that a young child lives in before it acquires language. As my memory of what I could do and the skills I had learned interacted with and influenced the area of my brain that was the focus of my waking thoughts, I reintegrated my personality and became fully conscious. Only then did I know who I was.

'This often happens as people wake up, but we accept that we are disorientated by sleep, so it is not a problem.' Karl explained. The implication of this, is that many sleepy people have known the warm bliss of unawareness of self that seems to be at the centre of much religious belief, but have put it down to the pleasures of drowsiness.

Later I read more of Karl's work on memory, and how it creates consciousness. Human memory works in a different way to the digital computer memory. It is non-representational. This means that, within our heads, memories occur when we make a match between the electrical activity of our brain and the trigger signals that we get from the environment.

Karl had written of how we all experience this phenomena.

Events dimly remembered become vivid, when we return to the scene of the experience. Meeting old friends, hearing familiar music, rereading a long-neglected topic, all call forth reconstructive power thought long gone. We are little aware of the amount of our memory that is carried 'out there' – not in our brains but in our homes, jobs, and libraries. Given these highly structured inputs, the machinery of our brains can restructure – reconstruct – a remembrance from the bits and dabs actually stored in the head. ... For education, the moral is clear: instruction (shared discovery of structure) should supplement teaching (showing).[1]

Karl's thought – that we change and develop as the structure of our brain changes to accommodate concepts we are learning – is profound. It seems to echo the methods used by Masonic ritual to impart learning. Its implication is that we develop our personality by physical changes taking place in the structure of our brains. But what sort of changes occur? What role do brain activity, and the memories we create, play in determining personality? Do these types of process happen during Masonic ritual? How does Masonic ritual change our brains? It seemed to be a process similar to a child growing into an adult – something Karl knew a lot about. Karl had said that a baby, in the early days of its life, experiences primary consciousness. Yet at this time it has three times as many separate brain cells as there are people alive in the whole world.

'How do we grow from an almost unaware new-born baby to a fully aware adult?' I asked him.

He took hold of his wife's hand and play-acted counting her fingers, obviously enjoying the chance to touch her.

'If I set out to count each individual neuron, and am fast enough to check each object off at the rate of one a second, it will take me around thirty million years to complete the full numeration.'

'Should we order pudding first?' asked the practical Andrej.

Karl grinned across at Andrej and me. He looked pleased that he had encouraged us to visualise the awesome complexity of even a baby's brain.

But I was still puzzled. Does the ritual of Freemasonry provide ways to help us change the way our brains work? Are these changes for the better?

Later on there was a further treat in store. We were all invited for a private viewing of a fascinating artifact at the local Masonic temple, which is home to Lodge Kirkwall Kilwinning.

We walked together from the harbour up the narrow winding High Street towards the Cathedral of St Magnus, before turning down the side road where the Masonic temple is to be found. We entered by a side door and were welcomed by senior members of the Lodge. They escorted us up the stairs to the temple and pointed to what looked like a large roll of carpet hung on a spindle high on the west wall of the Lodge.

'That is the Kirkwall Scroll,' our hosts proudly announced.

The Brethren of Lodge Kirkwall Kilwinning take excellent care of this ancient document. When we saw it, it was kept high on the west wall of the temple. It was protected from direct sunlight within the darkness of the temple, and access to it was guarded from casual visitors; even invited guests viewed it only by prior appointment. (Unfortunately it now has to be stored in a safe vault, after it received a great deal of unwelcome publicity and extravagant claims for its origins.) We were all extremely impressed with the quality and preservation of the scroll and grateful to the Brethren and Officers of the Lodge for allowing us to see it.

But what is it?

It appears to be an enormous sheet of canvas and could well be the earliest documentary evidence of the beginnings of Masonic symbolism. But how did it come to be hanging on the wall of a Masonic temple in Kirkwall?

To find out that I needed to understand the history of Lodge Kirkwall Kilwinning and how it came to own the scroll.

The Origins of the Scroll

The Kirkwall Scroll, is made of three pieces of strong linen (some suggest sailcloth) sewn together and hand-painted throughout. The complete hanging cloth is 18ft 6in long and 5ft 6in wide. It consists of a centre strip 4ft wide painted with around a hundred Masonic symbols, and two outer strips which seem to be maps. These appear to have been cut from a single strip of material before being sewn to the outer edges of the centre strip.

Many of the inscriptions on the scroll are written in an old Masonic code widely used in Scotland for Masonic gravestone inscriptions; it is also sometimes known as the Enochian Alphabet, in certain degrees of the Ancient and Accepted Rite. In the second scene of the Scroll, counting upwards, an altar is shown standing on a black–and white pavement with a coded inscription. Part of that inscription decodes as:

I am hath sent me unto you. I am that I am.
I am the Rose of Sharon and the Lily of the Valley.
I am that I am or I will be that I will be.

In a talk on the Kirkwall Scroll given to Lodge Kirkwall Kilwinning in 1976 Bro. James Flett said:

When I joined our Lodge many years ago there was at that time a very old Brother who occasionally visited the Lodge meetings at the advanced age of over 90. On one occasion I asked him if he could tell me anything about the Scroll. He said he did not know very much about it except that at his Initiation it lay on the centre of the Lodge room floor when he was a young lad of 20.[2]

I believe the Scroll is an early Tracing-board that was intended by its creators to be unrolled, section by section, as the relevant degrees were being worked. Other writers have made the point that the

Scroll is too long for the floor area of the existing Kirkwall Temple, and the previous building – the Tolbooth, on the Kirk Green in front of St Magnus Cathedral – was even smaller. However, if my view of its purpose is correct, it would never have needed to be fully unrolled.

What is not in doubt is that the Kirkwall Scroll has been in the care of the Lodge for a long time, at least since 1786. Many theories about its purpose and meaning have been put forward, but these have mainly come from groups which have preconceived agendas for the Scroll's role in history.

George William Speth (1847–1901) was one of those with forthright views on the matter. He was a founder and secretary of the highly opinionated Quatuor Coronati Lodge, and this self-styled 'premier' lodge of research has a long track record of supporting the party line on the London origins of Freemasonry that the Duke of Sussex laid down when he forced the formation of the United Grand Lodge of England on to the reluctant Masons of England and Wales in 1813.[3] As editor of its house journal, *Ars Quatuor Coronatorum* (AQC), Speth was duty bound to support the rather absurd belief that Freemasonry appeared in London in 1717. It is supposed to have started when a group of bored gentlemen toured the local building sites asking the workmen if they had any interesting rituals which their 'betters' could use for moral improvement – a theory with all the charm and credibility of a situation comedy script.

In 1897 Speth, ready to uphold the Quatuor Coronati tradition of dismissing early Masonic documentation in Scotland, decided to investigate the Kirkwall Scroll. He commissioned an article from an Orkney Mason, Archdeacon Craven, about the major treasure of Kirkwall's Lodge. This was published in volume 10 of AQC, along with

Speth's own opinions about the Scroll. Without even seeing it for himself, Speth decided that it was a lodge floorcloth from 'the first half of the eighteenth century, or very little later', so making sure the myth of Freemasonry beginning in London in 1717 remained unchallenged.

In the 1920s another member of Quatuor Coronati, William Reginald Day, who also belonged to the Sydney Research Lodge in New South Wales, tackled the Scroll again, and wrote an article for AQC (vol. 38, 1925). Day said he had looked closely at the structure and subject matter of the scroll – although it seems he looked more closely at Speth's article than the Scroll itself. Unsurprisingly he finds clues to the cloth's date, claiming to find 'the arms of the Grand Lodge of the Antients' – but the Antients' coat of arms did not feature a five-pointed star and an all-seeing eye in the sky under the arch. How Day failed to notice these differences remains a mystery. Using this rather weak similarity, Day asserts that the Scroll is of a later date than 1751, especially as he sees other traces of Antient influence, which he does not specify and neither I nor the Brethren of Kirkwall Kilwinning I consulted could see. Once more AQC maintained the myth of Freemasonry being invented in London in 1717 and safely dismissed any thoughts of a Scottish origin for the Craft.

Day also claimed to have found (in cipher) three verbatim quotations from the King James Bible (those quoted above), and uses them to place the scroll after 1611. However, I cannot find those exact words in my copy of the King James, only fragments interspersed with other phrases. Still, following the time-honoured Quatuor Coronati attitude of dismissing all things Scottish, Bro. Day used this 'evidence' to assert that the Kirkwall cloth was a modern work of art, and he advanced the idea that an Orcadian Mason called

William Graham, who worked in London as a house painter and later returned to Orkney, painted the Scroll himself on a large spread of canvas.

There the matter stood until 21 July 2000, when an article appeared in both The Times and the Daily Telegraph. It was written by Orkney journalist Kath Gourlay who reported the results of scientific tests carried out on the Scroll.

The results of radiocarbon dating carried out on a rare wall hanging have shocked members of a Masonic lodge in the Orkney Islands, who have been told that their document is a medieval treasure worth several million pounds. ... radio-carbon dating of the scroll points to the huge 18-ft sailcloth hanging as being fifteenth-century.[4]

Here the mystery deepens. There are two radiocarbon dates for the scroll. One for the centre section and a quite different one for the outer sections. Kath Gourlay reports this as follows:

Contact with the University of Oxford Research laboratory, which did the radiocarbon dating, adds to the mystery by supporting both dates.

'We analysed material from the Kirkwall Scroll on two separate occasions,' says a spokesman from the Archaeology and History of Art department which carried out the work. 'You have to allow a certain margin of error in calibrating carbon content, and the first sample, taken from the outside edge of the material, was possibly eighteenth- or early nineteenth-century (1780–1840). The second piece, which came from the central panel, produced a much older date – fifteenth- or early sixteenth-century (1400–1530).'[5]

The 280-year difference in age between the central strip and the two side strips makes Day's claim that William Graham painted the whole cloth extremely unlikely. Graham, who presented the Scroll to Lodge Kirkwall Kilwinning in 1786, would have first to have obtained two strips of cloth, one new and the other 280 years old; then he would have had to cut the new cloth in two and sew the two half-strips to the outside of the older cloth before starting to paint. Why bother? If he wanted a wider strip of canvas he could just have sewn the new strip alongside the old to obtain the greater width. So the radiocarbon evidence suggests that if he added the outer strips, he did so because he wanted to preserve the inner cloth but disguise it, improve it, or change it in some way. I will explore why Graham may have wanted to do this later in this chapter.

I contacted the Lodge to enquire if any observable difference in the weave between the central strip and the outer edges had been detected on the back of the cloth, as the front of the Scroll is coated with a thick layer of paint, and no cloth pattern is visible. A venerable Brother replied:

It appears all three panels have been backed with some form of cloth that extends the full width of the Scroll. Its age is uncertain but this smooth lining is not modern. Unfortunately, this negates access to the back of the painted sides and thus it is impossible to compare the weave and textures of all three panels. The ridges where the panels are sewn together can be clearly seen and touched, confirming the Scroll is of three vertical panels.

The fact the painted cloth has been backed with a stronger cloth, in the same way that a woollen rug is backed with hessian, suggests it was intended to be rolled out as floorcloth, rather than displayed as a hanging.

But the radiocarbon-dating evidence renders unsustainable the claim put forward by writer Andrew Sinclair that there is a fifteenth-century secret hidden in the outer (map) sides of the Scroll. Nor is it possible for the Scroll to have been part of Kirkwall's heritage 'from the late fourteenth century, when Prince Henry St Clair became the Earl of Orkney', as he also claimed. There is no trace of Freemasonry in Kirkwall before 1736, so Sinclair's theory also ignores the question of who stored this Masonic artifact for over two hundred years?

The outer sections of the scroll do date from the time of William Graham, so Day may be right in claiming he painted that, but the centre strip is older. With the rediscovered knowledge of the sevenfold path of Freemasonry, which Wilmshurst writes about and which I traced in the first seven chapters of this book, a possible rationale began to form in my mind.

The tradition of the Tracing-board grew out of an older practice: that of drawing the key symbols of a degree on the floor of the lodge-room. In the days before lodges owned their own temples, the symbols of the degree to be worked would be drawn on the floor of the lodge and later erased by the candidate. Wilmshurst explained it thus in a series of lodge lectures he gave in 1929. The notes he made for these talks say:

In earlier days, when the Craft was not a popular social institution but a serious discipline in a philosophic and sacred science, instruction was not treated casually. The Board was not, as now, a product of the Masonic furnisher's factory; it was the most revered symbol in the Lodge; it was a diagram which every Brother was taught to draw for himself, so that both his hand and his understanding might be trained in Masonic work. The literary records show that at each Lodge meeting the Board of the Degree about to be worked was actually drawn from memory with chalk and charcoal on the floor of the Lodge by the Master, who from previous practice was able to do this quickly and accurately. In advancing from West to East during the Ceremony, the Candidate took the steps of the Degree over the diagram. The diagram was explained to him as an integral part of the Ceremony, and, before being restored to his personal comforts, he was required to expunge it with a mop and pail of water, so that uninitiated eyes might not see it and that he might learn a first lesson in humility and secrecy.

In course of the 18th century the drawing of the diagram from memory upon the ground was superseded by the use first of painted floor-cloths and afterwards by wooden boards resting on trestles, on which the diagram was permanently painted.

The boards are cryptic prescriptions of a world-old science, taught and practised in secret in all ages by the few spiritually ripe and courageous enough for following a higher path of life than is possible as yet to the popular world. The detailed interpretation of their symbolism is necessarily difficult, for symbols always comprise so much more than can be verbally explained, and so few Masons have as yet educated themselves in the language of ancient esoteric symbolism.

The central strip of the Kirkwall Scroll fits this description. It shows seven panels, each describing a step leading from the west to the east (it would unroll from the bottom to the top). It begins with the basic symbols of the Craft; the central, pivotal step shows a tomb, symbolising the death of the ego; and the sequence progresses to an idyllic vision of the ecstatic bliss of the centre. A continuity of vision is maintained, from the sun, the moon and stars and the vision of the rising of a lozenge-shaped all-seeing eye in the first step, to an ordered arrangement of the heavens with the symbols repeated showing the stars rearranged as pillars around the moon as the centre. This well-structured sky stands above a final scene of oneness with nature. Each scene in this floorcloth fits the spiritual steps Wilmshurst describes in his writings. He talks of the seven steps that I have described following in the first seven chapters of this book.

But, if the Kirkwall Scroll is an early Masonic floorcloth showing the steps of this spiritual path, where was it created, and how did it pass into the ownership of William Graham? One thing known about Graham is that he was a member of an itinerant lodge that was No. 128 on the roll of the Antient Grand Lodge, and which, not enjoying the luxury of its own temple, met in various London pubs: a room would be hired for the evening and then set up for the ceremony. Wilmshurst gives the clue in his comment that, in these circumstances, early lodges used floorcloths. The centre strip of the Kirkwall Scroll is just such a floorcloth. But Lodge No. 128 (it did not have a name) was formed in 1750, so the cloth pre-dates its formation by about 220 years.

I argue in the Hiram Key series of books that modern Freemasonry began at Roslin, as William St Clair, the last Norse earl of Orkney, was building the chapel there. If, as these books outline, William gave the operative masons rituals, then when they dispersed they took with them the tradition of the 'Mason Word' (a secret password known only to Master Masons).* A geographical study of the earliest

---

*For a fuller discussion of the Mason Word see Lomas & Knight (1966).

mentions of Masonic lodges shows them to have spread out from a centre near the Firth of Forth, where William St Clair built Rosslyn Chapel.[6]

The earliest written reference to a Masonic lodge found in a non-Masonic source occurs in Aberdeen in 1483. At this time the choir of the burgh church of St Nicholas was being rebuilt. The estates of William St Clair had been broken up after his death on 3 July 1480, and the masons who worked on Rosslyn Chapel were dispersed from the village of Roslin. It does not seem impossible, or even unlikely, that some of those masons would have sought work in Aberdeen. At least six masons were part of a lodge in Aberdeen at this time. Prof. David Stevenson of St Andrews University reports that the minutes of Aberdeen Burgh Council record that the Burgh Council was called in to settle a dispute between 'six masownys of the lurge'. Fines were laid down for offences, with provision for exclusion from the lodge for repeat offences.[7]

Aberdeen Lodge recorded its rituals and traditions of history when James VI's Master of Works, William Schaw, set up a formal Lodge system in 1599. This encouraged the lodges to write down their governing statutes, and those drawn up by Aberdeen show that the lodge was familiar with the Mason Word well over a hundred years before London Freemasons supposedly learned the rituals of Freemasonry from their local building sites:

Wee Masiter Meassones and entered prentises all of ws wnder subscryvers doe heir protest and vowe as hitherto wee have done at our entrie, wen we received the benefit of the Measson word, that wee shall own this honourable Lodge at all occationes except those who can give ane Lawful excuse or sickness or out of towne.[8]

This is evidence that a lodge of Masons existed in Aberdeen at the time the middle section of the Kirkwall Scroll was created. This Lodge first becomes visible within three years of the death of William St Clair of Roslin. Although I have argued elsewhere that he began the rituals of Freemasonry, I think it highly unlikely that St Clair had anything to do with creating this scroll. It is crudely and simply painted, which suggests it is far more likely to be the work of operative masons such as those who formed that early Lodge of Aberdeen. If they wanted to continue practising and teaching any rituals that they had been first taught during the building at Roslin, then the creation of a floorcloth showing the main steps and symbols makes sense. And whoever did paint the Scroll was in right at the start of Freemasonry.

Could the Kirkwall Scroll be an ancient floorcloth from Aberdeen? The date of the earliest record of the Lodge (1483) fits with the radiocarbon dating of the Scroll (1400–1530), and Aberdeen has traditionally maintained close ties with Orkney. But how might a scroll created by early Masons in Aberdeen have come into the ownership of William Graham, so that he could pass it on to the Lodge in Kirkwall? Could it have been through the agency of William's father, Stromness merchant trader Alexander Graham?

During the eighteenth century a privileged group of lairds got rich by trading kelp-slag, the calcined ashes of certain varieties of brown seaweed (kelp). Orkney had vast reserves of seaweed, but harvesting and processing it was labour-intensive. The landowners, who were used to taking their rents in kind, soon realised that by insisting on taking it in the form of labour to harvest kelp, they had a ready, if not willing, source of cheap workers.

The kelp was cut at low tide, using sickles, and heaped on the beach to dry. The dry weed was then burned to form kelp-slag, which was a major raw material for the production of alum and other alkali products. Prices for it began to rise in 1760, when alum factories were set up on the Firth of Forth, and when the new industrialists of Tyneside started to pay good money for reliable supplies of alkali, a boom was born. This bonanza lasted from 1770 to 1830, with 60,000 tons of kelp-slag per annum being shipped at a price of £20 per ton. Historian Willie Thomson says of this period:

> *The instinct of trade permeated all classes from the highest to the lowest.*
> *Repeated efforts were made to confine its benefits to the burgesses of*
> *Kirkwall (who included most of the landowners), and to prohibit the*
> *activities of pedlars and country people who traded in a small way with*
> *visiting shipping. The Country Acts not only forbade trafficking, but*
> *regarded it as barely distinguishable from theft and begging.*[9]

But it was the Orkney estate owners who benefited most from this unexpected boon of the industrial revolution. Their tenants worked the land and harvested the kelp as part of the cost of keeping a roof over their heads (only after the rent in kind was paid could they work to feed themselves), so kelp-processing costs were part of the landowners' rent-rolls, and the Kirkwall kelp-masters netted profits of around a million pounds a year. The rich prospered and did their best to make sure they guarded their privileges. During the run of bad harvests from 1782 to 1785 many tenants died of famine on West Mainland, where there is no kelp, but the 'generous' kelp lairds advanced credit to their kelp-harvesting tenants to ensure their labour force survived the famine. When the debts were called in they reaped the benefits in reduced production costs, and so increased their profits. Thomson estimates that during this period the lairds made three times as much from kelp production as they earned from the rental income of their estates.

Of course, with such vast profits to be made, there were battles about who should benefit. As a royal burgh, Kirkwall held a royal monopoly on trade with Orkney. Only Kirkwall burgesses had the right to import and export. But this position was not accepted by the rising merchant class of Stromness. The Hamnavoe Sound offered far easier access to Atlantic shipping and was attracting business from the Hudson's Bay Company and North Atlantic whaling ships. Kirkwall's burgesses wanted to tax the trade of the thriving new port, but they ran into a singularly bloody-minded opponent in the shape of Alexander Graham (sometimes spelt Graeme in older texts). Orkney historian Willie Thomson said of him:

Matters came to a head in 1742, when Alexander Graham and a number of fellow Stromness merchants received an assessment from Kirkwall magistrates. Graham was required to pay a mere £16 Scots, but Kirkwall was to find him a stubborn, single-minded and litigious opponent, ultimately willing to ruin himself and his family for principle, or perhaps just sheer obstinacy. ... The case dragged on for sixteen years through local courts, to the Court of Sessions and eventually to the House of Lords, where Alexander Graham was ultimately victorious.[10]

Despite his persistence and his ultimate victory, though, Alexander Graham was not awarded costs. So he went on to lose more money in unsuccessful attempts to recover his costs through a House of Lords' ruling.

His son William, meanwhile, was living in London, where he made a good living as a house painter. He joined his local Freemasonic lodge, No 128 in the Atholl or Antient Constitution,★ which before 1771 met at the Red Horse Inn in Old Bond Street, and from 1771 to 1793 met at the Crown and Feathers public house in Holborn.[11] (After the creation of the United Grand Lodge of England the lodge number passed to Lodge Prince Edwin, which meets in Bury in the Masonic Province of East Lancashire. That Lodge is still listed under this roll number.) William Graham was described by his friends as 'Mason-mad', and in 1785, when he came home to Orkney to take up the post of Customs Officer for the burgh of Kirkwall, he wanted to continue to work his Masonry.[12]

Orkney had just suffered its third bad harvest in a row, and the landowning members of Lodge Kirkwall Kilwinning and its Master, James Traill, were coining in profits from the kelp boom. And during the same boom years vessels from Stromness would ship out heavy with kelp-slag. They would sail down the east coast of Scotland to the Firth of Forth, unload the slag at Leith and return to collect a cargo of coal from Inverness before sailing back to Orkney. This route involved a regular stopover at Aberdeen. Moreover, Stromness ships also traded in what Orkney historian Willie Thomson, describes as 'small luxuries' – he lists such examples as gloves, paper, tobacco, golf clubs, sealing wax and white sugar.[13] Significantly, William's father, Alexander, was trading in such small luxuries with ships passing through Aberdeen.

★The Atholl, or Ancient, Constitution was a breakaway group of Masons, unhappy with the Grand Lodge of London's Hanoverian leanings, who felt the Hanoverians had betrayed the ancient Scottish teachings of Freemasonry. In 1748 they set up their own Grand Lodge under the Duke of Atholl's patronage and worked a ritual they claimed was truer to 'Ancient Freemasonry'. They called Masons of the Grand Lodge of London 'the Moderns', and were themselves known as 'the Ancients'. See Lomas (2002), p272.

Consequently, he could well have had the opportunity to acquire a Masonic floorcloth from that long-established Masonic centre (often Masonic relics pass into the hands of relatives who are non-Masons, and in such circumstances may end up being sold). His son William, a 'Mason-mad' exile in London and a member of an Atholl lodge which followed the Scottish traditions of Masonry, would certainly have recognised the value of such a floorcloth. And, as Alexander spent a considerable time in London while his dispute with the Burghers of Kirkwall was heard in the House of Lords, I suspect it was at this time that he could have given the Scroll to his son. So there is a feasible way for William to have come by the Scroll.

But how did Lodge Kirkwall Kilwinning come to have in its care the oldest documentary evidence of the early beliefs and symbols of Freemasonry? To answer that, I needed to look at the early history of the Lodge.

Freemasonry Comes to Orkney

On Monday 1 October 1736 Freemasonry began in Kirkwall. Two visitors arrived at Tankerness House at the invitation of four burghers of Kirkwall: Alexander Baikie, James Berrihill, James Mackay and Robert Sutherland. Both visitors were Freemasons. One was John, the father of James Berrihill, and a member of Lodge Stirling, the other was William Meldrum of Lodge Dunfermline.[14]

Alexander Baikie was a merchant and shipbuilder. His grandfather, Thomas Baikie, had made his fortune building the trading vessels known as 'great boats', craft about 30 ft long, propelled by six oars and two masts of sails, that could carry up to seven tons of cargo among the islands of Orkney, Shetland, or even as far afield as

Norway. By 1736 the Baikies were successful merchants and landowners, and Alexander's brother James was Provost, the chief officer of the Royal Burgh of Kirkwall.[15] Alexander, though, had his own plans for achieving status: he wanted to set up a lodge of Freemasons in Kirkwall. If he couldn't match the civic influence of his brother, then perhaps he could build another support group in the form of a Masonic lodge. Freemasonry in Scotland had a history of Royal patronage from the time of James VI, and there were rumours that a new Grand Lodge was soon to be formed in Edinburgh.

His visitors that October evening were members of well-established and influential Freemasonic lodges. Perhaps more importantly for Alexander Baikie, both the lodges of Stirling and Dunfermline were signatories to the Schaw Statutes of 1601, the credentials which confirmed Royal patronage for Freemasonry.* These state documents also confirmed the hereditary rights of the St Clair Earls of Roslin to be patrons of Freemasonry:

> *From aige to aige it hes bene obervit amangs ws that the lairds of Roslin hes ever bene patrones and protectors of ws and our previleges.*[16]

This link to the political patronage of both the Crown of Scotland and the Earls of Roslin mattered to Baikie because William St Clair of Roslin – the original patron and protector of Freemasons affirmed by James VI's Master of Works, William Schaw – had also been Earl of Orkney, having been thus ennobled by Eric VII of Norway and Denmark in 1434. The early minutes of Lodge Kirkwall Kilwinning confirm the social importance of this connection to the founders of the Lodge.

*For a fuller discussiion, see Lomas (2002).

An Orkney Earl, William St Clair, is recorded as holding the appointment of Patron of the Masons of Scotland about 1430 and 1440, which is a period before the transfer of our islands to Scotland in 1468. This position was hereditary, and was held by the descendants of this Earl until 1736, when the last William St Clair, having no son to claim his honours, placed his resignation before the Grand Lodge of Scotland which had been inaugurated that year.[17]

Is the fact that a lodge was founded in Orkney just before the creation of the Grand Lodge of Scotland a coincidence? It was formed by Masons from two lodges which had supported the St Clair claim to patronage in the Charter of 1601 and were also founder lodges of the new Grand Lodge of Scotland. John Berrihill, as a member of Lodge Stirling, must have been aware of moves to create a Grand Lodge of Scotland later that year, and he would have known it was planned to offer the role of Grand Master Mason to William St Clair of Roslin. (The Grand Lodge of Scotland was formed on the feast of St John in December 1736, two months after the setting up of Lodge Kirkwall Kilwinning.) As an Orcadian, Berrihill would also be aware of the Norse links with Orkney and with the St Clairs of Roslin. Be that as it may, the strategy was successful, the timing perfect. Even the choice of name shows political skill. Lodge Mother Kilwinning was the only other source of Masonic patronage; it had stood out from the initial formation of Grand Lodge and reserved its right to warrant daughter lodges. So, by incorporating Kilwinning into their Lodge's name, the newly made Masons of Kirkwall left open the possibility of seeking a warrant from Lodge Mother Kilwinning in Ayrshire if the 'lairds of Roslin' failed to support them. One way or another they were determined to make their mark on Kirkwall society.

That October evening Lodge Kirkwall Kilwinning was established when the visiting Masons from Lodges Stirling and Dunfermline imparted the secrets of the 'Mason Word' to James Mackay, Alexander Baikie, Robert Sutherland and John Berrihill. These four then became Master, Wardens and Keeper of Box (what we now call Secretary and Treasurer) of the new Lodge. At once they requested a warrant from the newly formed Grand Lodge of Scotland. And they were successful. (That warrant, signed by William St Clair of Roslin, the first Grand Master Mason of the Grand Lodge of Scotland, still hangs in the temple at Kirkwall, and on the night of my visit with Karl Pribram it was shown to us with great pride.) The first by-law of the new Lodge fixed the date for the election of its officers:

... and that their shall be ane election of office bearers yearly upon St John's Day being the twentie seventh day of Decr. as is the order of the foresaid Ludge.[18]

Lodge Kirkwall Kilwinning was to become a meeting place for the great and the good of Kirkwall. Alexander's brother James, the Provost of Kirkwall, followed him into the Mastership of the Lodge, and a year later Mungo Graham, one of the many well-heeled descendants of Bishop George Graham, took the Master's chair. Clearly Mastership of the Lodge was an honour highly sought after by the lairds and minor gentry of Kirkwall. James Flett quotes a note in the Lodge minutes in a discussion of the timing of meetings of the Lodge, where he says:

Few meetings were held throughout the year, as the membership of the Lodge consisted largely of the landed proprietors of Orkney — such notable names as that of Baikie, Traill, Graham, Moodie, Riddoch and Young being conspicuous. During the seasons of the year when their respective estates required their personal supervision they devoted their energies to their advancement and resided in their country houses. About Lammas, when the long dull northern winters set in, they returned to their town residences in Kirkwall and helped to enliven the burgh and while away the long evenings by attending many a ball and party in the old Town Hall on Broad Street, and no doubt a Masonic meeting offered a welcome relaxation from estate affairs and civic duties.[19]

One of the duties of the Lodge was to organise Masonic Balls, and by the early nineteenth century this important task was carried out by a Special Committee. It was responsible to the Master of the Lodge for 'regulating the annual Ball to be given to the ladies and gentlemen of Kirkwall'.[20] Clearly the social role of the Lodge in Orkney society was important.

William Graham's return to Orkney in 1785 set off a saga of wooing, rejection and reconciliation with these worthies that would not be out of place in any modern soap opera. It starts with the 'Mason-mad' Graham visiting Lodge Kirkwall Kilwinning for the installation of the new Master, Robert Baikie. He was invited by Baikie and soon asked the Brethren to accept him as a joining member of the Lodge. The minutes for Tuesday 27 December 1785 record:

Bro. William Graham, visiting Brother from Lodge No. 128, Ancient Constitution of England, was at his own desire admitted to become a member of this Lodge.[21]

Robert Baikie had political ambitions and hoped to displace Charles Dundas, the sitting MP, for a seat in the House of Commons. The seat he wanted represented a rotten burgh, controlled by 27 voters, at least half of whom were what Orkney historian Willie Thomson calls 'faggot voters'. (To get a vote all you needed was ownership of a parcel of land worth at least £400, and factions increased their share of the vote by splitting their land into a number of fictitious lots in the names of reliable dependants.) Among these faggot voters Thomson lists the name of Graham. [22]

It seems Graham and Baikie were made for each other. Graham wanted to be accepted by the Masonic lairds of Kirkwall, and Baikie wanted an extra vote which was in Graham's gift. A month later the intensity of the wooing increased when Graham presented Robert Baikie and the Lodge with a Masonic treasure, the Kirkwall Scroll. The minutes for 27 January 1786 record:

The Master presented to the Lodge a floorcloth, gifted to the Brethren by Bro. William Graham of 128 of the Ancient Constitution of England.

In the parliamentary election of 1780 Robert Baikie bought enough votes to get himself elected as MP for Orkney. And from 1785 to 1787 William Graham was a rising star in Lodge Kirkwall Kilwinning. He was reported as being 'not an installed office holder but filling vacancies when occasion arose'. In 1787 he got the socially important task of arranging the St John's Day Ball.[23] The pair were riding high.

Then Baikie was expelled from his parliamentary seat for what Willie Thomson calls 'sharp practice'.[24] His fall from parliamentary grace was echoed by a withdrawal of the goodwill of the Lodge, which distanced itself from him; he was allowed to remain a member but did not hold office again. Baikie's protégé Graham also fell from favour with the Lodge. In 1789 Graham proposed six candidates for membership of Kirkwall Kilwinning. All were friends of his and tradesmen of the Incorporated Trades of Kirkwall. Whether they were involved in the unspecified 'sharp practices' of Past Master of the Lodge Robert Baikie is not mentioned in the Lodge minutes, but all were rejected. This was a grave social slight for Graham.

By 1791 Graham had given up all hope of becoming Master of Lodge Kirkwall Kilwinning and had seen his influence slip in line with the fortunes of his sponsor. So he decided to create a new focus for influence in Kirkwall: he applied to Grand Lodge for a warrant to form a new lodge, to be known as St Paul's Lodge of Kirkwall.

On 21 January 1791, in his capacity as Master-Elect of the St Paul's Lodge, he wrote to the Right Worshipful Master of Kirkwall Kilwinning, Bro. William Manson, inviting him and his Brethren to attend the consecration of the new lodge at the house of Bro. George Rendall at 12 noon sharp.[25] None of them accepted, but they kept hold of the Scroll. Graham then thumbed his nose at the 'toffs' of Kirkwall Kilwinning by admitting his six rejected candidates to the new lodge.

The Brethren of Lodge Kirkwall Kilwinning were annoyed. They summoned Graham to appear before their court to explain himself, but he refused to submit to their judgment. They then expelled him and refused to allow members of his new lodge to attend their lodge as visitors. Graham appealed to Grand Lodge to support his position, which it duly did, but it was a full year before any member of Kirkwall Kilwinning accepted Graham's invitation to visit the new lodge. Then Bro. Archibald Stewart visited St Paul's and was made welcome. Heartened by this attention, Graham wrote to the Master of Kirkwall Kilwinning suggesting that the lodges shared their Masonic rooms. But the then Master, Andrew Baikie (a cousin of the disgraced Robert), probably wanting to avoid being tainted by the ill-odour of his relative's cronies, rejected the suggestion. Graham was not reconciled with Kirkwall Kilwinning until 1812, when he made a final bequest, leaving to the Lodge his last remaining Masonic treasures – a ceremonial shroud, known a Mort Cloth, and various books. His will said:

Renunciation of Mort Cloth and Book of Ancient Constitution of Free and Accepted Masons by William Graham in favour of the members of the Kirkwall Kilwinning Lodge.

Know all men by these presents that I, William Graham, Tide-master in the Customs of Kirkwall, do hereby make, give over and bequeath from me my heirs and successors To and in favour of the Kirkwall Kilwinning Mason Lodge for the regard that I have for the Ancient fraternity my Mort Cloth and Book of Ancient Constitution of Free and Accepted Masons and I desire that the same after being used at my burial shall be immediately delivered up to Doctor Andrew Munro to be by him presented to the members of that Lodge and by this to be used as shall appear best.

Done by me at Kirkwall, this ninth day of April, Eighteen Hundred and Twelve before Witnesses Andrew Louttit, Shoemaker in Kirkwall, and David Eunson, Vinter there,

Will. Graham.[26]

Why such a change of heart? There is a clue in the phrase 'I desire that the same after being used at my burial': Graham wanted a full

Masonic funeral, and it seems he thought the older lodge would be better set up to take charge of it. To encourage them to do so, he left them his remaining Masonic treasure from No. 128, his Atholl Book of Constitutions. His mort cloth is a bit of a puzzle, but Graham had also been a strong proponent of religious freedom, even though this fervour backfired on him. In 1796 he had supported the formation of what was known as an Anti-Burgher congregation. They practised an extreme form of Presbyterianism and decided to split from the established Presbyterian church because of a dispute between the Kirkwall Incorporated Trades (a guild of Kirkwall tradesmen) and the Cathedral Session (the body governing St Magnus Cathedral) over the charges made for the use of the Cathedral mort cloth (a pall to be spread over a coffin) that was hired out for funerals. Graham, acting as Master of the Lodge of St Paul's, laid the foundation stone of the Anti-Burgher meeting hall with full Masonic ritual. The minutes of Kirkwall Kilwinning had this to say:

It is necessary further to remark that this new Society of St Paul's Lodge had not been incorporated many months when it was resolved among them, on Mr Graham's motion, to establish an Anti-Burgher meeting house in Kirkwall. The plan of the foundations being arranged and the execution of the work being about to commence, Graham with his promiscuous brethren, which by this time had become very numerous, proceeded to lay the Foundation Stone, when Graham, after performing a great many antique tricks, kneeled down, made a long prayer, and dedicated this Church to their Titular Saint, and then with his brethren paraded the streets of this place to no small amusement of the public.[27]

But the issues worrying the new Anti-Burgher Church soon became more than just the cost of hiring a ceremonial shroud. Shortly afterwards their newly appointed minister encouraged his congregation to pass a rule prohibiting Freemasons from continuing or becoming members of the sect. That move cost Graham many members, and he appealed to Lodge Kirkwall Kilwinning to support St Paul's in a move to appeal against this extreme Presbyterian ruling that the Masonic Oath and connections with Freemasonry were a cause for excommunication.

Was the bequest of his own mort cloth Graham's final apology for his attempt to split Freemasonry in Kirkwall by founding a separate lodge? Perhaps that is how it was taken, for the Lodge of St Paul did not long survive the death of its founding Master, while Kirkwall Kilwinning still meets in the centre of Kirkwall.

So ended William Graham's 26-year love affair with Lodge Kirkwall Kilwinning. On his deathbed he was reconciled with his first love, the love to whom he had given his greatest treasure, an early floorcloth, as a betrothal gift.

There remains, though, the question of why William might want to disguise this old Masonic floorcloth by adding outer panels?

The reason can be seen in the difference between the mythical traditions of London and Orkney. Orcadians would notice the visual references to Norse Goddess worship, that the cloth contained, whilst London Masons would only see Eve in the garden. Until 1468 C.E. Orkney remained Norse. The Norse were not generally Christianised until the early twelfth century, and they worshipped a range of Gods and Goddesses, one of their favourites being the Goddess who gave her name to Friday, Freyja's day. The images and stories of Freyja would be little known in London but were part of the pre-Christian heritage of Orkney. This distinction remained until recent times, as Speth, in his 1897 article, said of the Kirkwall Scroll:

> *The central panels speak for themselves. They commence at the top with Eve and the animals in the Garden of Eden – but why Adam is omitted would be difficult to say, and end at the bottom with the Craft degrees.* 28

Apart from the problem that Speth has reversed the order of scenes, not realising how the floorcloth would be unfurled, he has no Norse knowledge. In Orkney, the depiction of a naked female sitting before a backdrop of hills under an apple tree, surrounded by the adoring beasts of the sky, sea and field does not speak of Eve, it says Freyja. Only the addition of the obviously Biblical side panels makes the top of the scroll look at all like Eve in the garden of Eden. William Graham must have realised this. Was this why he decided to add Biblical-looking side pieces – to make it more acceptable to Kirkwall Masons? James Flett, in his history of Lodge Kirkwall Kilwinning says:

> *Remember the distrust and superstitious awe with which Freemasonry was held by a large majority of the populace. … The rulers of Kirkwall in those days of superstition had a way of governing all and sundry with the 'iron fist'. In fact the Town Council and the Church held supreme sway over all Orkney. The most trivial breaches of the law were dealt with by magistrates too often in a cruel manner, and without doubt, they glaringly overstepped their authority on many occasions. … The Church as a body was not always impartial when meting out*

justice to offenders and looked upon the secret society of Freemasons with little favour.[29]

So just what old Scottish and Norse beliefs was William Graham trying to disguise by Christianising this old Masonic floorcloth?

The Role of the Goddess Freyja

Professor Hilda Ellis Davidson explains what the Norse believed about a supreme Goddess:

> *The literary sources tend to give the impression of one supreme and powerful goddess who might be regarded as wife or mistress of her worshipper. If he were a king, her cult would become part of the state religion, and she would receive official worship as part of the state religion along with the leading gods. In Scandinavian tradition the main goddess appears to be Freyja.*[30]

Temples to Freyja were extremely important to the Norse Jarls who built them. They believed that their political power depended on protecting these sacred buildings. When Olaf Tryggvason wanted to overthrow Jarl Hakon of Halogaland, the de facto king of Norway in the late tenth century, he did it by breaking down the image of Freyja from the temple where Hakon worshipped. Tryggvason dragged the image of the goddess out from her temple behind his horse, eventually breaking it up and burning it to dishonour his rival.[31]

A temple to Freyja was built at Trondheim by Sir William St Clair's ancestors, and it was from them that he derived his claim to the Norse Earldom of Orkney. But there are further points of Masonic interest about this temple. First, it was eastward-facing and had two pillars at its entrance. This was discovered when this temple was excavated during repairs to the floor of the medieval church dedicated to the Virgin Mary which later Christians built on top of it. Under these pillars a series of tiny pictures impressed into gold foil had been deliberately buried.[32] One is of particular Masonic interest, since it shows two strange beings in a five-pointed embrace.

When I first saw this image I thought it looked rather like two fish carrying out a Third Degree ceremony in a Masonic lodge: one looks like a male fish and the other a female. The metal gold was sacred to Freyja. Here is an image, carefully pressed into gold and ritually buried under the pillar foundations of the temple of Freyja in the ancient Jarldom of Møre, in what is now Trondheim. This temple was used for worship by Jarl Hakon, who believed he was the husband of the goddess.

Fig 5: Gold sheet with two impressed fingers
This was buried under a pillar at the entrance to the Temple of Freyja in Trondheim.

In *The Book of Hiram*, Chris Knight and I used evidence from Phoenician archaeology, the writings of contemporaries and inscriptions deciphered from the tombs of long-dead Phoenician kings to reconstruct the cycle of kingship that involved a king marrying a Goddess to become a god himself. And we pointed out their similarity to the rituals of Freemasonry.

We now knew that our Grand Master Hiram, King of Tyre, held the following religious belief: every year Baal, the son of Baalat and El, dies in the autumn equinox and is reborn at the vernal equinox. Checking out the dates given by Josephus, we know that Hiram of Tyre was conceived at the vernal Equinox and born at the Winter Solstice, when Venus rose close before the Sun. This made him a son of Venus. When his father died, Hiram had to change from being the Son of the Goddess to embracing her in marriage. This raised him from a Prince to a King.

As Baal, he entered the Temple of Venus on the eve of the autumnal equinox and ritually but only symbolically died, acting out his role as Baal. He was laid to rest, his feet pointing East and his head West, in the darkness of the inner sanctum of the Temple. Just before dawn Venus rose as the bright Morning Star, and as the light of the Goddess shone down, between the two pillars of the porchway, through the dormer and into the temple, the High Priestess, the light of Venus now back-lighting the whiteness of her body against the darkness of the sanctum, raised Hiram, the new king, in a wifely embrace. The embrace we could see depicted in the ritual picture found at the Temple of Venus at Møre. The embrace we had both experienced when we became Master Masons. But why a five-pointed embrace?

The planet Venus, as she moves around the sky, touches the path of the Sun (the Zodiac) in just five places. So the High Priestess of Baalat

personifies the Goddess as she comes to her husband at dawn, just as he
rises from below the dark earth.

First she reaches down to take his hand, then she places her right foot
against his. Two priests of El, who celebrate the Sun at his zenith and
setting, assisted her to pivot the king forward out of the cold embrace of
his grave into the warm embrace of the Goddess. As Hiram is lifted by
the priests of El, the High Priestess presses her right knee against his, she
pulls him tightly to her breast and completely embraces him, throwing her
arm across his shoulders to reach down his back as she breathes the secret
words of kingship, into his ear.

So the new king embraces the Goddess in the five-pointed embrace,
which can be seen each generation in the higher reaches of heaven, and
his power is established. This is the secret knowledge which Solomon
bought so dearly from Hiram, King of Tyre, and the detail has been
preserved in the weird and ancient rituals of Freemasonry. [33]

But there is another link between the cult of Freyja and early
Freemasonry. All the key events of the start of Scottish Freemasonry
take place on the Feast day of St John the Evangelist – 27 December.
Here was another coincidence. Just as Christianity had seized the site
of Freyja's temple and built a church to the Virgin Mary on top of it,
so they had taken the feast day of Freyja's birth, 27 December, and
renamed it in favour of St John. So, did St John become one of the
patron saints of Masons because his name was attached to a key date
in the calendar of the Norse-aware William St Clair? In Rosslyn
Chapel he incorporated many symbols, some Christian, some Jewish,
but many drawn from the pre-Christian beliefs of his Norse ancestors,
and his Norse ancestry was important to him (it was his family links
to the Jarldom of Møre that gave him the Earldom of Orkney).

At all events, all the early evidence of Scottish Freemasonry talks of the importance of decisions taken at meetings of Masons on the Feast of St John on 27 December. Of William Schaw and his first meeting of Scottish Masons which led to the creation of the modern Lodge system defined in the Schaw Statutes, David Stevenson says:

It is highly likely that William Schaw had convened his meeting of master masons on 27 December, the most important day in the Masonic Calendar, and it was as a result of the discussions then held that the First Schaw Statutes were drafted and agreed the following day.[34]

But there is another odd link between the rituals of Freyja and the rituals of Freemasonry: the manner in which a candidate is prepared for Initiation. The candidate is blindfolded and ritually threatened with death by strangulation and stabbing. This form of human sacrifice has a long history in western Europe, with supporting evidence coming from its bogs, the last resting places of many such offerings to Freyja.

A Candidate Properly Prepared

In 1963 Dr Alfred Dieck, of Hanover University, carried out a survey of all the preserved bog bodies found in north-west Europe: 690 in all.[35] The oldest were from the Mesolithic period, making them at least 5,000 years old, and the most recent were soldiers killed in the Masurian Lakes region of Poland during World War 1. But the majority of these bog people date from between 500 B.C.E. and 100 C.E., and there are a number of common features about the way they met their ends. They were offered as human sacrifices.[36]

P.V. Glob, Professor of Archaeology at Aarhus University in Denmark, made a detailed study of the way these people died.

Surveying the vast corpus of finds from Denmark's Early Iron Age and relating our knowledge to the numerous discoveries of bog people's deposition it emerges clearly that the circumstances of the bog people's deposition show nothing in common with normal burial customs, but on the contrary have the characteristics of sacrificial deposits. Probably, then, the bog people were offered to the same powers as the other bog finds, and belong to the gods.[37]

And in his *Germanicus* the Roman historian Tacitus said of the religion of the tribes of north-west Europe 2,000 years ago:

They do not consider it compatible with the greatness of the heavenly powers to confine their gods within four walls or to represent them in the likeness of a human face. They consecrate groves and coppices, and give the name God to that secret presence which they can see only in awe and adoration.[38]

There is a special way to kill a person who is to be sacrificed to the Goddess. When Walfred, an English Christian missionary, broke down Her images in Uppsala in 1070 the local believers promptly strangled him, and his body was thrown into the bog.[39] In his case this was a punishment for heresy and blasphemy against the Goddess, but in the case of the formal sacrifices of earlier times a more complex ritual was followed.

Tacitus tells how these honoured emissaries to the Goddess were chosen by lot.

A branch cut from an apple tree is divided up into small splinters. Each of these is marked with a distinctive sign, so that they can be distinguished from others. They are then thrown blindfold and at random on to a white cloth. [40]

Whoever drew the long twig was the chosen one. This method is confirmed by an archaeological find made at Borre Fen, in Denmark's Himmerland region. Beneath the body of a woman, killed in the ritual way, were found a number of slivers of apple wood, which, Glob says, 'could indicate a casting of lots which sealed her fate and brought her into the bog as a human sacrifice'. [41]

In 1946 there was another find in a Himmerland bog, near Rebild Skovhuse. It was a carved wooden figure of Freyja with its sex enhanced as a V-shaped incision in the area of the lap. [42] Was this a representation of the goddess whom people drew slivers of apple wood to be with?

At the beginning of the era of the bog people it was not a male but a female god that was dominant; and her servant, who fulfilled the role of male deity, had to be sacrificed at the completion of the journeyings so that the cycle of nature might be supported and helped forward. [43]

The chosen sacrifice was fed a ceremonial meal of a sort of porridge. It was made of a mixture of grains. Detailed botanical investigation of the stomach contents of a sacrificial victim found at Tollund, Denmark, showed it to consist of a gruel of barley, linseed, 'gold-of-pleasure' and knotweed. [44] This meal seems ceremonial, containing no traces of meat, which is known to have been part of the normal diet of the Danes at that time. Dr Helbaek, who carried out the tests, thought that the meal was eaten about 24 hours before death. Although the mix of seeds varied between victims, knotweed is a common factor.

The victims often had their eyes bound and were either naked or had a rough sheepskin or linen cloak about their shoulders. Pollen studies of the peat immediately below bog body finds discovered in the last fifty years have shown that most of the sacrifices took place in winter.[45] The method of dispatch was twofold; the victims were stabbed and strangled, then they were thrown into the waters of the bog. It would seem that the noose around a candidate's neck that Masons call a cable tow has a long history.

> *The rope nooses, which many of the bog people carry round their necks and which caused their deaths, are a further sign of sacrifice to the goddess. ... They are replicas of the twisted neck-rings which are the mark of honour of the goddess, and a sign of consecration to her. The neck-ring is expressly the sign of the fertility goddess ... at the end of the Bronze Age. ... The rope noose round the dead bog man's neck should be seen as a neck-ring and so as the pass which carries him over the threshold of death and delivers him into the possession of the goddess, consecrating him to her for all time.*[46]

Hilda Ellis Davidson says of this deity, that she 'was held to possess power over life and death'. Fortunately a detailed description of the method of sacrifice survives. In 922 C.E. a chief of the Rus tribe from Scandinavia died in Bulghar, a port on the River Volga, just at the time that an Arab embassy including a scholar by the name of Ibn Fadlan was visiting the local king. Ibn Fadlan – known as 'the truth-teller', because of his reputation as a reliable reporter – took great interest in strange religious customs, and he witnessed and recorded the chief's funeral rites. These included the sacrifice of a young woman to the Goddess.[47] The sacrifice was carried out by an old priestess, whom Ibn Fadlan called 'the Angel of Death', and her two younger assistants, called her 'daughters'. The fact the dead chief was far from home on a trading expedition suggests either that the priestesses of the Goddess must have travelled with him, or else there must have been a shrine to the goddess established in Bulghar, which was on a regular trade route. Ibn Fadlan, although a truth-teller is not all-knowing, and he does not mention how the sinister 'Angel of Death' came to be there at the time of the funeral – but her presence is perhaps some indication of the importance of the goddess religions to the seafaring Scandinavians.

Hilda Ellis Davidson said of the young woman whose sacrifice was a key element in the Norse funeral:

We know there were a number of woman slaves. … It was these who were asked if anyone would volunteer to act as the wife of the chieftain and to die at his funeral, and one girl agreed to this.[48]

Her role in the ritual, which Ibn Fadlan assures us she carried out eagerly, involved considerable effort to learn complex ritual. Only a religious incentive could be used in these circumstances, since material rewards mean little if you are to die. Was she being offered a chance to become one with the Goddess? A chance to be taken into a state of bliss in a place beyond death? A chance to win the eternal favour of the Goddess? Ibn Fadlan does not know, but the lure of supernatural reward must have been strong to overcome the fear of death and the process of dying. Let us return to the truth-teller's account of that process.

First the body of the dead chief was buried for nine days. During this time his sacrificial 'wife' was escorted by the Angel of Death and her daughters, and treated as a princess. She spent her time eating, drinking and singing songs of celebration about her future. After nine days the body was dug up, dressed in new finery and laid on a couch aboard a ship pulled up on to the shore for the purpose. The chief was provided with food and drink, animals were killed to accompany him – a dog, two horses, a cock and a hen – and his 'wife' dispatched the hen by cutting off its head. She had sexual intercourse with his closest kinsmen, to consummate her marriage. Then she sang a complex song of farewell to her female companions in which she described seeing her dead parents and her kinsfolk standing with her new husband in a fair green Paradise and preparing to go to meet them. This complete, she gave her arm rings to the Angel of Death and her finger rings to the daughters before drinking many cups of strong 'wedding ale'.

She was then taken into the pavilion or tent where the dead man lay. The Angel of Death put a running noose around her neck, and two attendants strangled her while the old priestess stabbed her in the heart.

The boat was burnt to ashes and a mound erected over it. Ellis Davidson likens Ibn Fadlan's account of a ship funeral with one excavated at Oseberg in southern Norway, and dated to about 850 C.E. It showed many of the features of this funerary ritual, except that the boat had been buried, not burnt. The boat contained beds for the bodies of the chief and his wife which had fine hangings.

Many female characters, some from the Otherworld, are depicted on the hangings, indicating a strong link between the goddess and the realm of death. There is also much symbolism associated with the Goddess Freyja.[49]

Norse Beliefs and Early Freemasonry

Over a whole series of books I have developed an hypothesis that modern Freemasonry was created by William St Clair during the building of the Chapel at Roslin. I believe that he drew on various religious traditions, such as Enochian Judaism, Phoenician Goddess worship, Christianity and the Norse mythology of Freyja.

The Kirkwall Scroll, dating from the earliest days of Freemasonry, uses the symbolism of a path towards what is known today in Freemasonry as 'the centre' This is a state of being which is at one with creation. But this, the oldest symbolic document describing the purpose of Masonic ritual, uses the metaphor of a Norse Deity. Freyja was dear to William St Clair's ancestors. Would it not be appropriate for him to use Her as a symbol of the 'God experience' which is the focus of Freemasonry?

The symbolic path that Walter Wilmshurst said is the purpose of Freemasonry is also found on the oldest symbolic document of Masonry. The oldest part of the Kirkwall Scroll shows the symbolic spiritual journey of Freemasonry and has been radiocarbon dated to round 1490 C.E. This is the time when Freemasonry was established in Scotland by the St Clairs of Roslin. But the Scroll itself is too crude to have been commissioned by William St Clair, the chapel builder. Its date suggests it may have been created by one of the earliest lodges of Freemasons, trying to make sure the spiritual secrets of their new Order survived and flourished. And my bet is that it was created in Aberdeen, during the rebuilding of the choir of the burgh church of St Nicholas.

If this idea is correct, then the path of Freemasonry evolved from a mix of some of the oldest teachings on spiritual growth. We Masons have inherited a treasure from our Ancient Brethren, but how should we use it, and how pass it on 'unsullied' to future generations? That is the final question I need to address as I complete my quest to understand why Freemasonry appeals to me. What responsibility do I and my brother Masons have, to preserve the teaching of the Craft?

[1] Pribram (1969), p. 78.
[2] Flett (1976), p. 5.
[3] Lomas (2002), chap. 12.
[4] Gourlay (2000).
[5] Gourlay (2000).
[6] Lomas & Knight (1996), p. 358.
[7] Stevenson (1988), p. 15.
[8] The Original Statutes of the Lodge of Aberdeen, Grand Lodge of Scotland.
[9] Thomson (1987), p. 209.
[10] Thomson (1987), p. 219.
[11] Lane's List.
[12] Flett (1976), p. 47.
[13] Thomson (1987), pp. 207–9.
[14] Flett (1976), p. 5.
[15] Thomson (1987), p. 5.
[16] Stevenson (1988), p. 34.
[17] Flett (1976), p. 4.
[18] Flett (1976), p. 5.
[19] Flett (1976), p. 68.
[20] Flett (1976), p. 69.
[21] Flett (1976), p. 155.
[22] Thomson (1987), p. 233.
[23] Flett (1976), p. 33.
[24] Thomson (1987), p. 233.
[25] Flett (1976), p. 33.
[26] Flett (1976), p. 63.
[27] Flett (1976), p. 48.
[28] Speth & Craven (1897).
[29] Flett (1976), p. 6.
[30] Ellis Davidson (1993), p. 48.

[31] Ellis Davidson (1993), p. 126.
[32] Liden (1969), pp. 23–32.
[33] Lomas & Knight (2004), p. 158.
[34] Stevenson (1988), p. 47.
[35] Dieck (1963).
[36] Glob (1971), p. 22.
[37] Glob (1971), p. 108.
[38] Tacitus (1980), p. 109.
[39] Adam of Bremen ([1070] 2002).
[40] Tacitus (1980), p. 109.
[41] Glob (1971), p. 22.
[42] Glob (1971), p. 108.
[43] Glob (1971), p. 132.
[44] Helbaek (1950), p. 164.
[45] Jorgensen (1958), p. 119.
[46] Glob (1971), p. 119.
[47] Smyser (1965).
[48] Ellis Davidson (1998), p 164.
[49] Ellis Davidson (1998), p. 167.

Chapter Thirteen

Where Now for Freemasonry?

Looking Backwards for a Way Forward

This book has been about my search for a meaning in Masonry, and an attempt to try to explain why such a weird ritualistic system can be so satisfying to take part in. That quest began a few weeks before my Initiation on 27 January 1988. It took me forward to studies of brain function that nobody had even thought of until sixteen years after I was initiated, and back five hundred years to the earliest Masonic artifact.

At first the way was confusing. I spent many years looking at the beginnings of Freemasonry before I stumbled across a golden thread of belief. It connected the unknown artist who created the Kirkwall Scroll to an Edwardian solicitor who spent his spare time pondering the mysteries of Masonry. Both understood the deep power of symbolism. Both used it to map out a path to the real secret at the centre of Masonry: knowledge of yourself.

On a small piece of salmon-pink notepaper stuffed in the back of a red-bound legal notebook I found this handwritten note by Walter Wilmshurst, dated June 1908:

The body of a human is the greatest marvel of creation, and can be made the most delicate instrument in the world. It is the God-given instrument of living science and its perfecting is an integral part of Masonic training.

It goes on to speak of the great issue at the centre of my quest.

I believe there is a science of sciences, and this I hold to be the science of Masonic Initiation. ... There are perfected men, who in varying degrees possess this science, and are therefore kin with the living intelligences of the universe, who are the natural modes of the divine mind.

Wilmshurst believed he had found a direct telephone line to god. And, although as a scientist I find this unlikely, it is an issue about which I have no quarrel with him. There is no objective way to say which of us is right.

I believe in the laws of physics. To me the only miracle is the fact there are no miracles. I share with Newton and Einstein in accepting that a scientist has a sense of universal causation. My religious feelings take a form Einstein described as:

Rapturous amazement at the harmony of natural law, which reveals an intelligence of such superiority that, compared with it, all the systematic thinking and acting of human beings is an utterly insignificant reflection. [1]

This feeling is a subjective state of my brain that can be reproduced in a laboratory or a thunderstorm. It can even be induced by meditating on Masonic symbols, as Walter Wilmshurst taught me. We share this view of the purpose of Masonry with our ancient Brother who painted the Kirkwall Scroll. On the seventh step of this mystical floorcloth he encourages the Masonic pilgrim to view the world as a place of harmony and oneness with creation. A naked female sits under a fruiting tree, looking out over the animals of the sky, sea and field as they live in accord under the benevolent gaze of the sun, moon and stars. The Bright Morning Star is replaced by a symbol which, if seen on pottery from level III of the Neolithic city of Çatal Hüyük in Anatolia, would be interpreted as the vulva of the Lady of the Beasts.[2] This mother goddess ruled over wolves and lions, grain and birth, and is associated with mountains. By the ninth century C.E. she was known to the Norse as Freyja, and her symbol was the apple tree.[3] But that is too long a story to tell in this book.

The link between William St Clair, the founder of Freemasonry, and the Knights Templar has been contentious since The Hiram Key came out. I am happy that the hypothesis laid out in that book is strong enough to stand on its own merits, and detailed discussion of it is also beyond the scope of this present volume. But there is no question that William St Clair's family built an east-facing temple with two pillars at its entrance. This building was in Trondheim, a key city of the Møre region of Norway.[4] As I have already mentioned, it was destroyed around 1000 C.E. by Olaf Tryggvason as part of a series of battles which resulted in William's ancestor Rognwald of Mørc becoming Jarl of Orkney. In time, William would inherit Orkney as an Earldom, just before the Kirkwall Scroll was painted.

The painter of the Kirkwall Scroll shows his vision of oneness with the centre as oneness with a goddess. Was this the Norse goddess Freyja? When I look at the Scroll I like to think the figure in the seventh panel is her, but it might mean more to you to see the figure as Eve in the Garden of Eden. That is the flexibility of a symbol: it speaks on many levels, and we should not rush to enforce a particular definition on any Masonic symbol.

But, moving on to the question of the reality or otherwise of a god, which it might seem I have tacitly accepted in this book, does a common human experience of a state of transcendental awareness mean that god exists? There is no way to tell. If a god or goddess exists, and it does not want to break the laws of physics, then this is the only way it can communicate with us. Einstein talks of 'the harmony of natural law, which reveals an intelligence of such superiority that, compared with it, all the systematic thinking and acting of human beings is an utterly insignificant reflection'. If there is such a being, it cannot randomly break its own laws, or it ceases to maintain that harmony of natural law. So its only remaining means of contact with humanity is via the state of mind that Persinger calls the 'God experience'.

The painter of the Kirkwall Scroll thinks of a Goddess experience. And Walter Wilmshurst, twentieth-century pillar of the United Grand Lodge of England, Past Assistant Grand Director of Ceremonies, Past Provincial Senior Grand Warden of the Province of Yorkshire West Riding, and President of the Masonic Study Circle, agrees with this widely uncelebrated Scottish artist. In an unpublished lecture he explained why Freemasons are called 'sons of the widow'.

All Initiates have a common mother. In Egypt she was called Isis, the universal widow. Do not be frightened of a so-called pagan name. Names change, but reality endures. Later she came to be called 'the Jerusalem above that is the Mother of us all'. The Hermetic texts call her the Virgin Mother of the world, the collective over-soul of Humanity, out of which each of us has sprung as her individualised offspring and to whose breast we shall all one day be gathered back again into unity. She is called a Widow because of the calamity that left her severed from her true Centre and Spouse. She mourns for her children, who are scattered in discord.

An ancient Hermetic oracle declared that to lift that Widow's veil spells death. Nothing mortal can look upon her face and live. The death meant was of the kind implied in our Third Degree, the death of all that is vain, unworthy, unreal, in yourself. Only what is immortal in you can gaze upon immortality unveiled, and none who has lifted the veil of the Goddess can thereafter continue to live as before. Your old self, your old life, dies and, just as in our ceremony the Candidate is made to turn and gaze back upon the emblems of mortality, so for the true Master Mason there comes the time when you look back upon your former self as upon the memory of a dream that troubled yet passed with the night. Thenceforward you enter upon a new life with the light of your own Morning Star your guide.

Walter Wilmshurst did not know about the Kirkwall Scroll. What a great pity he never saw this ancient Masonic proof of his vision of the transcendental experience that lies at the centre of Freemasonry. This marvellous state of mind may well be a wonderful experience, but it does not prove or disprove the existence of a deity. In the light of this insight, Freemasonry is wise to say, 'Every person's opinions are their own private property, and the rights of all to maintain their own are perfectly equal'.

The 'God experience' feels real, but that does not prove it is real. Dreams feel real when we have them, but when we wake we know them to be unreal. You could argue, as some mystics have, that what is less real is contained within that which is more real. Just as a dream is contained within the mind of the dreamer, so the 'God experience' is more real than our subjective awareness of self that seems to be contained within the oneness of transcendental bliss.[5]

There is a brain state, which can be reached accidentally or deliberately, that causes transcendental awareness. But we have no way to measure its reality. Our sense of reality is based entirely on how our brains process the external signals they receive, so we have no way of knowing if we are perceiving actual reality, or if we are creating a false impression from an unusual sequence of nerve impulses. The tool for measuring the state, and the organ for judging the reality of that state are the same. Hence, there is no external criterion by which to distinguish reality from delusion.

Newberg and D'Aquili say:

Although the notion of a reality more real than the one in which we live is difficult to accept without personal experience, when the mind drops its subjective preoccupation with the needs of the self and the material distractions of the world, it can perceive this greater reality. Mystical reality holds, and neurology does not contradict it, that beneath the mind's perceptions of thoughts, memories, emotions, and objects, beneath the subjective awareness we think of as self, there is a deeper self, a state of pure awareness that sees beyond the limits of subject and object, and rests in a universe where all things are one.[6]

The physical gains of reaching this deeper self are real. They are lower blood pressure, a decrease in heart rate, a lower rate of respiration, reduced levels of cortisol and a boost to the immune system. Persinger worried about the intolerant side effects of this state of mind, but said that it is useful, if religious fanaticism does not overwhelm its benefits. Freemasonry is the only spiritual system

I know that has evolved away from the risk of religious intolerance. It teaches you how to contact the centre, to experience oneness with creation, but it does not tell you what religious beliefs you must hold; all it asks is that you accept that there is a sense of order in the universe. It is as open to the scientist as it is to the religious mystic. And it gives both of them a shared symbolic system to enable them to talk about their insights into the human spirit without offending each other's belief systems.

Wilmshurst said:

Masonry is not a secular society. It is a house of the spirit. It is to be lived in the spirit as well as in the ritual. We who live it know that the sacred law of life itself, like our ceremonies that are dramatised images of that life, subjects us to repeated tests. Those who do not pass the tests remain self-inhibited from moving towards larger knowledge and deeper experience of that veiled at the centre of Masonic allegory.

The purpose of Freemasonry is to help its members become initiates in the Science of Life. If you want to know yourself, then Freemasonry offers a path to that knowledge. It is a spiritual adventure, fit for the athletic and adventurous mind.

But before you seek to explore the spiritual depths of the Craft, you should first sit down and weigh the cost. See that you are ready to build upon a rock, not on an unstable personal foundation. The initiate suffers mental anguish. Progress in Masonic science involves great changes to yourself, your normal mental outlook and your ways of living. The prizes are immense, yet remember they are not for yourself. Initiation involves exterminating your sense of personal self-hood to become a self-less instrument for the diffusion of light, wisdom and love to all beings. If you follow this course you will be building a temple of a perfected humanity.[7]

When you sense the light of the centre you realise a great sense of control over what would otherwise be the whims of fate. You feel that you are not alone in the cosmos, and your life becomes part of an intelligible plan. You know, deep in the tangle of your limbic system, that goodness can triumph, and even death has a purpose. This holds true whether there really is a deeper reality, or even if it is just a perception generated by an odd brain state. Either way, you realise that all religions and the gods they define are just ways of interpreting the transcendental bliss that mystics have known through the ages.

Freemasonry has evolved a spiritual system that does not have the superstitious baggage of most religions. But it is falling prey to the same failings that are destroying the church in modern Western society. It is losing track of its purpose and suffering a destructive failure to defend its core beliefs.

Blind Mother Nature has used a kind of intellectual sieve to create brains and intelligences which are increasingly competent to deal with the laws of nature. As human intelligence evolved, so the individuals who got the best opportunities to breed, and pass on their genes, were the ones whose brains helped them first to understand, later to predict and finally to exploit natural laws. Nature filtered out those individuals whose brains were not complex enough to learn. This is a process driven by an on-going interaction between consciousness and the physical world. As evolutionary biologist Stephen Jay Gould says:

Human cultural change is an entirely distinct process operating under radically different principles that do allow for the strong possibility of a driven trend to what we may legitimately call technological progress.[8]

This progress created a resonance between our brains and the universe which might explain something that puzzled Einstein when he said, 'the most incomprehensible property of the universe is that it is so comprehensible'.[9]

The next time you watch a candidate, prepared in the ancient Norse way as a sacrifice to the threefold goddess of Trondheim, ponder on how lucky the Craft is to have preserved a strand of this ancient wisdom. Our symbolism and myth draws on many sources: Enochian Judaism, early craft guilds, Egyptian builders, Phoenician traders and Norse temple-builders. The myths have been honed over thousands of years to nurture the human spirit. By maintaining and practising our ritual you can benefit your own harmony of mind, and preserve this great gift for future generations. But only if the Craft encourages and welcomes young people to join and learn.

The Future of Masonry?

There seems to be a new awareness of the spiritual self-improvement aspect of the Craft, and that it can fill a spiritual need which is not always met by religion. A difficulty scientists have with religion is the need to accept doctrines which are less than logical. Yet, as I have mentioned earlier, research shows that the spiritual practices which religions offer do improve people's state of happiness.

It may soon become possible, by surgical or chemical intervention, to improve those parts of the brain we consider worth improving and inhibit those functions which may be responsible for the dangers and contradictions facing modern society. Indeed, that is the purpose of Freemasonry: to help us learn how to live comfortably in balance with the stark reality of the cosmos.

I am heartened by the success of women's Freemasonry in Wales and England. It is growing and recruiting younger professional women into its ranks, and I wish the Sistren well. Clearly it is meeting a spiritual need and doing it well. Would that male Freemasonry were so successful.

But even ailing male Freemasonry has seen an upturn in recruitment, though this is not enough. Male Freemasonry has a real problem. Its natural conservatism combines with vested interests entrenched by long usage. This mind-set makes it difficult for young men to accept its outdated hierarchical attitudes; there are too many competing claims on the time of the younger generation for them to want to enter a system which does not bother to explain its purpose. But it could. Freemasonry is a heritage of ancient spiritual teaching, and it is held in trust by the present generation to pass on to our sons and daughters.

We saw in Part Two that there is a range of spiritual responses to be expected from shared ritual. There is room in Freemasonry for many types of lodges – for example we have lodges which share an interest in scouting, in amateur radio, or in the Internet. There is scope to develop more 'shared-interest' lodges, where members receive the spiritual uplift of the ritual and then move on to discuss their shared hobbies at the after-proceedings. However, we have a symbolic system which has evolved over hundreds of years to lift the spirit, so we should never water down the ritual and make arbitrary changes to it. Shared hobbies, by themselves, will not be enough to sustain us. We need the spiritual path that the ritual offers us, no matter how near or how far we may choose to follow it.

Wilmshurst warns us:

The popular idea of a successful lodge is one that has many members, works rituals every meeting, has many candidates, and a strong social programme.

These things have their worth, but the original idea of a lodge is quite different. It is a small community devoting itself in privacy to corporate work of a philosophical nature. This is for the intellectual development and spiritual perfecting of its members. Social amenities should be secondary incidents. It is desirable to practise these ideas if you want to revive the spiritual dimension of the Craft. [10]

The strength and worth of a lodge does not depend upon numbers and popular attractions. It rests on the quality of the corporate life of its members. It depends on their united and consistent co-operation towards a common ideal. Its success relies on their ability to form a group consciousness.

The Craft is an ancient discipline that is adapted for people who live in the real world and discharge domestic and secular duties. It is not like an enclosed order; it does not call upon you to follow any uniform rule of life, but leaves you to live your life in your own way. However, it helps you acquire ways to harmonise your outward and inward lives, and, as Wilmshurst's work shows, it lays down three definite guidelines that constitute a rule of life:

1. It emphasises continual obedience to Moral Law.
2. It calls for 'daily progress in Masonic Science' by following some form of helpful study, reflection or meditative practice adapted to one's taste and temperament.
3. It provides the symbolism of the working tools and the Tracing-boards for daily contemplation and reflection.

Wilmshurst advised us to pay attention to these points. Especially to our use of the symbolic working tools and Tracing-boards, which he said 'cannot be too closely or too often pondered upon and applied'.

However, there is little point in attracting new members and then failing them by not educating them in the spiritual tradition of the Craft. Lodges of Instruction must do more than endlessly rehearse ceremonies. New Masons need a forum to discuss the working tools, the Tracing-boards and the landmarks of the Order. Ideally, these should be informal seminars, vehicles to share ideas. They should meet on the level, without badges of office or trappings of rank. In an open seminar you must be ready to argue your case, submit to cross-examination and justify your beliefs. You may even have to change your view. But if Freemasons fail to do this, our Order will lose the respect of the next generation. New members may join but they will not stay, and Masonry will die. The educational programme for new Masons which the Grand Lodge of Queensland, Australia, has put in place is an example of good practice in this area. Freemasonry needs more such initiatives.

Remember what Wilmshurst said about Masonic education.

Throughout the ages the aspirant to Initiation has found it essential to pass under the personal tuition of some expert teacher who knows the way and can give him help suited to his personal requirements. Hence the Craft, following this traditional method, declares that every new Apprentice shall find a Master and from him gain instruction. For the opened lodge was never intended to be a place for instruction; it is a place for corporate realisation of the truths in which we are to be instructed privately elsewhere.

It rests not only upon the moral duty of every more advanced Brother to help the less advanced, but upon the spiritual principle that whoever has freely received must as freely give, that no one is initiated for his private advantage but must pass on his light to someone below him on the life-ladder.[11]

As a member of a lodge you value that membership. But, if you want to grow spiritually, you must do more. You are invited to co-operate actively and systematically with every other Brother in a concerted effort to realise your lodge as an organic unity of minds. It should be more than a temporary association of persons. The ritual should give a lift to your spirit and refresh you to face the outside world. The ancient, although unenforceable, penalties not only link you with a more brutal past world, they focus your mind on the reality of existence and warn that progress involves risk and effort. We should not restrict the use of these powerful emotional tools of ritual simply to satisfy the superstitious fears of people who have hostile and intolerant agendas to promote. Freemasons have as much natural right to practise their spiritual ways as any religion, and we should insist on our freedom of belief. Remember the words written by American Masons in the Declaration of Independence:

We hold these truths to be self-evident, that all men are created equal, that they are endowed by their Creator with certain unalienable Rights, that among these are Life, Liberty and the pursuit of Happiness. – That to secure these rights, Governments are instituted among Men, deriving their just powers from the consent of the governed.

Freemasons should insist on their right to pursue happiness in their own way, free from persecution. And yet Freemasonry should avoid becoming stuck in an authoritarian way of thinking. It sometimes behaves like a paternal Victorian business. The dangers and possibilities can be seen by looking at how similar organisations have grown and prospered. Computing-Tabulating-Recording Ltd (CTR) was in a shambolic condition when Thomas Watson became its President in 1914. It was a hierarchical mix of three disparate companies, Herman Hollerith's Tabulating Machine Company, and Charles Ranlett Flint's International Time Recording Company and Computing Scale Company of America. Most financial analysts of the time didn't give the resultant muddle much chance of surviving, let alone prospering.

At his first meeting with all the managers of the merged companies Thomas Watson, the new company president, showed them what he called 'The Man Proposition.'

He wrote this list on a flip-chart:

The Manufacturer
General Manager
Sales Manager
Sales Man
Service Man
Factory Manager
Factory Man
Office Manager
Office Man

Let his biographer Kevin Maney take up the story:

Then Watson crossed out all of the letters of the job titles except for the word Man. Watson said that everybody in the company was important and every man was equal. 'We are just men,' Watson continued. 'Men standing together, shoulder to shoulder, all working for one common good.'[12]

Using this philosophy Watson turned the ailing CTR into the enormously successful IBM.

Likewise, Freemasons working together can make our Order thrive. An example of good practice is to be found in Scottish Freemasonry, which has no individual rank higher than Brother. The Most Worshipful, the Grand Master Mason, Brother Buggins is still Brother Buggins; it is the office of Grand Master Mason which is most worshipful. We live in an age where all young professionals understand and use the concept of the 'flat organisation' that Watson used to build IBM. Watson preached working together 'on the level', and this is just what our ritual teaches us to do.

Freemasonry does need to modernise. It must adapt its times and modes of meeting to fit in with the limited spare time of the younger generation it wants to encourage to join. Young professionals, when they first join a lodge, do not want to spend their limited spare time as unpaid bar-keepers or waiters. The more progressive lodges hire bar staff and waitresses, rather than alienating new members by trying to force them into acting as stewards. That system may have worked in more subservient times, but it has no future if Freemasonry wants to recruit and retain new blood. However, revising its social arrangements does not mean that Freemasonry should fiddle with the ritual, for Masonic ritual works well. If it ain't broke don't fix it!

There has already been too much arbitrary changing of ritual by appeasers who have butchered metaphors and removed symbolic actions that they did not understand, to fit in with the prejudices of bigots who are not Freemasons. The ritual is our heritage. It has evolved to meet the spiritual needs of Brethren and been refined by constant repetition. We should never allow it to be changed by self-appointed, ignorant censors, but only by the corporate spirit of the lodge. The ritual of a lodge belongs to that lodge and should be cherished and preserved.

Freemasonry has grown and prospered, despite years of problems and appeasement. This is because it is permeated by an unseen force that makes it work. Freemasons 'happily meet, happily part and happily meet again' because the culture of Masonry has an internal discipline which makes it continue. This secret force is the power of ritual, the key part of the spiritual reward of being a Mason.

Ritual turns a group of separate individuals into a living, regenerating corporate culture. It is the DNA of Freemasonry. As we saw in Part Two, ritual is a meme which evolves and grows. Over four centuries our evolving ritual has developed a spiritual reward to encourage Initiates to share their teaching. Each lodge contains its own set of ritual-DNA, the genes of its future existence. This pattern tells the members what to do and how to work with other lodges. This is the mechanism which has kept our Order a living, regenerating entity, and we interfere with it at our peril. Changing the ritual without understanding is like practising uncontrolled genetic engineering, or disrupting Masonry's chromosomes by irresponsibly bombarding its gonads with high-energy radiation. The results are unpredictable, but all outcomes have a high probability of creating monsters that can no longer reproduce themselves.

Freemasons do many things in their lodges that strike outsiders as unusual. Sometimes candidates disagree with our ideas and believe they know better ways. As long as the ritual is left to work its spiritual magic, this is not a problem. But we must always bear in mind that the power of the ritual lies in the way it has evolved to create a group mind out of a disparate huddle of individuals. We mess with this at the peril of our Order's long-term survival.

Physically we are separate individuals. We live in different places. We have our personal obligations and duties. But mentally we need to learn to become free Masons – by which I mean we should assert the freedom of our spirits to rise above the limitations of separateness and distance. When you join a lodge you agree to meet at a common centre, and there – literally and Masonically – you build, with the members of your Lodge, a mental community or group-mind. This is the real purpose of the Masonic art.

Your lodge-room is your psychological retreat. Every day, for at least a few moments, you can make a point to project your will in an effort to realise your corporate unity with the members of your Lodge. This will focus and refresh your spirit. Following the precedent of our lost Grand Master Hiram Abif, every day at the hour of high twelve, banish every other concern from your thoughts and visualise yourself and your fellow members gathered together in Lodge, in peace, concord, and charity with each other.

If the members of a lodge do this conscientiously and regularly, it brings about the following results:

1. In a mental but real sense the lodge will meet every day, not just at distant intervals.
2. It will increase the harmony of thought and the unity and concentration of purpose at the times when the lodge does meet physically. This will increase the enjoyment and benefit of the ritual.

3. The lodge-room will come to fulfil the purpose for which it was consecrated. It will form a focus point and storage place for its members' collective thoughts and aspirations.

Each member should contribute a daily quota to this concerted work at the lodge-room, and I would suggest you think of it as part of the daily 'Masonic labour' to which your obligation committed you. All Masons will recognise that this is the real use of the 24-in gauge, whether it is thought of as 'labour', 'refreshment', or 'prayer', and will probably find it includes all three terms.

Do not give up on this spiritual practice simply because it may feel futile or fanciful. You may experience no benefit from it at first. But, if you persist, you will get results. No candidate can enter a lodge without first meeting opposition and giving the proper knocks. In this higher sense of seeking to enter the lodge you may meet with barriers of inertia, diffidence or unbelief in yourself. These will only give way when you apply knocks of resolute effort to them.

And do not fall into the trap of thinking that this work is too feeble to be worth the effort. The desire to collaborate is itself a contribution and helps your spirit benefit. The more you develop that desire by practice, the greater will be your contribution. Meeting upon the level is the common aim.

If you are tempted to skip this regular meditation and reflection, then you short-change yourself and miss out on the therapeutic benefits of the ritual. If you cannot observe the practice precisely at noon, perform it as near to that time as you can. You can, of course, repeat it at other times of the day – or as often as you want – in addition to the appointment at high twelve. In this way you discipline yourself to take regular breaks when you actively relax.

Your Lodge will become a mental refuge from the pressures of daily life. You can mentally retreat there at will. If you follow up this practice with regular discussion at Lodge meetings you will draw from the common pool of thought-energy. Weaker and less efficient contributors are enriched by the more capable ones, and so are gradually raised to equality with them.

This book has looked at the spiritual lessons of the Craft, trying to separate them from the mass of outward moral teaching within which they are deliberately veiled. I have written of many philosophic secrets. Some may startle or even give offence to you, until you learn to receive their hidden wisdom with the simple vision of a child.

But if you follow the discipline and industry of the Masonic system, you will come to know the Blazing Star rising at your centre. Its self-convincing light will disclose to you all that now lies secret and unexplained.

But if we are to pass Freemasonry on to the next generation we must be more open about its purpose. Knowing it to be a system of societal and self development, we should take the performance of our rituals seriously and try to make sure that our ceremonies continue to work their spiritual magic for our initiates. I enjoy my Freemasonry and want to share and pass on the rituals and teaching which have benefited me.

Wilmshurst said:

The Craft's purpose is to help individuals reach the Initiate state. But do not imagine that Initiation is for your personal benefit. To make you complacent and self-satisfied is not the aim of the Craft. If you wish to understand this view, then consider these two facts.

Firstly, the path to attainment is of much too strenuous and painful a nature for the majority to take or even to wish to take it.

Secondly, this path involves the dying down and elimination of your sense of personal self-hood. To attain a higher state you will lose your present way of life before gaining one on a higher level.

To seek Initiation your motives must be altruistic. As an Initiate you will become enlightened when you become selfless and impersonal. You must dispel your own darkness. The uninitiated are blind to the limitation set by their egos, but the blind cannot lead the blind, save into ditches.

Initiates – individuals of vision and who know the Plan of Life – are needed for the world's guidance and salvation.[13]

Freemasonry works at many levels. You may join for the social aspects, but then find that you greatly enjoy the ritual working. The more you understand and practise, the more you begin to delight in the ceremonies. The real secrets of Freemasonry can only be lived, not given away or stolen; nothing you have read in this book will enable you to become a Mason, although it may encourage you to seek out a lodge and live the ritual for yourself.

Symbolic Explanations

I began this quest with a scientific analysis of the metaphor of Supreme Being. I want to close it by extending a temple metaphor first used by a great role model who continues to inspire me as a scientist, so as to illuminate the spiritual benefits of being made a Mason. In 1918, in a speech to the Physical Society in Berlin, Albert Einstein said:

In the temple of science are many mansions, and many indeed are they that dwell therein and the motives that have led them hither. Many take to science out of a joyful sense of superior intellectual power; science is their own special sport to which they look for vivid experience and the satisfaction of ambition; many others are to be found in the temple who have offered the products of their brains on this altar for purely utilitarian purposes. Were an angel of the Lord to come and drive all the people belonging to those two categories out of the temple, the assemblage would be seriously depleted. .... I am quite aware that we have just now light-heartedly expelled in imagination many excellent men who are largely responsible for the building of the temple of science. ... But of one thing I feel quite sure: if the types we have just expelled were the only types there were, the temple would never have come to be, any more than a forest can grow which consists of nothing but creepers. [14]

Einstein's analysis of motive can be applied to Freemasons. There are two ways of approaching the world. The first says that if you want a fulfilled and satisfying life, only you can make it happen. If you smile at somebody, they will smile back, and both of you will feel better about each other and the world. The more people do this, then the better the world becomes.

The second view says that the extent to which we are able to live a fulfilled and satisfying life depends entirely on the opportunities that the world gives us.

The first view says you must take personal responsibility for your own development and then help others to develop themselves. This leads to self-improvement. The second says either that there is no point in trying or that power groups must take social control of collective resources and make sure that all are treated equally. This can foster an acute awareness of oppression and control and create the impression that 'society' is to blame for the barrenness of many lives.

One view is about equality of opportunity, the other is about equality of reward, no matter how little or how much you contribute. The first view places inner development at the centre of progress, and the second gives priority to the outer world.

Both these views are extreme and unworkable. But then the question arises: 'where is the balance point, a point where the individual can live in harmony with society?' And that is a more complex question. Freemasonry offers an answer which seems to work. It says in its first ritual lesson to a newly made Mason:

Now you have been made a Mason you have a duty to spend time studying the basis of the sacred law, and in attempting to understand its standards of accuracy and equity before applying its dictates to your actions in life, towards the Cosmos, your fellow humans and to yourself.

In approaching the cosmos you should try to regain and retain the childish awe with which you first beheld the magnificence of the eternal heavens. By studying the precision of its movements you will be enabled to discover sources of consolation and sustenance.

You should act towards your fellow humans upon the square, by offering support and charity to the distressed in such a manner as you would expect them to behave to you were you ever to be in need.

Within yourself you should endeavour to become disciplined in your use of your physical and intellectual faculties in their fullest energy, thereby enabling you to exert all aspects of your talents to their best advantage.

Masons are citizens of the world, and as such should provide good role models in the discharge of their civil duties, they should never propose nor accept any act that is intended to subvert the accord and harmony of society; should obey the laws of any state in which they live and which offers them its guardianship; and, finally, never forget that there is in their hearts, a sacred and indissoluble attachment to that country which gave them birth and infant nurture.

As a human being I urge you to apply these thoughts to all domestic and public acts of merit. Let Prudence steer you; Temperance moderate you; Fortitude bolster you; and Justice inform all your achievements. Be most heedful to defend, to their highest lustre, those truly Masonic ornaments which have already been well exemplified, Benevolence and Charity.

In this book I have taken you on a journey of inquiry into the spiritual aspects of Freemasonry. I set out to turn the Hiram Key. But Masonic truths are traditionally illuminated by symbols, so I have drawn a symbol of the Hiram Key which represents my truth and feelings about Masonry. The symbol is threefold, and I will describe it from my scientist's viewpoint, although you may choose to interpret it differently.

The head of the key, the part I hold to turn it, is made up of the mystic sign. The square represents the independence of the brain's autonomous systems of arousal and quiescence. The compass symbolises a tool to measure, control and understand their responses. Together the square and compasses combine to form the lozenge-shaped handle for the key. It is linked by a square-section shaft to the symbol of the centre, the shape which engages with and unlocks the Glory there. It is a circle bounded by two pillars and represents the balance between light and darkness, good and bad, arousal and quiescence, the centre and the periphery. At the middle of the circle is the point from which you can no longer err.

I have tried to explain what I have discovered about the spiritual dimension of the Masonic method and how the initiatory system works in practice. I hope that what I have described may reveal

Fig 6: How I see the symbol of the Hiram Key

something of the invaluable light and wisdom concealed within our system. There is nothing hid which shall not be revealed in due course and to the properly prepared. The increasing anxiety of so many Brethren today to realise more fully the true content and purpose of our Order is a sign that the Light of the Centre is gradually breaking over the Craft. May more of its members find the knowledge of the lost but genuine secrets of their being.

The future is now in the hands of the Masonic Fraternity. I hope this book helps you to take advantage of Masonic teaching and to enlarge the borders of your understanding about this momentous and underestimated subject. And that you succeed in inspiring the next generation to benefit from, and continue, its teaching.

If it is to survive into the next generation, Masonry must attract young blood. The continued decline of organised religion in the West, exacerbated by scientific scepticism about its need to believe in miracles, cuts many people off from the real benefits of spiritual growth. The vacuum left by the decline of moderate churches is filled either by weird and wonderful New Age beliefs or by despotic religious fundamentalism. We all have a genetic need to believe in something. Our brains, it would seem, have evolved to make some sort of belief inevitable. But we can have choice in what we decide to believe. It is not necessary that we must automatically become biased against science, intolerant of the beliefs of others, or fail to live in harmony with the cosmos to find spiritual satisfaction.

Freemasonry offers a tolerant, inclusive, spiritual banquet for the inner spiritual hunger we all feel. And it tries to function without fostering superstitious intolerance or persecuting the diversity of human belief. If you are a Mason already, I hope this book will encourage you to explore more of our Order's spiritual warmth and to guard its landmarks well. If you are not a Mason, perhaps what I have told you about this antient pathway of the human spirit, will encourage you to learn and live it for yourself.

[1] Einstein [(1949) 1956], p. 29.
[2] Gimbutas (2001), p. 107.
[3] Ellis Davidson (1998), p. 85.
[4] Liden (1969), pp. 23–32.
[5] Underhill (1923), pp. 1–29.
[6] Newberg, D'Aquili & Rause (2002), p. 178.
[7] Wilmshurst (ed. Lomas) (in press).
[8] Gould (1997), p. 219.
[9] Einstein [(1949) 1956], p. 29.
[10] Wilmshurst (ed. Lomas) (in press).
[11] Wilmshurst (ed. Lomas) (in press).
[12] Maney (2003), p. 55.
[13] Wilmshurst (ed. Lomas) (in press).
[14] Einstein [(1918) 1982], p.78.

Bibliography

Adam of Bremen ([1070] 2002) (trans. F.J. Tschan) *History of the Archbishops of Hamburg-Bremen* Chichester NY: Columbia University Press.

Alexander, F.M. (1969) (ed. E. Maisel) *The Alexander Technique. The Resurrection of the Body* New York: University Books.

Barlow W. (1991) *The Alexander Technique* Rochester Vt: Inner Traditions International.

Barth, F. (1975) *Ritual and Knowledge Among the Baktaman of New Guinea* New Haven Ct: Yale University Press.

Bastock, M. (1956) 'A gene mutation which changes a behavior pattern' *Evolution* 10, pp. 421–39.

—— (1967) *Courtship: An Ethological Study*, Chicago Il: Aldine Press.

Bastock, M. & A. Manning (1955) 'The courting of *Drosophila melanogaster*' *Behaviour* 8, pp. 85–111.

Bear, D.M. & P. Fedio (1977) 'Quantitative analysis of interictal behaviour in temporal lobe epilepsy' *Archives and Neurology* 34, pp. 454–67.

Blackledge, C. (2003) *The Story of V* London: Weidenfeld & Nicolson.

Blackmore S. (1999) *The Meme Machine*, Oxford: Oxford University Press.

Boyer, Pascal (2002) *Religion Explained* London: Vintage.

Brown, D. (2003) *The Da Vinci Code* London: Bantam.

Brown, W.M. (1980) 'Polymorphism in mitochondrial DNA of human as revealed by restriction endonuclease analysis', *Proceedings of the National Academy of Sciences of the USA*, 77, pp. 3605–9.

Campbell, J. (1988) *The Power of Myth* New York: Doubleday.

Carmichael, M.S., R. Humber, *et al.* (1987). 'Plasma oxytocin increases in the human sexual response' *Journal of Clinical Endocrinology and Metabolism* 64, p. 27.

Colbert, E.H. (1980) *Evolution of the Vertebrates: A history of the backboned animals through time* New York and Chichester: John Wiley.

Critchley, H.D., R. Elliott, C.J. Mathias, R.J. Dolan (2000) 'Neural activity relating to generation and representation of galvanic skin conductance responses: a functional magnetic resonance imaging study' *Journal of Neuroscience.* 15 April 2000 20 (8), pp. 3033–40.

D'Aquili, E.G. & A.B. Newberg (1993) 'Liminality, trance and unitary states in ritual and meditation' *Studia Liturgica* 23, pp. 2–34.

Dawkins, R. (1976) *The Selfish Gene* Oxford: Oxford University Press.

—— (1988) *The Blind Watchmaker* London: Penguin.

—— (1998) *Unweaving the Rainbow* London: Allen Lane.

—— (1999) *The Extended Phenotype* Oxford: Oxford University Press.

Dennett, D.C. (1990) 'Memes and the Exploitation of Imagination' *Journal of Aesthetics and Art Criticism* 48, pp. 127–35.

—— (1992) *Consciousness Explained*, London: Allen Lane.

Devereux, P. (2002) *Living Ancient Wisdom* London: Rider.

Dewhurst, K. & A.W. Beard (1970) 'Sudden religious conversion in temporal lobe epilepsy' *British Journal of Psychiatry* 117, pp. 497–507.

Diamond, J. (1997) *Guns, Germs and Steel: The fates of human societies* London: Vintage.

Dieck, A. (1963) 'Zum Problem der Hominidenmoorfunde (menschliche Moorleichen)' *Neue Ausgrabungen und Forschungen in Niedersachsen* 1, pp. 106–112.

Edelman, G.M. & G. Tononi (2000) *Consciousness: How Matter Becomes Imagination* London: Penguin.

Edwards, B. (1979) *Drawing on the Right Side of the Brain* London: Fontana/Collins.

—— (1987) *Drawing on the Artist Within* London: Collins.

Einstein, A. ([1918] 1982) Address to Berlin Physical Society on the occasion of Max Planck's 60th Birthday in Cal Seelig (ed.) *Ideas and Opinions: Albert Einstein* New York: Three Rivers Press.

—— ([1930] 1982) 'Religion and Science', in Cal Seelig (ed.) *Ideas and Opinions: Albert Einstein* New York: Three Rivers Press.

—— ([1941] 1982) 'Advancement of Science', in Cal Seelig (ed.) *Ideas and Opinions: Albert Einstein* New York: Three Rivers Press.

—— [(1949) 1956] (trans. A. Harris) *The World As I See It* New York: Philosophical Library.

Ellis Davidson, H. (1993) *The Lost Beliefs of Northern Europe* London: Routledge.

—— (1998) *Roles of the Northern Goddess* London: Routledge.

Fiske, A.P. & N. Haslam (1997) 'Is obsessive-compulsive disorder a pathology of the human disposition to perform socially meaningful rituals? Evidence of similar content' *Journal of Nervous and Mental Disease* 185 (4), pp. 211–22.

Flett, J. (1976) *Lodge Kirkwall Kilwinning No 38²* Lerwick: Shetland Times.

Forster, E.M. (1927) *Aspects of the Novel* London: Edward Arnold.

Fort Newton, J. (1921) *Builders: A Story and Study of Masonry* Whitefish Mt: Kessinger Publishing.

Freeman W.J. (1999) *How Brains Make Up Their Minds* London: Weidenfeld & Nicolson.

Galton, F. (1869) *Hereditary Genius, an Inquiry into its Laws and Consequences* London: Macmillan.

Gelihorn, E. & W.F. Kiely (1972) 'Mystical states of consciousness. Neurophysiological and clinical aspects' *Journal of Nervous and Mental Disease* 154, pp. 399–405.

Gimbutas, M. (2001) *The Language of the Goddess* London: Thames and Hudson.

Glob, P.V. (1971) *The Bog People* London: Paladin.

Gopnik A., A. Meltzoff & P. Kuhl (1999) *How Babies Think* London: Phoenix.

Gould, S.J. (1997) *Life's Grandeur: The Spread of Excellence from Plato to Darwin* London: Vintage,

Gourlay, K. (2000) 'Orkney scroll may be priceless relic' *The Times*, 21 July.

Hawking, S. (1988) *A Brief History of Time* London: Bantam.

Helbaek, H. (1950) 'Tollund-Mandens sidste Maaltid' *Aarbøger for nordisk Oldkyndighed og Historie 1950*, pp. 311–41. For information in English, see also www.silkeborgmueseum.dk/en/tollund.html (accessed October 2004).

Henderson, M. (2002) 'Scratches that trace the ascent of man' *The Times*, 11 January, p. 5.

Hodgkinson, L. (1988) *The Alexander Technique* London: Piatkus.

Jansky, J., *et al.* (2002) 'Orgasmic aura originates from the right hemisphere' *Neurology* 58 (January), pp. 302–4.

Jevning, R., R.K. Wallace & M. Beideback (1992) 'The physiology of meditation. A review', *Neuroscience and Biobehavioral Reviews*, 16, pp. 415–24.

Jorgensen, S. (1958) 'Grauballenmandens fundsted' *UML: åårbog for Jysk Arkææologisk Selskab* Aarhus: .

Johanson D.C. & M.A. Edey (1981) *Lucy: The Beginnings of Humankind* London: Granada.

Joseph, R. (1988) 'Dual mental functioning in a split brain patient' *Journal of Clinical Psychology* 44, pp. 770–9.

—— (1996) *Neuropsychiatry, Neuropsychology and Clinical Neuroscience* Baltimore MD and London: Williams & Wilkins.

Kandel, E. R., J.H. Schwartz & T.M. Jessell (2000) *Principles of Neural Science* (4th ed), New York and London: McGraw-Hill.

Komisaruk, B.R. & B. Whipple (2000) 'How does vaginal stimulation produce pleasure, pain and analgesia?' in R.B. Fillingim (ed.) *Sex, Gender and Pain*, Progress in Pain Research and Management, vol. 17, Seattle Wa: IASP Press.

Komisaruk, B.R., C.A. Gerdes & B. Whipple (1997) 'Complete spinal cord injury does not block perceptual responses to genital self-stimulation in woman', *Archives of Neurology* 35, pp. 1513–20.

Lane's List: Masonic Records 1717–1894 (2nd ed. 2000), Hinckley: Lewis Masonic.

Libet, B., A. Freeman, K. Sutherland (eds) (1999) *The Volitional Brain: Towards a Neuroscience of Free Will* Thorverton: Imprint Academic..

Liden, K. (1969) 'From Pagan Sanctuary to Christian Church: the excavation of Maere Church, Trondelag' *Norwegian Archeological Review* 2, pp. 23–32.

Lomas, R. (2002) *The Invisible College*, London: Headline.

—— (2003) *Freemasonry and the Birth of Modern Science*, Gloucester Ma: Fair Winds Press.

Lomas, R. & C. Knight (1996) *The Hiram Key* London: Arrow.

—— (1997) *The Second Messiah* London: Arrow.

—— (2000) *Uriel's Machine: The Ancient Origins of Science* London: Arrow.

—— (2004) *The Book of Hiram* London: Arrow.

Maney, K (2003) *The Maverick and His Machine:* Hoboken NJ and Chichester: John Wiley.

Marzi, C.A. (1986) 'Transfer of visual information after unilateral input to the brain', *Brain and Cognition*, 5, pp. 163–73.

McClelland, D. (1961) *The Achieving Society* Princeton NJ: Van Nostrand.

Moir, A. & D. Jessel (1989) *Brain Sex, The Real Differences Between Men & Women* London: Mandarin.

Morgan, E. (1972) *The Descent of Woman* London: Souvenir Press.

Newberg, A., E. D'Aquili & V. Rause (2002) *Why God Won't Go Away: Brain Science and the Biology of Belief* New York: Ballantine Books.

Newton I. ([1725] 1934) *Mathematical Principles of Natural Philosophy* Berkeley Ca: University of California Press.

North J: (1996) *Stonehenge, Neolithic Man and the Cosmos* London: HarperCollins.

Ornstein, R. (1991), *The Evolution of Consciousness* New York and London: Touchstone Books.

Orwell, G. (1968) *The Collected Essays, Journalism, and Letters of George Orwell* vol. 2: *My Country, Right or Left* New York: Harcourt, Brace & World.

Penfield, W. & P. Perot (1963) 'The brain's record of auditory and visual experience', *Brain*, 86, pp. 595–695.

Persinger, M.A. (1983) 'Religious and Mystical Experiences as artifacts of temporal lobe function. A General Hypothesis' *Perceptual and Motor Skills* 60, pp. 827–30.

—— (1984) 'People who report religious experiences may also display enhanced temporal-lobe signs' *Perceptual and Motor Skills* 58, pp. 127–33.

—— (1987) *Neuropsychological Bases of God Beliefs* New York: Praeger.

—— (1993) 'Vertorial cerebral hemisphericity as differential sources for the sensed presence, mystical experiences and religious conversions' *Perceptual and Motor Skills*, 76, pp. 915–30.

Pert, C.B. (1998) *Molecules of Emotion* London: Simon and Schuster.

Pincus, Jonathan H. & Gary J. Tucker (1978) *Behavioural Neurology* Oxford: Oxford University Press.

Pinker, S: (1994) *The Language Instinct* London: Allen Lane.

Pribram, K.H. (1969) *On the Biology of Learning* New York: Harcourt, Brace & World.

—— (1974) 'How is it that sensing so much we can do so little?' in (F.O. Schmitt & F.G. Worden eds) *The Neurosciences, Third Study Program* Cambridge Ma and London: MIT Press, pp. 249–61.

Raine, A., M.S. Buchsbaum & J. Stanley (1994) 'Selective reductions in prefrontal glucose metabolism in murderers', *Biological Psychiatry*, 29, pp. 14–25.

Ramachandran, V.S., & S. Blakeslee (1999) *Phantoms in the Brain* London: Fourth Estate.

Ramachandran, V. S., W.S. Hirstein, K.C. Armel, E. Tecoma & V. Iragui (1997) 'The neural basis of religious experience', *Proceedings of the Annual Conference of the Society of Neuroscience*, vol. 23, abstract 519.1.

Reanney, D. (1995) *The Death of Forever* London: Souvenir Press.

Sinclair, A. (2000) *The Secret Scroll* London: Sinclair-Stevenson.

Speth, G.W. & W. Craven (1897) 'The Kirkwall Scroll' *Ars Quatuor Coronatorum* 10, pp. 27–31.

Squire, C. (1912) *Celtic Myth and Legend, Poetry and Romance* London: Gresham.

Stevenson, D. (1988) *The Origins of Freemasonry* Cambridge: Cambridge University Press.

Smyser, H.M. (1965) 'Ibn Fadla's account of the Rus' in J.B. Bessinger Jr and R.P. Creed (eds) *Medieval and Linguistic Studies in Honour of Francis Beabody Magoun, Jr* London: Allen & Unwin.

Tacitus (1980) *Germanicus* London: Penguin.

Temple, R. (1991) *He Who Saw Everything: A verse translation of the epic of Gilgamesh* London: Rider.

Thom, R. (trans D.H. Fowler) (1975) *Structural Stability and Morphogenesis: An outline of a general theory of models* Menlo Park Ca: Benjamin/Cummings.

Thomson, W.P.L. (1987) *History of Orkney* Edinburgh: Mercat Press.

The Times (2002) Renéé Thom Obituary, 26 October.

Turner, V.W. (1969) *The Ritual Process: Structure and anti-structure* Chicago Il: Aldine Publishing.

Underhill, E. (1923) *Mysticism. A Study of the Nature and Development of Man's Spiritual Consciousness* London: Methuen.

Van de Castle, R. L. (1994) *Our Dreaming Mind* London: Aquarian.

Wachtmeister, C. & M. Enquist (1999) 'The Evolution of Female Coyness – Trading Time for Information' *Ethology* 105 (11), pp. 983–92.

Wilmshurst, W.L. (1922) *The Meaning of Masonry* London: William Rider.

—— (1924) 'Notes on Cosmic Consciousness', typescript of article for *The Occult Review* March.

—— (1925) 'The Fundamental Philosophic Secrets within Masonry', paper read to London Masonic Study Circle (unpublished MS).

—— Unpublished journal notes 1889–1939.

—— (ed. R. Lomas) (in press) *The Secret Science of Masonic Initiation* Hinckley: Lewis Masonic.

Wilson, C. (1990) *The Craft of the Novel* Bath: Ashgrove Press.

—— (2004) *Dreaming to Some Purpose* London: Century.

Worthington, E.L., T.A. Kurusu, M.E. McCullough & S.J. Sandage (1996) 'Empirical research on religion and psycho-therapeutic processes and outcomes. A ten-year review and research prospectus' *Psychological Bulletin* 119, pp. 448–87.

Index